Cultural Calisthenics

ROBERT BRUSTEIN

CULTURAL CALISTHENICS

Writings on Race, Politics, and Theatre

Ivan R. Dee
Chicago 1998

CULTURAL CALISTHENICS. Copyright © 1998 by Robert Brustein. All rights reserved, including the right to reproduce this book or portions thereof in any form. For information, address: Ivan R. Dee, Publisher, 1332 North Halsted Street, Chicago 60622. Manufactured in the United States of America and printed on acid-free paper.

Library of Congress Cataloging-in-Publication Data:
Brustein, Robert Sanford, 1927–
    Cultural calisthenics : writings on race, politics, and theatre /
Robert Brustein.
        p.   cm.
    Includes index.
    ISBN 1-56663-220-X (alk. paper)
    1. Theater—Reviews.   2. Theater and society.   I. Title.
PN1707.B75   1998
792—dc21   98-29317

To Doreen

Ah, love, let us be true
To one another! for the world, which seems
To lie before us like a land of dreams,
So various, so beautiful, so new,
Hath really neither joy, nor love, nor light,
Nor certitude, nor peace, nor help for pain;
And we are here as on a darkling plain
Swept with confused alarms of struggle and flight,
Where ignorant armies clash by night.
—Matthew Arnold, "Dover Beach"

Acknowledgments

Most of these articles and reviews were first published in *The New Republic*, with the following exceptions: "Coercive Philanthropy" originally appeared, in a shorter version, on the op-ed page of the *New York Times*, as did "Gardens and Showcases"; "A Modest Proposal for the NEA" originally appeared in *Newsweek*; and the two Diaries were first published in the Microsoft Internet magazine *Slate*. "Christopher Durang" and "Eugene Ionesco" were written as introductions to their books. "The Decline of Serious Culture" began as a lecture given at Michigan State University and was later included in a collection published by Cornell University Press.

I wish to thank my editors at these various magazines and publishing houses for helping to detect errors and improve my prose, but especially James Wood, Alex Star, and Leon Wieseltier at *The New Republic*; Lynn Kasper at the American Repertory Theatre; and Ivan R. Dee. There are countless others, including my wife Doreen Beinart, who have been of invaluable aid to me in my writing. But in the interests of brevity, I can only thank them collectively and anonymously.

Contents

Cultural Calisthenics

Introduction

This book will be published in a year that marks my forty-fifth anniversary as a critic of American culture, a phenomenon I have watched primarily through the prism of the American theatre. A person who devotes so much time to what so many now consider a peripheral activity in our country must strike people as a little cracked. And I confess that I sometimes feel a bit like Don Quixote, riding my aisle seat as if it were Rocinante, pursuing an old-fashioned illusion into the harsh glare of a neon reality.

It's hard to explain why such a ride is still an exhilarating trip for me, why I continue to feel that initial rush of excitement over the rising of a show curtain. Unlike some of my long-suffering colleagues, I don't find my labors as a theatre critic to be any hardship, despite my many years at the task and the low proportion of worthy productions. I think the reason for such equanimity is that the quality of any single dramatic work has always been of less interest to me than the cultural atmosphere it breathes—what Lionel Trilling called "the haunted air." The ephemeral nature of the theatre, the fact that it is so evanescent and quotidian, often makes it a more accurate barometer of our day-to-day existence than many more permanent records. Our best playwrights consciously take the temperature of their age. The lesser writers do it unconsciously. Hamlet calls players the abstracts and brief chronicles of the time. He might have said the same thing about plays.

My greatest satisfaction, of course, comes from seeing a great play in a powerful production. But even bad evenings in the theatre can tell us something about who we are, where we are, and where we are going at any given moment. I don't think I've ever written a notice to which I didn't eventually attach a judgment of value. I'm an opinionated man. But after all these years of passing judgment, the thing that gives me most pride (or shame) is not the accuracy of my critical opinions. It is whether or not I have accurately analyzed the cultural soil in which the play was germinated.

In the past that soil was often nourished by such social concerns as Marxist revolution, political justice, racial equality, and the Vietnam War. Today it is being irrigated by issues of cultural diversity, gay rights, women's issues, and political correctness. Every thirty years, it would seem, the drama is reconditioned, refurbished, and hauled into the field like a piece of artillery—"drama as weapon." In the thirties and forties this weapon was aimed against totalitarianism abroad and on behalf of economic equality at home; in the sixties against an unjust foreign war and on behalf of civil liberties; in the nineties against the spreading plague of AIDS and on behalf of equal rights for minorities, gays, and women (aside from Tony Kushner, American playwrights seem curiously uninterested these days in international issues).

These are genuine problems which have involved creative people in a lot of strenuous calisthenics as they stretch their tendons and flex their muscles preparing to wrestle with political agendas from the left and the right. I've been doing some bench presses and chin-ups myself in an effort to keep these exercises in perspective. I believe that plays must be engaged with the social and political issues of the time, but I continue to hold the admittedly unfashionable view that no major work of art ever changed society, however it succeeded in changing consciousness. It is true that *Uncle Tom's Cabin* constituted a strong argument on behalf of the abolitionist cause, just as *Waiting for Lefty* aroused a lot of theatre audiences to express solidarity with some striking taxicab drivers. But such works are of interest today largely as historical curiosities. The American plays that have lasted are not those originally conceived as instruments of propaganda. They are plays that have aspired to be works of art, preeminently the brooding apolitical dramas of O'Neill.

Today's activist plays, like those of the past, can certainly help to allay our sense of loneliness during bad political times. But I think it wishful to believe that such drama represents an effective agency for reforming the body politic, much less altering the history of dramatic literature. Chekhov wrote: "Great writers and artists must deal with politics only in order to put up a defense against politics," by which he meant that (1) it was the writer's obligation to contest narrow interpretations of reality, and that (2) art provided one of the best alternatives to what Orwell was later to call "the smelly little orthodoxies that are nowadays contending for our souls." For who, if not the artist, was in a position to appreciate the ambiguities and complexities, the surprises and contingencies, of everyday life? "I am not a liberal and not a conservative," Chekhov wrote in a famous letter to Suvorin, "not an evolutionist, nor a monk, nor indifferent to the world. I would like to be a free artist—and that is all."

The operative word in that passage is "free." Chekhov wrote under threat of severe censorship—he knew how art could be made tongue-tied by authority. He also knew how ideological thinking could clog the creative imagination. But he insisted on writing from his own perception of things, without allegiance to any creed, philosophy, or faction. This is not to say that Chekhov possessed no political sympathies. Although profoundly suspicious of revolutionary movements and radical programs, he was a firm believer in political reform. But the objectives he espoused in his role as citizen, he steadfastly refused to propose as an artist, always criticizing "tendencies" in creative work, always urging the reader or spectator to act as his own judge and jury.

Many today, believing that every human activity is political, declare this kind of disinterestedness a snare and a delusion. I believe they are wrong. Although absolute impartiality probably doesn't exist in nature, it remains an indispensable ideal. We must continue to pursue the truth, however elusive, through the most impenetrable ideological thickets.

I write these words, admittedly, from a position that is hardly impartial. For if the nature of my critical work requires me to be a detached observer, my anxieties about the future of free expression keep forcing me back into the exercise room to join the calisthenics. Unlike many of my fellow critics, who are under no obligation to reveal the principles that inform their opinions, I often feel obliged to disclose the extra-aesthetic reasons why I like or dislike a play. And that may explain why my writing is often identified with controversy. It wasn't enough to say I found the ending of August Wilson's *The Piano Lesson* crude and contrived. I also had to blurt out some troublesome generalizations about what I perceived to be Wilson's narrow view of the black experience. Out of that swirled the charges and countercharges that eventually led to the debate between us at Town Hall in New York.

Similarly, I am not satisfied simply to evaluate a production at a resident theatre. I also want to look at that production in the context of the theatre's goals and purposes, the audience's expectations, the other plays in the season, indeed the whole construct of planning and funding for the arts. I admit a vested interest here, since I lead a non-profit institution that is also trying to stay solvent (and honest) in a difficult climate. When the National Endowment for the Arts is threatened with extinction or has its funds severely cut, or when Jesse Helms tries to impose content restrictions on government grants, I start pumping iron, aroused for a number of reasons, both subjective and objective. I fear for my theatre. I fear for the whole resident theatre movement. I fear for the nation.

I am both a critic and a practitioner. I try my best to practice what I preach, and I try to preach what I practice as well. This double function sometimes makes me vulnerable to charges of colliding interests. I assure you I am sensitive to these, and I have tried to flag those places in the book where my interests overlap. If I've missed a few, I apologize. I will try to be more careful in future. But don't expect me to be so repentant I would give up my criticism or my practice. I'm having too much fun.

A word about organization. The first section of *Cultural Calisthenics* is devoted to essays about the racial and political issues that have been troubling us of late. The middle two sections cover some of these issues in the context of reviews of theatre productions, originating both from home and abroad. And the final section is composed of essays about a number of artists important to the modern theatre. Most of these collected pieces have been prompted by occasions—plays, productions, biographies, and cultural controversies. I hope they also provide an occasion for enjoyable reading and provocative ideas.

R. B.

Cambridge, Massachusetts
June 1998

PART 1

POSITIONS: RACE AND POLITICS

Coercive Philanthropy

For a number of years now, American culture has been asked to shoulder obligations once considered the exclusive responsibility of American politics, and this has radically altered the way we now regard the arts. The activization of culture in recent times has come about, one suspects, because legislative solutions to the nation's social problems have been largely abandoned or tabled. Instead of developing adequate federal programs to combat homelessness, poverty, crime, disease, drug abuse, and racial tension, our governing bodies have responded with depleted federal subsidies, dwindling programs for the poor and unemployed, congressional boondoggles, and other instances of systemic inertia. Aside from the debates over competing health care programs, the most significant action advanced by liberals for solving America's more urgent social needs has been to increase the cultural representation of minority groups.

This state of affairs has a history that goes back to the Carter years, but it was clearly intensified during the Reagan-Bush administrations, with their neglect of economic inequities and indifference to social injustice. The powerful conservative revulsion against traditional liberalism led not only to a restructuring of national power but a redistribution of the country's wealth, while the burgeoning deficit and a growing taxpayers' revolt frightened lawmakers away from passing any incremental social programs. Add to these political and economic retrenchments a new ideological vacuum created by the collapse of the Soviet Union. Not only was Marxist economic theory discredited by the failure of communism, but so were the related though considerably milder platforms of socialism, liberal humanism, the welfare state, the New Deal, the Great Society, perhaps even the whole construct of democratic politics. For the first time in more than a hundred years, there exists no viable theoretical alternative to laissez-faire capitalism with its unregulated greed and unequal income structure, no collective idealism to temper unrestrained individualism, no Marx or Keynes to dispute with Adam Smith or Milton Friedman, not even a radical national magazine (if we discount the intellectually weakened *Nation* and *Dissent*) that still gives voice to opinion on the left.

This is not the place to debate the strengths and weaknesses of opposing political ideologies. What I am arguing, rather, is that the weakening of the political left and the absence of a genuine political dialectic has led to paralysis in an arena of social action usually serviced by legislation. It is because of this inertia that the nonprofit cultural sector is being pressed into compensatory service, as a way of sustaining hopes disappointed by the political system. The result is a scene that would be comical were it not so disheartening—a limping gaggle of have-not geese honking loudly for the same small handful of feed. Not only is America's underclass crippled by poverty and hopelessness, but federal money for artistic projects, always pitifully inadequate by comparison with other civilized countries, has been flat or diminishing since 1980, while the National Endowment for the Arts is threatened with extinction every time it spends two hundred dollars on a controversial grant. Staggering under massive deficits, and teetering on the edge of bankruptcy, our nonprofit cultural institutions are nevertheless being asked to validate themselves not through their creative contributions to civilization but on the basis of their community services. This condition was accurately predicted by Alexis de Tocqueville early in the nineteenth century when he expressed doubts about the possibility of serious art in the United States: "Democratic nations," he wrote in *Democracy in America*, "will habitually prefer the useful to the beautiful, and they will require that the beautiful be useful."

Current pressures on the arts to be useful cause funders to measure their value by outreach programs, children's projects, inner-city audience development, access for the handicapped, artists in schools, etc., in addition to demanding proofs of progress in achieving affirmative-action quotas among artistic personnel, board members, and audiences. This social utilitarian view of culture has some undeniable virtues. Certainly, few people of goodwill would dispute the artistic advantages of genuine multiculturalism or inter-culturalism in the arts (as opposed to unicultural programs primarily designed to empower single-issue groups). And there are unquestionably deep humanitarian impulses governing the new philanthropy. Given the limited resources available for both social and cultural programs, the civic-minded agencies that disburse grant money no doubt sincerely believe that a single dollar can fulfill a double purpose, just as many contemporary artists would prefer their works to function not only as a form of self-expression but also for the public good.

Looked at in the long perspective, however, the push to transform culture into an agency of social welfare is doomed to failure. To demand that creative expression be a medium for promoting minority self-esteem may seem like a thrifty way to respond to the urgent needs of the underclasses. But whatever the immediate effects of such well-meaning civic experiments, they are not long-lasting. Works of art have occasionally been known to transform consciousness and alter individual destinies. They have rarely been known to change society. Culture is not designed to do the work of politics, nor will inspirational role models even begin to compensate for the unconscionable neglect of arts education in our schools. No wonder inner-city children prefer rap or salsa when so few qualified teachers have been employed by the system to expose them to serious theatre, art, or music. No wonder the infrequent visit of a performance artist or a dance company on a grant often leaves them baffled and sullen when no money exists for developing their imaginations. Effective projects like the Teachers and Writers Collaborative, in which poor kids are introduced to language and poetry by practicing poets, are rare and privately subsidized. Anything short of daily arts education in the public school curriculum will register as little more than tokenism. Indeed, such cosmetic procedures may even be exacerbating the problem since they tend to varnish the surface instead of probing root causes.

Whatever its impact on education, for philanthropy to administer nonprofit funding by utilitarian rather than traditional aesthetic criteria is almost certainly likely to doom the arts as we know them. It is very ominous indeed that the word "quality," the standard by which art has habitually been measured, is now avoided in the majority of funding circles, being considered a code word for racism and elitism. This is true not only in federal, state, and city cultural agencies, where one expects the arts to be subject to populist and egalitarian political pressures, but even in most private funding organizations. With a few lonely exceptions (most notably the Andrew W. Mellon Foundation and the Shubert Foundation), large and small private foundations now give their money not to general support as in the past but overwhelmingly to special programs conceived by the officers of the foundation. Active rather than receptive in relation to the choices of artists and the programming of artistic institutions, the foundation world is now engaged in what we can only regard as coercive philanthropy. Artists and institutions are obliged to follow the dictates of officious program directors, or be exiled to an economic Gulag.

The Lila Wallace–Reader's Digest Foundation, for example, which handed out $45 million to the arts in 1993, describes its three-year program for resident theatres in the following manner: "To expand their marketing efforts, mount new plays, broaden the ethnic makeup of their management, experiment with color-blind casting, increase community outreach activity and sponsor a variety of other programs designed to integrate the theatres into their communities," and also to encourage "dynamic interactions between artists and communities . . . to develop new audiences . . . [and] to address the interests of children and families." These are all benevolent social goals, but they are also all peripheral to the true work of most theatres. What the foundation fails to "expand" or "broaden" or "sponsor" is an artistic goal. As a result, the great preponderance of Wallace funds each year goes to increasing "the African-American audience" or "doubling the number of Asian Americans in the overall audience" or "increasing the number of Latino theatregoers to 40% of the audience" or deepening "the involvement of . . . Latino immigrants, emerging Latino business and professional leaders" or attracting "new theatre audiences from . . . Hispanic concert-goers and African-American concert-goers" or diversifying "through the addition of actors of color . . . with the input of its new African-American artistic associate" or including "greater promotion within the African-American community" or developing "new audiences from New York City's Asian-American communities," and so on (I quote a few typical citations from recent grants). Only one award last year went to an institution proposing a project with any artistic dimensions, and that one was designed to broaden the base of childrens' audiences.

Similarly the Rockefeller Foundation, once among the most enlightened supporters of artists and artistic institutions in America, now disburses about $15 million annually, mostly to scholarship but also to arts projects indistinguishable from its equal opportunity and social science research grant recipients. Rockefeller's arts and humanities division describes its mission as encouraging scholars and artists "whose work can advance international and intercultural understanding in the United States . . . extending international and intercultural scholarship and increasing artistic experimentation across cultures." It should be noted that "international and intercultural understanding" no longer includes any understanding of Europe. To judge by the grants, the phrase refers almost exclusively to African, Asian, and, especially, Hispanic countries and cultures. (Only eight of eighty-seven grants could be construed as escaping these categories.)

As a result, Rockefeller's three granting categories advance such noble objectives as "Extending International and Intercultural Scholarship," "Fortifying Institutions of the Civil Society," and "Increasing Artistic Experimentation Across Cultures," while the grants go almost overwhelmingly to African-American, Native American, Asian, and Latino artists or institutions engaged in social objectives (Rockefeller's largest grant in recent years, amounting to almost $2 million, was awarded to the "Intercultural Film/Video Program" in order to enable visual artists not to experiment with new visions or advance film and video techniques but rather to "create work that explores cultural diversity"). One is not surprised to learn that Rockefeller is considering a new play initiative designed to fund works that deal with an issue the program directors call "conflict resolution." Heaven help the playwright with other issues in mind.

As for the Ford Foundation, whose enlightened arts division under W. McNeil Lowry was largely responsible for the massive explosion of American nonprofit dance, theatre, symphony, and opera companies since the sixties (including many racially diverse institutions), the lion's share of program budgets now goes to urban and rural poverty, education, governance and public policy, and international affairs. This is entirely understandable, given such pressing needs at home and abroad. But once again a reduced arts budget—$5.5 million in 1993, out of $54 million for education and culture—goes to institutions devising projects similar to the foundation's civil rights and social justice programs. Ford describes its arts division as pursuing two goals, "cultural diversity and strengthening creativity in the performing arts," and adds, "Both goals have become increasingly interconnected, particularly since mainstream arts institutions have become more interested in culturally diverse art and audiences in recent years. At the same time, much of the new performing art the Foundation has supported has been that of minority artists and arts organizations."

Rockefeller also claims that a new "interest in culturally diverse art and audiences" exists among mainstream arts organizations. One might question whether this new "interest" is quite as widespread as recent foundation applications would suggest. Has this passion for culturally diverse art arisen spontaneously, or is it the result of external pressures, notably a desperate need to qualify for subsidies? Whatever the answer, there is no doubt that a lockstep mentality is ruling today's funding fashions where the flavors of the year (or decade) are cultural diversity and multiculturalism. Examples of this can be furnished from any number of private foundations—not to mention federal, state, and civic funding agencies, and private corporations such as AT&T. In a recent issue of *Corporate Philanthropy Report*, a contributions manager bluntly states: "We no longer 'support' the arts. We *use* the arts in innovative ways to support the social causes chosen by our company." The entire arts budget of the Nathan Cummings Foundation (approximately $800,000) goes to what the officers call "culturally specific arts institutions" and "community-based arts organizations." Well, at least it goes directly to minority organizations and not to coercing mainstream institutions into changing their nature.

Even the John and Catherine T. MacArthur grants, originally devoted to identifying and rewarding American "genius" regardless of race or ethnic background, now has a largely multicultural agenda under its new program director, Catharine Stimpson. As a result, of the four grants awarded to performing artists this year (three to gifted people of color), the only white male recipient is listed as a "theatre arts educator," whose main qualification for genius was to have founded "a theatre company for inner-city children of Manhattan's Clinton Neighborhood and the Times Square welfare hotels." This project is no doubt of significant value, and its director deserves support, recognition, and funding. But the question remains: Is this award for a "genius" or for a deeply committed social worker?

It is difficult to criticize this kind of philanthropy without being accused of insensitivity to minority artists. But it may be a serious error to assume that all the foundation dollars being poured into developing inner-city audiences are successfully democratizing American culture. What we need is some rigorous documentation regarding the impact of these grants. And, indeed, advance reports of a survey commissioned by the Lila Wallace–Reader's Digest Foundation suggest that what typically attracts minority audiences to the arts is not mass infusions of audience development money, or even special racial or ethnic projects. Rather it is the *quality* of the art itself.

Whatever its success in the minority community, the new coercive philanthropy is having a demoralizing effect on artists and artistic institutions. The entire cultural world is bending itself into contortions in order to find the right shape for grants under the new criteria. (Like other institutions that poorly perform the new calisthenics, my own theatre has received no money for its customary activities from Ford, Wallace, or Rockefeller for more than four years.)

And the pressure comes from many directions. Recently a report issued by the American Symphony Orchestra League threatened the constituency of this service organization with loss of funding if orchestra programs didn't start to "reflect more closely the cultural mix, needs, and interests of their communities." In order to accommodate cultural diversity, in short, institutions of high culture were being asked to include popular, folk, and racial-ethnic expressions in their classical repertoire, as if there were not sufficient outlets for this music in the popular culture. In a typical stab at conformity with the new orthodoxy, a major symphony orchestra management recently invited its own inquisitor. It hired a "Diversity Initiative Consultant," who issued a memorandum to that symphony's "family" in the form of a questionnaire designed to induce "cultural awareness" and "to elicit your perceptions of the organizational culture and diversity of cultures in your work environment."

The dopey questions were framed in a benevolent enough fashion ("Have you realized that your own upbringing was not the same as other races or cultures?" "Have you avoided people of a different or certain racial, ethnic, or cultural group?"). But I trust I am not alone in detecting a certain Orwellian cast to these diversity experts who roam the corridors testing everyone's sensitivity to racial slights. When they enter the corridors of culture, they inspire an atmosphere of fear, constraint, and mistrust. It may not be long before anxious employees, prodded by the batons of vigilant thought police, will be fingering fellow workers who neglect to display sufficient "tolerance" or "sensitivity" as measured by such politically correct indicators.

This insinuation of politics into culture comes at a time when tribalism has begun to shatter our national identity, when the melting pot has turned into a seething cauldron. It is only natural, under such conditions, that philanthropy should rush to the aid of racial, ethnic, and sexual groups clamoring for recognition through the agency of creative expression. But the thing about a group with special interests is that in order to achieve power, influence, strength, and unity, it must display a common front. And this often means suppressing the singularity of its individual members and denying what is shared with others—neither good conditions for creating the idiosyncrasy and universality associated with great art.

What seems to get lost in all this separatist clamor for cultural identity is that the most pressing American issue today is not race or gender or ethnicity but rather what it has always been—the inequitable distribution of the nation's resources, which is an issue of class. This makes our concentration on culture as an open door to equality and opportunity look like a diversion from the pressing economic problems that afflict our more indigent citizens. It reminds me of how, beginning in the fifties, our attention was distracted from the depredations of an unregulated economy and focused on the evils of network television. Thirty years ago, in an article called "The Madison Avenue Villain," I argued that since the whole purpose of the mass media was to peddle consumer goods, to hold the account executive or the TV packager responsible for brutalizing mass culture was to blame the salesman for the defective products of his company. In short, by concentrating on the "wasteland" of mass culture instead of the economic necessities that were driving it, we were effectively blocking a remedy, which could only be political.

Much the same thing seems to be happening today, except that while we are still blaming the failures of our mass society on mass culture (consider the debates over TV violence), we are now asking high culture to compensate for the failures of our affluent society. But by forcing artistic expression to become a conduit for social justice and equal opportunity instead of achieving these goals through the political system, we are at the same time distracting our artists and absolving our politicians. Indeed, it seems to be an American habit to analyze a problem correctly and then come up with the wrong solution.

The right solution, I believe, will only be found when we recognize that we are all members of the same family and that the whole society bears responsibility for the woes of its more indigent relatives. This means responding to unemployment and its consequences in crime and drug abuse with a strong legislative initiative like that employed in the thirties by Roosevelt and the New Deal—a new Civilian Conservation Corps to turn gun-toting inner-city youth into skilled artisans repairing roads and building bridges, a reformed welfare system that emphasizes the dignity of work, a public educational system devoted to teaching subjects and developing skills rather than promoting diversity and managing crowd control, and, yes, a federal works project to provide opportunities for anyone who seeks employment, including artists. All this, of course, requires pots of money and goes directly against the grain of the new mean-spirited, Republican-dominated Congress. But we Americans, for all our complaining, are now the most undertaxed citizens in the Western world, and we are in a deepening crisis that needs attention. It will not be resolved by demolishing the small fragile culture we still have.

1994

A Modest Proposal for the NEA

The National Endowment of the Arts, like its sister agency the National Endowment for the Humanities, once again faces the prospect of annihilation—at the very least a significant reduction in funds—by the new Republican-led Congress. Government-supported arts programs, despite their minimal drain on the federal budget, have always been a furball in the throats of conservatives, who generally find them dominated by "elitists," "liberals," "perverts," "weirdos," and other low forms of American life. In the Gingrich era, the NEA now faces the same congressional euthanasia that doomed the arts program of the New Deal's short-lived Federal Works Project in the thirties.

Many of those calling for an end to the NEA claim they don't oppose the arts. They simply want the arts (along with the humanities and public television) to be supported exclusively by private money. "Privatization" would throw back artistic and humanistic expression entirely on the charitable impulses of individuals, corporations, and foundations, most of whom have their own agendas. And since those who control the purse strings often dictate how the money is spent, this could spell the end of many valuable artistic institutions that refuse to be coerced by the current guidelines.

Still, given the current climate, there is much to be said in favor of severing the NEA's ties with Congress. For one thing, it would free this agency from the humiliating treatment it suffers at the hands of its political opponents every time the NEA comes up for renewal or reappropriation. How could this valuable agency be genuinely "privatized" without losing its capacity to fund all deserving art?

One idea making the rounds is that the National Endowment for the Arts (as well as the National Endowment for the Humanities) should begin to accumulate a genuine endowment, similar to those now helping to drive the private American university. Ideally this endowment would have to be sizable enough to generate ample annual interest, enough to supply generous subsidies to all deserving artists and artistic institutions. It would have to provide sufficient funds to make arts subsidy independent once and for all, not just from public censorship and opprobrium but from foundation fashions, corporate self-interest, and capricious individual giving.

It may well be asked how Congress could be asked to appropriate funds for what it considers unruly performance artists and obscene photographers—funds not in the millions but the billions—when it bridles over the measly allotment the NEA presently receives. The money would not come from public funds. It would be derived from the artists themselves through the avenue of royalties, the only requirement being a change in the copyright laws.

Royalties are commonly paid to creative people by producers, theatre, dance, and opera companies, and others until fifty years following the death of the author. After that date, all published works enter the public domain and are free from payment. Supposing artistic royality payments were to continue after fifty years, collected directly by the NEA (literary and scholarly royalties could be similarly collected by the NEH). Thus instead of paying 6 percent of gross receipts to the O'Neill estate for the rights to perform *Strange Interlude*, as is customary, a theatre company would send its royalty check to the NEA after the play enters the public domain. In the same way, after *The Sun Also Rises* enters the public domain, the book's publisher would send a royalty check to the National Endowment for the Humanities in order to subsidize the work of other writers and scholars.

This may strike some observers as a hidden tax burden on non-profit artistic institutions, already groaning under substantial deficits. But such institutions have traditionally paid royalties for new works, and the new payments need not be retroactive. Only works entering the public domain after the date of the change in copyright law would pay royalties under this system. Since such classical literature as the plays of Shakespeare and the novels of Hawthorne, and such ballets as *Swan Lake*, could still be performed or published free, those institutions finding such payments burdensome need only publish and produce classics exempt from royalties.

Were the copyright laws changed to accommodate this idea, a sizable endowment would rapidly accumulate. To give an example, a single nonprofit theatre with five or six hundred seats typically pays a playwright about twenty thousand dollars (representing a 6 percent royalty over a four-week run). Multiply that figure by the number of theatres producing plays falling into the public domain and you have some idea of how quickly the National Endowment could grow.

The moral advantage of the idea is that those providing primary support for living artists (and scholars) would be dead artists (and scholars). No longer would legislators be able to argue that the federal government should not fund artistic expression because it isn't enjoyed or endorsed by the entire population. No longer would private foundations be able to dictate artistic content on the basis of restrictive guidelines. Free from fashion, favor, and influence, receiving the kinds of subsidies enjoyed by most civilized countries in the world, American artists would be in a position to write their own declaration of independence—from censorship and repression.

1995

Subsidized Separatism

August Wilson's keynote address at the TCG (Theatre Communications Group) Conference in late June 1996, later published as "The
Ground on Which I Stand," was greeted with a standing ovation by
the various resident theatre people attending, though some found it
divisive and disturbing. Since I was not present at the conference, I
was hardly in a position to express my own reactions, though word
leaked back to me that chief among the malefactors identified in Wilson's broadside—his "snipers" and "naysayers" and "cultural imperialists"—was myself.

Wilson's rambling jeremiad is essentially an effort to accentuate
the achievements of black theatre, which he claims to be supreme
today though "often accomplished amid adverse and hostile conditions." "Black theatre is alive, it is vibrant, it is vital," he says. But not
all its practitioners are following the proper path. In the same speech
Wilson manages to express his disdain for black "crossover artists"
who, "like house slaves entertaining the white master and his guests,"
manage to "slant their material for white consumption." He rebukes
white foundations for failing to create and subsidize black theatre
companies. And he characterizes the idea of "color-blind casting" as
"a tool of the Cultural Imperialists"—"the same idea of assimilation
that black Americans have been rejecting for the past 300 years."

If you hear echoes in this of 1960s radicalism, particularly the language of black nationalism, your ears are not deceiving you. And
Wilson is hardly reluctant to admit his militant inheritance. Testify-
ing that the black power movement was "the kiln in which I was
fired," he proclaims that its concern with "self-determination, self-
respect and self-defense" are the values that govern his life. He claims
that "I am what is known, at least among the followers and supporters
of Marcus Garvey, as a 'race man.' " He announces that the ground
on which he stands was pioneered "by Nat Turner, by Denmark

Vesey, by Martin Delaney, Marcus Garvey and the Honorable Elijah Muhammad"—rebels or separatists all, some proponents of a return to Africa. Conspicuous by its absence is the name of Martin Luther King, among many other honored black Americans for whom the idea of integration has not been considered anathema.

The foundation of this long tirade is Wilson's insistence on black culture, particularly black theatre, not only as an unparalleled achievement but also a singular and discrete experience of life. It is an experience that cannot be fully absorbed or understood by white people, much less criticized by them: "We cannot allow others to have authority over our cultural and spiritual products," he says. "We need to develop guidelines of the protection of our cultural property, our contributions and the influence they accrue." Whites and blacks can occupy the same country, but they cannot occupy the same ground. "Where is the common ground in the horrifics of lynching? Where is the common ground in the policeman's bullet? Where is the common ground in the hull or the deck of a slave ship . . . ?" He describes "black conduct and manners as part of a system that is fueled by its own philosophy, mythology, history, creative motif, social organization and ethos." He deplores the presence of a black actor in a non-black play, standing on the stage "as part of a social milieu that has denied him his gods, his humanity, his mores, his ideas of himself and the world he lives in. . . ." Indeed, he considers the very idea of an all-black production of *Death of a Salesman* to be "an assault on our presence . . . an insult to our intelligence."

This is the language of self-segregation. At times, it is true, Wilson is willing to concede that blacks and whites breathe the same air and partake of certain "commonalities" of culture. Among these "commonalities" he mentions food, though even that admission is weirdly exclusionary. Black people have had to be satisfied with the leavings of the pig. Yet blacks and whites "share a common experience with the pig as opposed to say Muslims and Jews, who do not share that experience." (Black Muslims? Reform Jews?) It is also true that, in the rolling cadences that bring his speech to its climax, Wilson concedes the American theatre's power to "inform about the human condition, its power to heal, its power to hold the mirror as 'twere up to nature, its power to uncover the truths we wrestle from uncertain and sometimes unyielding realities." Even this boiler-plate rhetoric, however, for all its afterthought references to the unifying nature of the theatre, fails to compensate for the divisive nature of his remarks. Perhaps some future student of syntax will analyze how Wilson's vacillating use of the word "we" in the same paragraph (first inclusive: "We have to do it together," then exclusive: "We are brave and we are boisterous") betrays his ambivalent sense of American identity. This ambivalence makes for some confusing assertions. "We are black and beautiful. . . . We are not separatists. . . . We are Africans. We are Americans."

Furthermore, Wilson's insistence on the strength and uniqueness of a proud black culture is oddly inconsistent with his notion that blacks are "victims of the counting houses who hold from us ways to develop and support our talents." This inconsistency grows more glaring when Wilson directs his biblical fury toward some of these "counting houses" (his name for the funding agencies) and concludes that "the economics are reserved as privilege to the overwhelming abundance of institutions that promote and perpetrate white culture." He notes that of the sixty-six League of Resident Theatres (LORT) only one can be considered black. And in an impassioned if curious appeal for subsidized separatism, he sees no contradiction in demanding that white foundations take the responsibility for founding as well as funding black theatres, as if theatre companies were the creation of philanthropic agencies rather than the indigenous outgrowths of dedicated artists and supporting communities.

I'm not at all certain any more what constitutes a "black" or "white" theatre. Both the precarious Negro Ensemble Company and the thriving Crossroads Theater fit Wilson's exclusive definition clearly enough. But how does one describe the New York Public Theater and Atlanta Alliance Theater under their black directors George C. Wolfe and Kenneth Leon? Or the Yale Repertory Theatre and Syracuse Stage when they were led by such black directors as Lloyd Richards and Tazewell Thompson? Most American theatres today, like many American cities—indeed like many Americans—are racially mixed. Are black actors now to perform only black parts written by black playwrights? Will James Earl Jones no longer have a chance to play Judge Brack or Darth Vader? Must we bar Andre Braugher and Denzel Washington from enacting the Shakespearean monarchs? Is Othello to be an unacceptable opportunity for Morgan

Freeman or Laurence Fishburne? Will Athol Fugard be told he cannot take a colored role in his own plays? No more voodoo *Macbeths* or all-black *Godots*? No more efforts on behalf of nontraditional casting and integrated theatre companies? Must history be rolled back to the days of segregated theatres?

I fear Wilson is displaying a failure of memory—I hesitate to say a failure of gratitude—when he charges nonprofit resident theatres with using "sociological criteria" in choosing plays that "traditionally exclude blacks." All of his own plays were originated and produced by a large consortium of mainstream institutions, including the Yale Repertory Theatre, the Huntington, the American Conservatory Theater, the Goodman, the Mark Taper, and others. Wilson's pervasive tone of victimization, in fact, is oddly inappropriate for a playwright whose six LORT-generated plays, after completing the resident theatre circuit, all found their way to Broadway, where they won two Pulitzer Prizes, five New York Drama Critics Circle awards, and I don't know how many Tonys, besides generating enormous box office income for the playwright (from white and black audiences alike). Is a man who has garnered such extraordinary media attention (not to mention every conceivable playwriting fellowship) really in a position to say that blacks are being excluded from the American theatre or that these institutions only "preserve, promote, and perpetuate white culture"? Has he read any foundation reports lately? Does he have any idea of the proportion of grants, both public and private, that are exclusively reserved for inner-city audience development and multicultural activities in resident theatres?

I am the only villain identified by name in Wilson's speech. He makes reference to my article "Diversity and Unity," but there are also hidden allusions to what I wrote in "The Options of Multiculturalism," my unfavorable review of his play *The Piano Lesson*, and my *Times* op-ed piece on coercive foundation funding. Wilson specifically attacks what he calls my "surprisingly sophomoric assumption" that the present funding climate is characterized by confused standards and sociological rather than aesthetic criteria. I confess to believing that most foundations (by their own admission) no longer make artistic quality their primary consideration. But I categorically deny I ever said that "the practice of extending invitations to a national banquet from which a lot of hungry people have been excluded" (my phrase, uncredited) establishes (his phrase) "a presumption of inferiority of the work of minority artists."

Wilson's charge, with its nasty imputations of racism, is intended to characterize a review of two minority playwrights who, in my estimation, met the highest standards, and without being exclusionary. "Drenched in their own cultural juices," I wrote, "they are nevertheless capable of telling stories that include us all, thus proving again that the theatre works best as a unifying rather than a segregating medium." I was talking about transcendence, about recognizing that the greatest art embraces a common humanity. Although Wilson might dismiss such playwrights—the younger generation of black writers like Anna Deavere Smith and OyamO and Suzan-Lori Parks—as "crossover artists" entertaining the slave owner and his guests, my article was a plea to minority playwrights like himself to acknowledge, without any loss of racial consciousness, that they belong, as artists, to the same human family as everyone else.

Some people may remember that, almost alone among white critics, I have expressed reservations about Wilson's plays. This was an aesthetic judgment, not a racial one. While I admire Wilson's control of character and dialogue, a lot of his writing has seemed to me weakly structured, badly edited, prosaic, and overwritten. Consider, for instance, *Seven Guitars*, which I didn't review (I left after four guitars). I don't think it exposes "the values of white Americans based on their European ancestors" to believe that a conventionally realistic play needs an animating event, and that, however colorful its subject matter, it cannot ramble willy-nilly for one act lasting two and a half hours without establishing a line of action. My less technical objection has been that, by choosing to chronicle the oppression of black people through each of the decades, Wilson has fallen into a monotonous tone of victimization which happens to be the leitmotif of his TCG speech.

I am also disturbed by other attitudes reflected in that speech, notably that only the black experience inspires the work of black artists. In "The Options of Multiculturalism," I suggested that, while Wilson has announced he will never allow a white director to stage his plays, a backyard drama like his *Fences* shows the considerable influence of white playwrights, particularly Arthur Miller's *All My Sons*. (It may be that Wilson's anger over this conjecture ricochets into his ferocious attack on the *New York Times* for allegedly underplaying the influence of black singers on Michael Bolton—something he calls an "intent to maim.")

It is perfectly possible that I am wrong in my assessments. And I can understand how a playwright, no matter how highly praised by mainstream critics, can smart under adverse criticism, even in a relatively small-circulation periodical such as *The New Republic*. It is also no doubt painful to him that *Seven Guitars* lost the Tony this year to *Master Class*. But that is no justification for wheeling out the creaky juggernaut of black power to roll over anyone who makes a negative judgment on his plays. Indeed, Wilson seems to suggest occasionally that the only true critical function is boosterism. For at the same time Wilson is questioning the very idea of critical opinions ("The true critic does not sit in judgment . . . the critic has an important responsibility to guide and encourage . . . growth"), he is announcing that every African American, contrary to Du Bois's idea of "the talented tenth," is artistically gifted: "All God's children got talent." This is progressive-school nonsense. The greatest tribute that a critic can pay to a playwright such as Wilson is to judge and analyze his work by the same criteria as anybody else's work.

Wilson writes: "I stand myself and my art squarely on the self-defining ground of the slave quarters." Isn't it time to acknowledge that, for all the grim uncompleted racial business in this country, those quarters have long been razed to the ground? Isn't there some kind of statute of limitations on white guilt and white reparations? Isn't it possible to recognize that there is a difference between losing your freedom and losing a Tony, between toting a bale of cotton and bearing the burden of an unfavorable review? To say that whites can't understand black culture because their ancestors were not enslaved is almost as problematical as saying that Wilson can't understand the writings of a Jew because he hasn't experienced life under the pharaohs. Many brilliant black artists and intellectuals—Albert Murray, Ralph Ellison, Henry Louis Gates, Shelby Steele, and others—have repudiated the "ethnographic fallacy" that one writer's peculiar experiences can represent a whole social category. This tribalist approach, as Diane Ravitch has written, "confuses race with culture, as though everyone with the same skin color had the same culture and history."

August Wilson is more comfortable writing plays than apostolic decrees. His speech is melancholy testimony to the rabid identity politics and poisonous racial consciousness that have been infecting our country in recent years. Although Wilson would deny it, such sentiments represent a reverse form of the old politics of division, an appeal for socially approved and foundation-funded separatism. I don't think Martin Luther King ever imagined an America where playwrights such as August Wilson would be demanding, under the pretense of calling for healing and unity, an entirely separate stage for black theatre artists. What next? Separate schools? Separate washrooms? Separate drinking fountains?

1996

More Noise Than Funk

(Bring in 'Da Noise, Bring in 'Da Funk)

Bring in 'Da Noise, Bring in 'Da Funk has been playing to packed houses at the New York Public Theater for some weeks now, and soon will be selling out on Broadway. Subtitled "A Tap/Dance Discourse on the Staying Power of the Beat," the evening has been conceived and directed by the talented George C. Wolfe and choreographed by the brilliant young dancer Savion Glover, who also performs. With four frenetic tappers pounding the stage floor to splinters, two galvanized drummers whacking away as if possessed, and a powerful jazz singer screeching at high decibel levels, the show has the capacity to induce a state of pandemonium, perhaps at the cost of your ear drums. At the performance I attended, people rose to their feet and roared, and I am bound to report that even those remaining seated seemed totally enthralled by the evening's dynamics.

But *Noise/Funk* aspires to be considerably more than a work of rousing entertainment. The trademark of the show is *'Da Beat* (as identified in an overhead stage projection). And with 'Da Beat serving as a metaphor for African-American history, and tap as its singular racial inheritance, the evening is less an exhibition of black talent than a chronicle of black oppression, viewed through the prism of jazz dance. As such, *Noise/Funk* had a profoundly dispiriting effect on me, for all its theatrical expertise.

Like George C. Wolfe's *The Colored Museum*, *Noise/Funk* is a structure of historical episodes with satirical overtones—but unlike that youthful work (or the playwright's more mature *Jelly's Last Jam*), it displays not a whit of self-satire or self-examination. Instead, blacks are consistently paraded before us as victims of racial prejudice, while their primary forms of expression—rhythm, jazz, and tap dancing—are treated as African inheritances expropriated for commercial purposes by a venal white society.

There is no evidence whatever in this marathon display of victimology that tap is one of the few forms of American popular culture unimpeded by race or ethnicity. But, as a matter of fact, tap dancing originated (in the nineteenth century) as a compound of many percussive dance styles—not only African but English, Irish, and Scotch as well. During the Jazz Age, black street kids (known as "pickaninnies") often used to back up white singers like Sophie Tucker and Cosie Smith, and many of them matured into vaudeville stars. But in addition to such fabled black tap dancers as Buck and Bubbles, the Nicholas Brothers, the Choclateers, Gregory Hines, the great Charles "Honi" Coles, and the immortal Bill "Bojangles" Robinson, tap was also the domain of many inspired white performers, notably Louis DaPron, Ruby Keeler, George Murphy, Ann Miller, Donald O'Connor, Fred Astaire, and Gene Kelly, among countless others.

Indeed, tap dancing was one of the very few expressions of American culture (jazz was another) that knew no racial divide. This is not to say, of course, that early show business was free of prejudice. All but a few blacks (celebrities like Ethel Waters, Joe Louis, and Bojangles himself) were habitually refused entrance to the Cotton Club, though it was situated right in the center of Harlem, on Lenox Avenue and 142nd Street. And it was years before black entertainers could perform on the vaudeville stage. But whatever their experience with prejudice, the early black entertainers were generally free of racial resentment. Leonard Reed, who invented the Shim Sham Shimmy, mingled with whites all his life and, except during his carnival days, rarely saw another black performer. His experience was not unusual. "I never thought of color," said the black dancer Willie Covan, "I honestly didn't think of no prejudice. White or colored. It didn't matter to me. No, all I thought about was dancin'."

Noise/Funk also thinks a lot about dancing, but what really obsesses its creators is color. In a satiric episode called "The Uncle Huck-a-Buck Song," a black hoofer (clearly modeled on Bill Robinson) has a dialogue with a white blonde doll called "Li'l Darlin'" (clearly modeled on Shirley Temple). The major issue between them is that Li'l Darlin' makes a lot more money than Uncle Huck-a-Buck. The truth is that the relationship between Bojangles and the child star Shirley Temple was one of intense mutual affection (and, yes, it is also true he always called her "darling"). Indeed, in the four films they made together, Robinson and Temple represented the first interracial couple in Hollywood history. Any resentment is the invention of latter-day revisionism where, in the mythology of modern black separatists, interracial friendship is either a form of Uncle Tomism or a façade concealing seething hatreds. Wolfe's Uncle Huck-a-Buck episode reminded me of LeRoi Jones's play *Jello* where Rochester threatens Jack Benny with a razor and steals all his money.

Wolfe satirizes whites not only for stealing black art forms but also for their own feeble cultural expressions. One brief moment, for example, features a particularly gleeful send-up of classical ballet, with one of the tappers getting up on his toes and mincing across the stage. But the best black tap dancers, artists like Fayard Nicholas for example, created a style that fused tap, fantastic acrobatics, and balletic leaps and turns, while Bill Robinson danced on his toes all the time. Fred Astaire's contribution to the form was his extraordinary capacity to unite the grace of ballroom dancing with the electric beat of tap. Even his walk—the springy lope of a cheetah preparing to run—was a special form of dance. And the late great Gene Kelly managed to combine the calisthenics of an acrobat with the athletic grace of a Martha Graham dancer, choreographing numbers with a cartoon mouse, with his own image, and with an umbrella while sloshing about in two inches of water.

Noise/Funk chooses to ignore these creative contributions, possibly because some have white origins, relying instead on a style of tap dancing that eventually comes to seem extremely repetitive. "In the beginning there was 'Da Beat," Wolfe's narrator declares at the start of the show as the sound of tapping is heard behind a blue show curtain. But 'Da Beat of *Noise/Funk* rarely varies in rhythm. This kind of beat is best described as "tap rap," because, like hip-hop, it is angry, staccato, and percussive, as if the dancers were stomping on the faces of their oppressors. (The music by Anne Duquesnay, Zane Mark, and Daryl Waters is similarly limited in its rhythm and melodic line.) As for the lyrics, and the narrative spoken by Reg E. Gaines, they are often rendered incomprehensible by the unbalanced mix of the amplification system. Too much coherent speech or song is swamped by the loud cadences of 'Da Beat. Through the hands and feet of the four ecstatic dancers and the two tireless drummers pummeling white plastic tubs, the cultural links with continental Africa are clearly established. But unlike tap rap, African drums were also a form of telegraphic communication.

In the beginning was 'Da Beat, in this revisionist version of *Genesis*, and in the beginning there were also slave ships, which begat whippings, lynchings, beggary, unemployment, imprisonment, drug addiction, race riots, lootings, and "burn baby burn"—in short, the epical history of racial injustice in white America. In its two-hour journey from the seventeenth century to the present, *Noise/Funk* leaves no racist issue untouched. Blacks are ordered off trolley cars by white conductors, dragged into the streets and beaten by white policemen, exploited by white businessmen. And they also resist the white power structure. A drug dealer testifies that he'd rather sell crack than work for the minimum wage. Al Sharpton and Louis Farrakhan make obligatory appearances (naturally, there is no mention of Martin Luther King).

All this is true but not the whole truth. *Noise/Funk* would have been a stronger work had it looked beyond its own narrow confines. It might have included some sign of how things have improved for some black people, some acknowledgment of the successes of the growing black middle classes, some hint of how blacks are now being represented in the universities, the media, and the professions. Oh yes, there is one character representing Colin Powell (and carrying his new book) who comes on stage to dance with street kids. But even he ends up giving the finger (to a passing taxicab). The evening concludes with the performers taking confessional turns, *Chorus Line*-style, to describe their personal histories, the influence of their families, and their debt to dancing ("Tap sort of like saved me"). No allusion to affirmative action, no evidence of any of the efforts being made by white society to atone for past injustices.

All of this is admittedly well performed by the cast, and expertly directed by Wolfe, using projections to facilitate his whirlwind trip through history. But the major effect of the evening is to reinforce the old stereotype that black folks have a great sense of rhythm. As for whites, they are left with a great and lonely sense of apartness. Aside from that little blonde doll, no nonblacks are represented in this expurgated History of Tap, and none is even mentioned except as a purveyor of oppression.

Of course large pockets of racism still exist in our country. But the entertainment world in general, and the theatre in particular, have been chief among those agencies trying to break down the remaining boundaries between the races. There is no doubt that some black leaders have been preaching separatism and exclusion, and one must concede that black anger sells very well these days to guilty white audiences. But there are other audiences, including some of those rising so readily to their feet at the close of *Noise/Funk*, who are beginning to find these ritual expressions of anger a little opportunistic and not a little boring.

Aside from being producer of one of the largest theatrical empires in the country, George C. Wolfe has participated in a number of high-royalty Broadway hits. Rather than take his instruction on the subject of racial inequality, we might do well to listen to Ellen Stewart of La Mama, a black woman who has fought all her life to preserve her fragile but invaluable theatrical enterprise—with very little help from the white liberal society. Indeed, the Carter administration sliced her NEA funding in half because they didn't find it "American" enough.

"Many times I have been called in and asked," Stewart said in a recent interview, " 'Why don't you do more for your race? You could be funded differently. Why don't you do so-called American playwrights?' But I think in world terms. I believe we are one race, and everybody is in that race." That kind of thinking, which refuses to make distinctions among artists on the basis of color or nationality or gender, which insists on inclusion rather than exclusion, is hardly fashionable with the current tribalism known as multiculturalism and cultural diversity. But it represents, as *Noise/Funk* does not, the only kind of thinking that can prepare the way for great art and build the path to a reconciled society.

1996

On Cultural Power

It might seem a little disingenuous for Theatre Communications Group, the sponsor of the occasion, to have called the Town Hall meeting between August Wilson and me a "discussion" rather than a debate, when the differences between us, particularly on the subjects of nontraditional casting and the place of black artists in the American theatre, have already been so hotly and publicly contested. But we are not really having a debate in the sense that any one man can score enough points to prevail over the other. The issues that divide us are so complicated, and have been around for so long in so many different guises, that nobody can hope to end an argument that has gone unresolved for centuries. It is our moderator Anna Deavere Smith's hope that we can come a little closer to each other's position through reasoned understanding. That is my hope too.

All of the disagreements expressed by August Wilson and myself are perceived to be over the emphasis on race in the American theatre. In a sense this is true, but in another sense, to reduce these differences to racial categories is to regard them too narrowly. Actually I believe our argument boils down to a philosophical dispute over the basic function of dramatic art. If I understand Mr. Wilson's position correctly, he regards theatre partly as an avenue to political and cultural power—a medium through which a large disadvantaged class can dramatize its past injustices and perhaps find redress through changes in the social or political system. This activist view of art has had a long and honorable history, dating back at least to Plato, who believed that the function of the artist—when that Greek idealist allowed the artist any function at all—was to create ethical models of character behavior which would help humankind evolve toward the ideal republic.

Aristotle in his *Poetics* rejected this idea, believing that the best drama, by which he meant tragedy, was essentially cathartic rather than activist in nature, being based on action that is fated rather than on character, which can be subject to change. I incline toward Aristotle's repudiation of Plato's political view of art. We have had some sour experience in the twentieth century regarding efforts to regulate or improve human nature through the agency of a political system: Nazi Germany, Soviet Russia, Iran under the Ayatollah, to name a few. Starting with Plato, who banished the artist from his ideal Republic, utopianists, even the best of them, have usually ended by suppressing free artistic expression. "All revolutions," as Eugene Ionesco wrote, "burn the libraries of Alexandria." Today in America we see a similar development in what is called political correctness—which in its overzealous crusade to purge our language of offensive terms sometimes seems to be leading to what one critic has called "freedom *from* speech."

Out of a conviction that freedom *of* speech is essential to creative invention and critical thought, a number of modern artists, both black and white, *whatever their beliefs as citizens of the state*, have rejected the concept of art as an ideological instrument. Ideological art is dedicated either to reinforcing the existing power structure (as in totalitarian regimes) or (as in most activist revolutionary expression) reforming and changing it. The alternative to ideological art was eloquently summed up by the Czech novelist Milan Kundera, when he said that his primary artistic function was to speak truth to power. *Speaking truth to power!* Isn't that why we revere the greatest dramatists from Aristophanes to Athol Fugard—and isn't that one of the reasons we cherish Shakespeare despite his incorrigible need to flatter the reigning English monarchs? Each of these writers displayed the courage to speak truth to power. Such truth tellers help to give physic to pomp and expose the corruptions of authority by revealing the reality behind human action and human motive—in short, the workings of the human soul, which has no color.

The great black writer James Baldwin, at least early in his career, also believed in speaking truth to power. In an essay called "Everybody's Protest Novel," he wrote, "Let us say that truth is meant to imply a devotion to the human being.... It is not to be confused with a devotion to a Cause; and Causes, as we know, are notoriously bloodthirsty." Note that neither Baldwin nor Kundera seems much interested in using the artistic process to *achieve* power. Indeed, behind their words is the implication that the true artist must shun power, because power systems are not only *not* instruments of truth. They may very well be the enemies of truth. Those who believe in art as a political weapon, as a method of empowering the disadvantaged, no doubt serve a useful social function. But sometimes at a cost. A passionate political purpose occasionally obliges these artists, in my opinion, to sacrifice individual truth for the collective good.

Of course, it is possible to justify such choices if the right ends are achieved. But look at the downside. While the arts at best are inclusive, ideological art is exclusive. The spectator is pressured to reach conclusions, coerced into choosing sides. Political art is usually a persuasive form of melodrama, the opposition of right and wrong—or shall we say black and white?—when the truth is usually grey. Any large group with a common purpose—whether it calls itself a commune, a community, a collective, a society, or a nation—has difficulty tolerating those nuances and subtleties and complications that characterize the search for the truth. Reality lies in the shadows rather than the sunlight, and large groups need certainty, not ambiguity. It was Bernard Shaw who told us, "Forty million Frenchmen *can't* be right." And it was Anton Chekhov, claiming to be "a free artist and nothing more," who said that his artistic obligation was not "to solve problems but simply to present them correctly."

I believe that the artist must be free to speak truth to political power, and that means black power as well. August Wilson stimulated considerable debate in his keynote address at the TCG conference in June by announcing that he was a "race man" who aligned himself with such separatists as Marcus Garvey and the Honorable Elijah Muhammad. He criticized certain unidentified black "crossover artists" who "like house slaves entertaining the white master and his guests," as he put it, prefer to "slant their material for white consumption." He properly applauded the achievements of black theatre professionals and correctly lamented the small number of professional black theatres in this country. But in perhaps his most controversial statement he called on all black actors to repudiate nontraditional or "color-blind casting" as "the same idea of assimilation that black Americans have been rejecting for the past 380 years."

Following the unicultural path Mr. Wilson has mapped out may prove a useful way to achieve black power. The question is whether it is the best advice to offer black theatre professionals who may not wish to cripple their careers for the sake of racial exclusivity.

My reply to Mr. Wilson's TCG speech was partly an effort to defend the rights of these artists to choose freely. It was also partly an effort to defend myself. In the same speech Mr. Wilson, hinting that I was racist, tried to paint me as an enemy of multiculturalism, as one who believes African-American theatre artists to be inferior, and as a Eurocentric critic adamantly opposed to black theatre. These charges are categorically false. My writings and actions are clear testimony to my support for the richness of multiculturalism so long as it is not a pretext for promoting race hatred or generating separatism. In my own career as founder and director of two nonprofit theatres, and as leader of training programs at Yale and Harvard, I have helped develop a number of gifted black artists, including such playwrights as OyamO, Lonnie Elder III, and Edgar White, such black directors as Walter Dallas (now head of Philadelphia's Freedom Theatre and the first director of Wilson's *Seven Guitars*), such black actors as Ben Halley, Jr., Franchelle Stewart Dorn, Charles Turner, Herb Downer, Starla Benford, David Allen Grier, and many others. In various Yale Repertory Theatre and American Repertory Theatre productions, I have worked with such black artists as Courtney Vance, Royal Miller, Maggie Rush, Rosalind Cash, Carmen de Lavallade, Cheryl Sutton, Lisa Vidal, Gilbert Price, Charles "Honi" Coles, Norman Matlock, Larry Marshall, and scores of others, many of them regular members of my resident companies. My theatres have produced or presented works by Suzan-Lori Parks, Derek Walcott, Adrienne Kennedy, the Negro Ensemble Company, and Anna Deavere Smith, many of whom I have also championed as a critic. Our commitment to color-blind nontraditional casting has been so stubborn and passionate that we risked being closed down through a court action by Samuel Beckett when he objected to our casting black company members Ben Halley and Rodney Scott Hudson in the ART production of *Endgame*.

While it is true I have not been enthusiastic about some of Mr. Wilson's plays, this is not the record of a person who denigrates the achievements of black artists. I salute these achievements both in black theatres and in mainstream theatres. And I find it not racist but the very opposite to demand the critic's right to apply the same standards to black theatre professionals as to anyone else.

I agree with August Wilson's appeal for more black theatres, though it is not entirely accurate to say that black theatre is discriminated against in America because only one out of sixty-six League of Resident Theatres can be called black. While the statistic is accurate, there are almost four hundred non-LORT theatres in the country that enjoy TCG membership, scores of which are black and receive funding from the National Endowment and other foundation sources (including Penumbra in St. Paul, where many of Mr. Wilson's works have been staged in secondary productions). I support his plea that foundations be more supportive of such theatres, assuming they have established records. This is a better course for the funding agencies than pouring their multicultural dollars into efforts to "diversify" the audiences of mainstream theatres. In fact, I strongly believe in general operating grants for all theatres of proven quality. But this support cannot be viewed as a form of entitlement. Black theatres should earn their foundation and corporate funding by the same criteria of value and community support as any other. If Mr. Wilson knows of a worthy black theatre that isn't being properly funded, he could give it instant recognition by rewarding it with one of his world premieres.

Although I see value in theatres that confine themselves to plays by black writers, I admit some difficulty in approving Mr. Wilson's appeal for the self-segregation of black artists in racial enclaves. If these artists excluded themselves from what Mr. Wilson calls the "Cultural Imperialists" and their "so-called classical values of European theatre," we would have been denied some very great performances, which represent the manifold achievements of nontraditional casting and true interculturalism. In fact, we would have been denied August Wilson's plays, all of which have been produced by the very mainstream nonprofit theatres he refers to as "Cultural Imperialists."

I had thought from certain of his recent letters and remarks that August Wilson would have liked to modify his position. If so, there would have been no "debate" between us. But he now seems as adamant as ever on the subject of excluding blacks from plays written by whites. However, since he recently denied ever saying he would never work with a white director, I must remind him of his 1990 op-ed piece in the *New York Times* called "I Want a Black Director," in which he refused to allow *Fences* to be filmed by a white man, adding this caveat: "Let's make a rule. Blacks don't direct Italian films. Italians don't direct Jewish films. Jews don't direct black American films." Wilson also extended this "rule" to his works for the theatre—rejecting Seattle Rep's Daniel Sullivan, for example, simply because he was white—out of a belief that only blacks could understand what he called "the specifics of the culture of black Americans." But, as a matter of fact, one of the best artworks I ever saw about the black experience was a film called *Fresh*. It was directed by an Israeli named Boaz Yakin. I suspect Mr. Wilson will call this an expropriation of black culture, as he once called George Gershwin's *Porgy and Bess* "a bastardizing of our music and our people." But the truth is not subject to racial generalizations, however they serve the aims of power. Indeed, in seeking to combat stereotypes, such generalizations may create another form of error, one that the black thinker Albert Murray called the "fallacy" of one man believing he can speak for his entire race. Many people in this country, including Mr. Wilson himself, are of mixed blood, and Eugene O'Neill, among others, has dramatized the tragic consequences of denying aspects of one's inheritance.

If no one person can speak for black Americans, no one person can speak for white people either. There is no such thing as a monolithic "Eurocentric" culture. The greatest modern European artists, like August Wilson himself, have almost invariably been rebels against the existing culture, not its proselytes and flunkies. I wrote a whole book about this, over thirty years ago, called *The Theatre of Revolt*. One of the subjects of that book, Jean Genet, when asked by an actor to write a play for blacks, replied, "But what exactly is a black? First of all, what's his color?" The same question might be asked about whites.

I understand how Wilson could fall into the ethnographic fallacy. I did the same thing myself not too long ago in a belief that the leading character in my musical *Shlemiel the First* could be played only by a Jew. Actually a truly wonderful Shlemiel, one who far exceeded my expectations for the part, proved to be a Gentile member of our company, the Maine-born Baptist Thomas Derrah, just as one of the most convincingly Jewish of the sages in that show was Vontress Mitchell, a black company member. It is a principle of theatrical art that it defies generalizations, being subject, like life itself, to surprises, reversals, and contradictions. General truths, Ibsen told us, have a shelf life of about twenty years, after which they become just as tired and worn out as any other convention. We speak a lot these days of cultural diversity, but true diversity lies in acknowledging that every human being is an individual, and not simply a member of a racial, ethnic, or sexual group. The variety of these individual differences is what bonds us all to the human family.

Ultimately, of course, the quarrel between Mr. Wilson and myself is not just over the function of art or the function of race in the theatre. It is over larger issues of inclusion versus exclusion, of integration versus separatism, of racial brotherhood versus racial division, which is to say the way of Martin Luther King and his followers versus the way of the young Malcolm X, Louis Farrakhan, and the Nation of Islam.

A great gulf still divides the races in this country, despite the significant strides of the last thirty years. It is an obligation of all men and women of goodwill to try to bridge that gulf and complete the still unfinished racial business of our nation. But I believe America will only begin to fulfill its promise when we acknowledge that we are individuals first, Americans second, and tribalists third, when we recognize that we are all the same species under the skin, when we understand that all human beings are responsible for each other, every mother's child.

Following our debate, Mr. Wilson announced that he was giving his early play Jitney *to the Crossroads Theatre in New Brunswick, a black resident company, before circulating it to mainstream theatres on its way to Broadway. I am cheered that something positive came out of our encounter.*

1997

Slate Diary #1

Wednesday, March 12

Yesterday a weighty log arrived from Theatre Communications Group, the sponsor of last January's debate between August Wilson and me at Town Hall. It contained scores of reports on the event from a great variety of newspapers and magazines. Leafing through this huge mass of Xeroxes made me realize, with a start, that the real quarrel was not between Wilson and me but rather between the two of us and the media. How difficult it is to get anything more than the simplest ideas reported accurately in the press. I was reminded of Arnold Weinstein's classic remark, upon refusing to be interviewed by a reporter, that the issue in question was too complicated "to survive the epistemological vicissitudes of journalism."

I can't speak for Wilson, but I just don't recognize my own position from the variety of reports in the *New York Times*, aside from William Grimes's objective account the morning after the debate. Paul Goldberger first muddied the waters in an earlier interview by imputing to me a belief that there was no place for all-black theatres in America. This he disputed, as well he might. So do I, as I made clear to him during the interview and later on in the debate.

Frank Rich weighed in a few days later in an op-ed column. Aside from calling us both "humorless," "decadent," "egomaniacal," and "tone-deaf," Rich rebuked me for "bragging about how many black people he has known." I had actually listed the black artists I had trained and worked with at my theatre, in an effort to illustrate the importance of color-blind casting. Rich's most puzzling charge is that in discussing racial issues, Wilson and I were ignoring the low estate of the American stage, when that is precisely what we have both devoted our lives to trying to improve.

1997

Slate Diary #2

Thursday, March 13

Additional material in today's mail suggested that there are others, besides Frank Rich, with a special agenda regarding the debate between August Wilson and me. The *Village Voice*, for example, dispatched four reporters to rebuke us for not debating the place of gays, lesbians, Asians, women, and other minorities in the theatre, a fifth later finding me guilty of being "old, misguided, and white." I humbly confess to most of these impurities; I promise to try to avoid them in the future.

The theatre journalist for the *Boston Globe* resented the fact that the debate had not been more contentious, and then, in a follow-up piece, grumbled (unconscious of any contradiction) that neither Wilson nor I had embraced the other's position. She was hardly alone in that last complaint. Dozens of commentators seemed unable to grasp the fact that, in Wilson's insistence on black actors working only in black theatres, and my call for nontraditional casting as well, we held conflicting points of view that could not be reconciled. But then we live in a country that believes not so much in teaching people how to swim as in advising them how to "get along" in the water, where togetherness is more valued than practice or principle.

A handful of analysts—among them Jack Kroll of *Newsweek*, Stanley Crouch of the *New York Daily News*, and John Simon of *New York* magazine—had no trouble grasping the issues. And it was comforting to receive strong supporting letters from a number of black intellectuals. But the great majority of commentators saw the debate through the prism of their own interests and ideologies. (Admittedly, so did I.) I've been criticized, by a growing crowd of relativists, for believing in universal values and embracing a single standard for art. The reports on the debate have forced me to admit the futility of sustaining artistic criteria in a politically correct age. Oh, the truth is out there, of course. And posterity no doubt will tell us what is valuable in the past, for history is the ultimate critic and arbiter. But our own time is almost totally blinded by subjective points of view.

1997

The Smashing of the Bell

Two tiny federal agencies, the pitifully underfunded National Endowment for the Arts and the National Endowment for the Humanities, are facing imminent extinction from mutinous Republican legislators, toadying to a rampaging Christian right. On July 14, 1995, Bastille Day, modern Jacobins in the House of Representatives (whose Committee for Public Safety is now called the Contract with America) took an irretrievable step. They agreed to a freshmen-sponsored proposal to the Interior Appropriations Bill that offered to make 40 percent cuts in the 1996 budgets and decapitate the Endowments entirely within two years. Meetings between the two legislative bodies might prolong the agony of these agencies a little longer, but, for all intents and purposes, the NEA and the NEH have been guillotined. Next on the block are the NEA- and NEH-sponsored achievements of the past thirty years. It is the end of a remarkable experiment, which for a time helped persuade the world that, despite itself and against all odds, our country might finally develop a civilization we could be proud of.

I no longer have the heart to argue the importance of government subsidy, however minimal, to the creative and intellectual life of this nation. After twenty-five years of disputation, my pen has run dry and my throat has gone hoarse. After auspicious beginnings and encouraging annual increases, we have watched the appropriations for the Endowments freeze, then diminish, and now disappear altogether. The mindless budget-cutting of this Republican Congress is making some of us ashamed to be Americans.

Both Chairman Sheldon Hackney of the NEH and Chairwoman Jane Alexander of the NEA are gracious and able personalities, who have worked tirelessly to save their agencies from the axe. But after meeting with each of them on a recent visit to Washington, after talking to their staffs, and after reading their brochures, I began to understand better why their efforts to save the Endowments were ultimately doomed to failure. The fact is that for the last two decades neither of these agencies has been allowed to establish or articulate a clear-cut policy or definition. Periodic hostages to congressional authorization and reappropriation, they were always prey to external pressures, whether from the left, in the form of multicultural panels with political agendas, or from the right, in the form of anticultural puritans with moral agendas, or simply from congressional demands to distribute funds on the basis of geography rather than merit. Gripped by a populist frenzy, few in Congress or the nation were equipped to appreciate the intrinsic importance of the arts and the humanities.

In recognition of this melancholy fact, the public testimony and published materials of Endowment chairpeople were always likely to emphasize not quality, excellence, imagination, and inspiration as criteria for funding, but rather such peripheral benefits as access, dissemination, bookbinding, inner-city outreach, arts education, and the impact of the arts and humanities on the local economy (hotels, parking lots, and restaurants). "The NEH is about democracy," wrote Hackney in an eloquent pamphlet called *Lasting Values in a Disposable World*, "about equal access and participation by the many, not the few." One understands the necessity for such populist rhetoric, and, of course, wide distribution is the goal of every artist and thinker. But not every great creative or critical work can generate immediate mass appeal.

The National Institutes of Health and the National Institute of Science do not have to apologize for distributing grants to scientists and researchers. Most laypeople understand how they eventually benefit from basic research. But forced to demonstrate their value to "the many, not the few," the NEH and NEA invariably have had to trot out wide-audience programs (like television documentaries) to justify their existence. In the rare cases when individual advances in art or intellect are mentioned, they are invariably encrypted within large invocations to "the human spirit" and "the human heritage."

This kind of elevated verbal reinforcement is the lingua franca of cultural administrators (I am often forced to use it myself). But if the importance of the arts and humanities is still not clear to this nation thirty years after the creation of the Endowments, then the struggle to preserve them is obviously hopeless. Who has been listening all this time? Who has been reading? Who has been thinking? In his office in the Old Post Office Building, the mild-mannered Sheldon Hackney has two warning signs: "Thou Shalt Not Whine" and "No Sniveling." I believe he has every right now to whine, snivel, scream, and stamp his foot. Certainly, delivering courteous speeches about the human spirit and the human heritage to people who believe the only function of government is to cut spending and reduce taxes is about as useful as reading Hegel to orangutans.

Anyway, it is clear that most legislators don't want to hear about the value of the Endowments. They just want to hear about their scandals. The thousands of NEA grants to symphonies, museums, and opera, dance, and theatre companies are of far less importance to them than a few hundred dollars transferred from a sheltering organization to a controversial performance artist, while the accomplishments of the NEH in furthering scholarship, criticism, and even TV documentaries fade before the single contested award for the establishment of history standards in the schools (an effort ironically initiated by the NEH's former chairwoman and currently fiercest critic, Lynne Cheney).

In the face of such persistent misrepresentation of their function, one wonders how Congress kept these agencies alive for so long. But a major difference between the past and now is that John F. Kennedy, Lyndon B. Johnson, and even Richard Nixon were willing to speak out fervently on behalf of the arts and humanities, while Bill Clinton uses the word "arts" as infrequently as Ronald Reagan used the word "AIDS." (It is true that Hillary did make one speech about the importance of the arts to the human spirit and the local economy that found its way onto the op-ed page of the *Times*.) Will Clinton veto the Interior Appropriations Bill? Certainly not for the sake of the NEH or the NEA, and not if the same lack of principle that weakens the president's foreign policy decisions hobbles or wobbles his domestic actions. His every move is measured by the armies of voters it might conscript, and the arts and humanities have fewer divisions than the pope.

Into this leadership vacuum has swarmed the budget-cutting servants of the religious right who, after the collapse of the Soviet Union, began to replace internal enemies like the Communists and their fellow travelers with artists and intellectuals, which is to say anyone still capable of independent thought. In the heated fantasies of conservatives, prefaces to arts catalogues replaced *Das Kapital* as demonized texts, and avant-garde artists like Robert Mapplethorpe, Andres Serrano, and Karen Finley assumed the subversive roles once assigned to Alger Hiss and the Rosenbergs.

Considering the hatred attracted by these individual artists, it might just have been possible to preserve the Endowments had they agreed to shut off funding to anything considered even mildly avant-garde or controversial. This desperate strategem was actually attempted under former NEA Chairman John Frohnmayer, with his notorious anti-obscenity pledge, until the courts ruled it unconstitutional. But aside from being an improper use of prior restraint, such an action would have effectively undermined a central purpose of the Endowments, which was not only to encourage established institutions and traditional scholarship but to help nudge forward the boundaries of art and thought. It is easy enough to celebrate such custodial NEH functions as editing and publishing the papers of Franklin, Washington, Jefferson, and Martin Luther King. But where is the dynamic critical reinterpretation that sheds new light on traditional texts? Similarly, "cutting edge" artists may be identified with the Antichrist in the minds of some legislators, but without them art would have no future.

It is the natural consequence of experimentation in the arts that it lead to occasional failure, of course, even to occasional scandal, though this has occurred far less frequently than reported. At the NEA fewer than forty out of thousands of grants—forty!—proved even remotely controversial. Naturally these were the ones that Donald Wildmon of the American Family Association and his letter-writing ilk seized upon to inflame the minds of right-wing congressmen. But who has ever bothered to compare the magnitude of Endowment sins with those of less stigmatized government agencies? Is anyone (other than a few libertarians and militia groups) calling for the abolition of the FBI because of Waco, or of the CIA because of Aldrich Ames, or of the Congress because of its destructive legislative actions, not least among them the axing of the Endowments?

Is it excessive to remind ourselves of Mao Tse-tung's Cultural Revolution? In 1966 the People's Republic of China, also under the name of "democracy," ridiculed artistic and intellectual expression and humiliated artists and intellectuals as "elitist" bearers of foreign ideas. Losing a few dollars in federal subsidy is hardly the same as outright censorship, imprisonment, or worse, but for artistic and intellectual institutions in this country economic strangulation can be just as lethal. The consequences will certainly be the same—the dumbing down of the entire nation.

Obviously individual poets, novelists, and scholars can always support their intellectual and creative habits by working at other jobs. T. S. Eliot found employment in a bank. Wallace Stevens helped run an insurance company. Faulkner and Fitzgerald went to Hollywood. But dance groups cannot take jobs in banks, or theatre companies find refuge in insurance offices. And it is nonsense to believe that private funds, which have been diminishing lately rather than increasing (and which are largely reserved for multicultural projects anyway), will compensate for the growing deficits caused by the collapse of the Endowments.

It doesn't take a prophet to see that we face the imminent loss of countless artistic and intellectual institutions, particularly the smaller ones, some of which depend for as much as 10 percent of their budgets on Endowment support. Oh, the dinosaurs will survive of course—cultural bastions like the Metropolitan Museum, the Boston Symphony, the San Francisco Opera. But a relatively modest company (like my own American Repertory Theatre in Cambridge, for example) will be able to sustain another major cut in subsidy only by doubling its ticket prices. This will make the theatre truly "elitist" in the sense that only the rich will now be able to afford a seat. To justify these high prices, the fare will inevitably become more commercial, thus completing a process, already widely advanced, of erasing the distinction between the nonprofit world, which is at least nominally devoted to art, and the profit world, which is entirely driven by the market. And the effort to build an alternative cultural system—democratic in the true sense of being available to anyone with an appetite for the imagination—will have come to an end.

One cannot begin to describe the climate of demoralization among those who have been struggling over the years to educate the minds and stimulate the imaginations of American citizens. Those efforts were experiencing considerable success, even in the theatre. Serious audiences were growing, serious playwrights were multiplying, and our country was finally developing a reputable culture. The Endowments were essential, not just for their comparatively small grants, not just because they helped to generate private funds from sluggish foundations, corporations, and individuals. They were important because at their best they served as the conscience of the field. Without them we are left to contemplate a culture without guidance, principle, or purpose.

This is a particularly squalid moment in our history, a moment filled with defeat and desolation. Running through my head is a passage in *Three Sisters* in which Chekhov compares Andrei Prozorov to a beautiful expensive bell, raised and educated with the help of countless people, then carelessly allowed to fall and smash. Lacking the financial support and the moral example of the Endowments, it will take at least another thirty years to raise such a bell again. But long before that time, thanks to our duly elected representatives, we will have regained our position as the dumbest and most Philistine democracy in the Western world.

1995

The Death of the Collective Ideal

Following a rampage by mutinous freshmen legislators in July, the Senate and the House have begun haggling over whether to eliminate the National Endowment for the Arts entirely, or simply to render it totally ineffective. After the House voted to slash the NEA budget to $99 million and axe it in two years, the Senate raised appropriations to $110 million without announcing a termination date. That sounds like an improvement, but Republican senators, in collusion with a number of Democrats, hedged the bill with so many "shalt nots" that it is doubtful any self-respecting artistic institution could live with it.

Amendments to the Senate version submitted by Jesse Helms (and endorsed, surprisingly, by Edward Kennedy) not only propose that nonprofit grantees agree to an obscenity clause barring offensive sexual representation, but forswear all subjects that "denigrate religion." A lower court ruling some years ago on similar NEA restrictions found them unconstitutional (the Clinton Justice Department is still considering whether to appeal that decision). Yet our legislators, like dysfunctional children who keep misreading the same passages over and over again, continue to misinterpret or disregard the intentions of the Founding Fathers.

Still more troubling, there are signs that the current Supreme Court may choose to disregard these intentions as well.* The Court's decision on Reagan's infamous "gag" rule, for example, found that the government was not suspending any freedoms by barring certain rights—the right (in this *Rust v. Sullivan* case) to discuss abortion in

---

*In June 1998 the Supreme Court actually did proceed to overturn the lower court's decision, ruling 8 to 1 that the obscenity clause in the NEA bill was indeed constitutional. In short, the First Amendment does not apply to the arts.

federally funded hospitals. Hospitals were always "free" not to accept federal funds. If the Helms restrictions are adopted by the full Congress, and supported by the Courts, refusing funds may be one of the last "freedoms" left to artists and artistic institutions. For some of us it will certainly be the only honorable option. Should my own theatre agree to these restrictions, for example, we would be obliged to cancel our season—at least three of our five proposed offerings, most notably Molière's *Tartuffe*, could be easily construed as "denigrating religion."

Indeed, for a few difficult years, and despite his friendship with Louis XIV, Molière got in deep trouble over that very same issue. Come to think of it, so did independent thinkers throughout history. On similar charges of "denigrating religion," Socrates was given hemlock, Jesus suffered on the Cross, Galileo faced excommunication, and Salman Rushdie is still being stalked by Iranian assassins. Have Jesse Helms and his Christian right cohorts forgotten that one of the reasons their ancestors came to this country was to seek refuge from narrow religious constraints? They are certainly ignoring the fact that our Constitution is founded on the separation of church and state.

If these issues are not soon resolved in a rational fashion, we must prepare ourselves for the death of the nonprofit cultural movement in America as we know it. Already a number of companies, mostly in dance (and notably the Joffrey Ballet), are throwing in the towel. Many deficit-ridden theatres will soon follow suit. And we may even lose some of our less-well-endowed opera companies, symphonies, and museums. The death of the nonprofit movement should come as no surprise. The remarkable thing is that it has managed to survive this long, considering how inimical the idea of not putting profit first has always been to the American system of values.

The concept of a culture driven by art and inspiration rather than by the cash register, a culture dependent on collective efforts rather than personal celebrity, always had a vaguely foreign ring to it. It challenged our traditional commitment to individualism, ignored the lure of the marketplace, perhaps even smelled of socialism, for God's sake. It was, therefore, only a matter of time before we would consign it to the same dustbin as the quaint old notion that in a civilized society we are all mutually responsible for one another.

I mention social welfare and cultural support together because it is no coincidence that the nonprofit movement in this country evolved and flourished during the same years as Kennedy's New Frontier and Johnson's Great Society (and, earlier, Roosevelt's New Deal). What they all shared was a common belief in community and a joint sense that, despite the generosity of private philanthropists, the only agency likely to show consistent concern for the well-being of most Americans was the government. Without federal involvement we would inevitably be reduced—as now we are—to a state of nature, which is to say a condition of unregulated greed and officially endorsed rapacity.

I don't mean to suggest that all those in the nonprofit sector are self-denying public servants. Creative expression is hardly selfless, and the creative life is famously driven by egoism and temperament. It has often been argued that the level of self-love among artists is higher than among most other mortals, which may help explain why in this country they are often the objects of such resentment. How many other Americans make their living performing tasks that satisfy their ego needs?

On the other hand, for years nonprofit artists found a way to sublimate impulses that might otherwise be construed as narcissistic into performances that entertained and stimulated audiences. Not on a mass scale—that appeal belonged to movie stars and rock idols—but rather on a local level where their following, if smaller, was often equally intense. It was in tight cohesive communities that actors, directors, singers, dancers, musicians, and performance artists were sufficiently valued to allow them to subordinate their individual careerism and undertake communal efforts on behalf of the public.

This at least was the declared purpose of the nonprofit membership, which in its ideal state flourished only for a few years. It was not long after—in the recession-driven seventies and eighties—that the marketplace began to compete for the talents of artists and artistic institutions and, more often than not, succeeded in winning them. I'm really talking about the theatre, which, though the weakest of the nonprofit structures, was nevertheless the movement's single innovation. Dance stayed relatively free of commercial incursions, having no great mass appeal (which may explain why dance companies are now the most seriously threatened by the collapse of federal funding).

Symphony orchestras, though also limited in popularity, were always fairly well supported by their communities. And the opera world was often buttressed by international stars with huge followings. Nonprofit theatre, on the other hand, almost from the beginning, was prey to the music of the marketplace, whether it called itself the lullaby of Broadway or the Hollywood serenade.

These commercial melodies were a form of pressure on the theatre to reclaim its seat on the Great White Way. Before World War II even the Group Theatre, for all its collective idealism, had to organize itself on a Broadway-oriented, box-office basis in order to survive (it survived for less than ten years). Only in the fifties and sixties, with the rise of such companies as the Arena in Washington, the Guthrie in Minneapolis, and the Trinity Rep in Providence, did the nonprofit theatre begin to challenge the hegemony of Broadway in a significant way, spreading into virtually every major urban center in the land.

Federal funding in alliance with corporate and individual contributions, private foundations, and subscription income had been responsible for the evolution of more than four hundred institutional theatres. Many of these employed permanent acting ensembles, performing—in the manner of dance and opera companies—in rotating repertory. But soon the fickle fashions of funding turned away from the theatre—or at least from general operating support—leaving these institutions with only one dependable source of funds, and only one artistic conscience, the NEA. Ranging from 1 to 10 percent of a theatre's budget, however, federal grants were never large enough to protect nonprofit theatres from deficits, and instead of increasing the NEA budget to compensate for other disappearing sources, government money was rapidly diminishing.

A few cities—notably Minneapolis, Chicago, Washington, San Francisco, and Louisville—were sufficiently proud of their theatres to support them properly. Many others began to founder. Before long these theatres were looking for alternative forms of survival—partnerships, bookings, retail shops, and corporate alliances equivalent to commercial announcements on National Public Radio. The most popular and lucrative approach—with Papp's *Chorus Line* as the significant model—was to transfer successful productions to the commercial theatre. Depending on the extent of control the originating theatre had over production, this was a marginally acceptable alternative to bankruptcy. (At least it was making money the old-fashioned way—by earning it.) Still, the search for potential Broadway product was largely responsible for a growing lack of risk in scheduling seasons. It certainly spelled the end of permanent companies among all but a handful of resident institutions. New York transfers broke the ranks of actors, shook their faith in the ideals of the company, and sent them into a commercial exile from which few were likely to return. Today the number of good actors available for company work is pitifully small.

The result of all this is a theatre in disarray, uncertain of its purpose, unclear about its identity, insecure about its survival, a theatre too weakened to lead its audiences and too confused to follow them. The future of nonprofit theatres in this country appears to be increasing commercialization, trivialization, or balkanization—in short, the end of the collective ideal. Meanwhile the media, in their ignorance of how the artistic process really functions and their insatiable hunger for product to write about, keep clamoring for hits which, in the present climate, are less and less likely to be produced.

It has often been said that every civilization gets the theatre it deserves. What we seem to be getting, through the crush of ineluctable social, economic, and legislative forces, is a theatre that will survive only by reverting to its former function as a watering hole for tired businessmen—appropriate enough for a nation whose elected representatives seem passionate only on behalf of businessmen and business interests.

1995

Gardens and Showcases

Years ago Robert Anderson remarked that a playwright can't make a living on Broadway, only a killing. For decades now, serious writers haven't even been able to make a killing. The commercial theatre may still be considered New York's primary tourist attraction, but out-of-town visitors largely patronize musical spectaculars. By the end of this season only eight straight plays will have opened on Broadway, and only one will have managed to recoup its initial investment.

As a result, the Broadway Initiatives Working Group—a consortium of theatre unions, commercial producers, and theatre owners working with the blessings of the city—is now trying to restore Broadway's former eminence as an incubator of new plays by reducing the risks to private capital investors. Chief among the suggestions being floated are tax abatements by the federal, state, and city governments. The city has already waived its commercial rent tax on Broadway theatres for the first year of a production. Now the Working Group seeks similar abatements on the taxing of sets, costumes, and properties, along with permission to sell the air rights over New York theatres.

Anything that can help the ailing Broadway economy should be welcomed. The question remains whether indirect subsidies to Broadway, however desirable for encouraging investments and increasing profits, is the proper way to ignite the creative spirit. It has been over thirty years since Broadway last functioned as a mecca for new plays, despite intermittent efforts to recapture the past. The Broadway Alliance, for example, gaining concessions from theatre owners and unions, managed to lower ticket prices on straight plays in the hope of attracting adventurous audiences. The result? Of the nine works produced under that contract, only two Terrence Mc-

Nally plays (*Love! Valour! Compassion!* and *Master Class*) returned their initial investment.

The independent producer Stuart Ostrow was able to create a commercial success out of David Henry Hwang's *M. Butterfly* without first trying it out in a noncommercial venue. But Ostrow's next Hwang play, *Face Value*, barely made it to Broadway. And while August Wilson's *Fences* and *The Piano Lesson* were modest hits, all of Wilson's other plays lost money for investors, despite Pulitzer Prizes and Critics Circle Awards. Even the hugely acclaimed *Angels in America* ended up in the red, primarily because of expensive rehearsal procedures. Rocco Landesman of Jujamcyn Theatres, along with James B. Freydberg and Max Weitzenhoffer, recently commissioned nine lively playwrights to write plays for the commercial stage. Four were delivered; three were staged by resident theatres; none found its way to Broadway.

If playwrights have become skeptical about their chances on Broadway, the problem lies with demographics. The audiences that used to flock to *Death of a Salesman* and *A Streetcar Named Desire* have either moved to Florida or transferred their allegiance to the Manhattan Theatre Club and the New York Public Theater, among other off-Broadway institutions. Fifty percent of the patrons for Broadway's new musicals come from out of town, a number that increases to 80 percent for the long-running blockbusters. As for native New Yorkers, if they show up at all, they usually limit patronage to works that celebrate their separate ethnic, racial, or sexual identities.

Perhaps it is time to acknowledge that, having lost its traditional audience, Broadway will never again be a home for new plays. Perhaps it is time for funding agencies to reconsider subsidies to the playwrights and to the off-Broadway theatres that were once in a better position to support them. It is true that the Working Group has invited three institutional theatres to join its consortium. Even that gesture is less for the purpose of encouraging creative experiment than for reducing financial risk.

Some may find it curious, in a period when the cultural buzz word is "privatization," that the for-profit theatre should be requesting indirect public subsidies for the sake of encouraging private investment. In the current climate, fellowships for playwrights have declined by 60 percent, and institutional theatres are languishing from dwindling federal and foundation grants. There was a time when individual playwrights received substantial help from a variety of sources, when resident theatres received major support for the development and presentation of new work. Out of those halcyon days came such dramatists as Jack Gelber, Edward Albee, Sam Shepard, David Rabe, David Mamet, Adrienne Kennedy, Arthur Kopit, Christopher Durang, Craig Lucas, Marsha Norman, and countless others—not to mention such innovative musicals as *Hair* and *A Chorus Line*, and, more recently, *Rent* and *Bring in 'Da Noise, Bring in 'Da Funk*.

Few of these artists' works were developed with the thought of profit or moving them to Broadway. But out of that creative ferment came the flowering of American theatre. If I may extend my overworked horticultural metaphor a little further, the playwright plants the seeds and the resident theatre nourishes the blossoms while Broadway, acting as the florist, occasionally plucks the splashiest bouquets. Everyone shares Broadway's nostalgia for its past glory. But it is getting things backward to renovate the flower shop while the plants are lying fallow for want of nurture and the seeds are beginning to rot for want of rain.

1996

Homogenized Diversity

(A Doll's House; How I Learned to Drive; Gross Indecency)

It's a melancholy paradox that every principle begets its polar opposite. Consider how the current mania for cultural diversity in the arts is creating political homogeneity and intellectual conformity. The theatre provides the most telling examples. It's as if a large majority of American playwrights, directors, actors, and producers had all attended the same schools, read the same books, met the same people, shared the same friends, voted for the same politicians, signed the same manifestos, reached the same conclusions.

As a result, we've been breathing the suffocating atmosphere of total consensus over the past decade or longer (as evidence, read any back issue of *American Theatre* magazine—its entire contents seem to have been written by the same woolly-minded social studies major). In such a world, all black people are fervently if angrily protesting racism, all women are passionately confronting sexist discrimination and sexual harassment, all gays are maintaining an identical nobility, laced with bitchy wit, in the face of desperate battles with homophobia and AIDS, and all white male oppressors are either confessing their guilt or persisting in their wicked ways. Contemporary theatre, in short, now features as many stock characters as *commedia dell'arte*. An art form wholly dependent on the element of surprise is now in the grip of mind-numbing predictability.

Even well-worn modern classics are being shaped to this Jell-O mold, as witness the Tony Award–winning production of *A Doll's House*. That many of its cast and its director are British suggests the problem is not defined by nationality—ideological conformity knows no boundaries. It's not that this particular *Doll's House* lacks surprise. It's just that the surprises are so driven by fashionable agendas. In the act of accepting her own Tony for best actress in the play, Janet McTeer joked that she had originally asked the producers to let her play Torvald. That, as a matter of fact, is exactly what she seems to be doing. The actor cast as her husband (Owen Teale), though virile enough, is no match for this strapping amazon. Rather than being terrorized by a domestic tyrant, like Ibsen's Nora, McTeer looks as if she could have broken the poor man into pieces over her knee. Perhaps, like Olivier and Richardson in *Othello*, McTeer and Teale ought to consider alternating their roles.

It's no reflection on the quality of her considerable acting abilities to say that McTeer has woefully misinterpreted her part. Every new production of a classic, of course, demands a fresh approach. But the reason for rethinking plays is to find your way back to the author's original intention, usually obscured under layers of orthodox piety. McTeer's resolutely ahistorical reinterpretation seems mainly designed to illustrate how a powerful woman can shatter glass ceilings.

Claire Bloom played Nora, quite properly, as a highly intelligent human being forced to act the mindless little squirrel whenever she had to ask her husband for a little pocket money. By kneeling and begging with her paws extended, she managed to shame every man in the house. McTeer's effect on male audience members, if my reaction is typical, is to raise their anxiety over her mental balance. At times I was tempted to rush to the nearest drugstore and fetch her some Valium. Giggly, hysterical, hyperactive, nervously fiddling with her blonde wig, riddled with crochets, tics, and nerves, biting her nails, McTeer comes on less as a woman in need of self-realization than a neurotic in need of group therapy. Strindberg would have adored her. She's the perfect realization of all his neurasthenic heroines, of what he scornfully called "the third sex." Strindberg might even have revised his sour view of Ibsen ("that Norwegian bluestocking") had he been able to watch McTeer transform Nora into his own Miss Julie.

It is true that Krogstad's threat to expose Nora's forgery plunges the poor woman into a state of dithers. But McTeer shows nervous symptoms from her very first entrance. By the time she gets to her tarantella dance, in fact, she's almost ready to be committed, since she's screaming like a banshee, hurling the tambourine, bouncing off the scenery. Torvald describes this dance as "too reckless, strictly speaking, it went beyond the bounds of art." He might have been characterizing McTeer's entire performance. Her final declaration, however, is a refreshing exception to the general twitching, being quiet, controlled, determined. She plays the scene as if it were the culmination of a serious emotional crisis, the kind that leads to a separation agreement. Still, McTeer's Nora would never have left her house or abandoned her children. She would have kicked her husband into the street and called a tough divorce lawyer. When she slams the door on her way out (actually, this famous slam is anticlimactic because the set is so ill-designed), she has hardly persuaded us she will try to realize herself through an independent life. Rather, she seems to be slamming the door on what's left of her husband's private parts.

Happily, a number of plays have recently opened that refuse to cater to ideological expectations. One of these is Jonathan Reynolds's bravely conceived and wittily written, if imperfectly crafted, *Stonewall Jackson's House*, a satire-within-a-satire on the whole sham of political correctness in the nonprofit theatre. In the first act a black woman begs a white couple to take her home as a slave. In the second she reveals herself to be the defiant author of the mind-boggling play in which this event occurs (thus exposing her white theatrical colleagues as pious liberal frauds). Another source of agreeable surprise is Paula Vogel's *How I Learned to Drive*. In *Hot 'n Throbbing*, an earlier play not yet seen in New York, Vogel scandalized some feminists by creating a pornographer who was not only decent of heart but female of gender. In her new play she is even more incendiary, conceiving a victim of sex abuse who actually comes to love her abuser. Despite its subject matter, *How I Learned to Drive* is neither a polemical play nor a feminist tract. Rather, it is a strange exotic love story—imagine Nabokov's *Lolita* if Humbert Humbert had been Lolita's uncle.

It was e. e. cummings, I believe, who first thought of stick-shift driving as a metaphor for sexual activity. Learning to drive for the pre-pubescent heroine L'il Bit is also equivalent to initiation into the mysteries of erotic experience ("Idling in the Neutral Gear," "Driving in First Gear" are some of the suggestive scene headings). L'il Bit is actually introduced to these mysteries by her Uncle Peck who has been in love with her since she was a baby. Stuck in an unsatisfactory marriage, Peck is slowly drinking himself to death. His only salvation is his passion for L'il Bit, to whom he actually proposes not only sex but marriage ("You've gone way over the line," responds the more grounded L'il Bit. "Family is family."). Curiously the word incest is never uttered in the play. Peck seems more worried about her tender age. Touching her body, examining her breasts, he postpones any attempt at full union until her eighteenth birthday (he is then forty-five), when he will no longer be guilty of statutory rape.

As the play moves along from 1962 to the present, weaving back and forth in time, Vogel creates an oddly lyric atmosphere, culminating, after Peck's death, in L'il Bit's final speech. She is thirty-five now, in her own car, and driving with authority and control. Looking in the rear mirror, she sees the ghost of Peck in the back seat. Repeating all the instructions he taught her, she enters a state of true transcendence. The car is moving smoothly along the road—"and then," she adds in the wonderfully elegiac tone that pervades the entire play, "and then I floor it."

This is a moving culmination of an exquisitely modulated production, sensitively directed by Mark Brokaw. And it is tenderly acted by Mary-Louise Parker as L'il Bit and David Morse as Peck. Morse—grey-haired, rugged, plagued by inner demons—maintains pretty much the same age throughout the action. But Parker brings her character through a variety of subtle changes from shy teenager to mature woman, and wallops us with the depth of her feeling. Despite the explosive subject matter, there isn't a judgmental moment in the entire evening. Effortlessly, Vogel moves her characters out of the provisional world of morality into the timeless world of art.

Moisés Kaufman's *Gross Indecency* does precisely the same thing. The conflict between art and morality, in fact, is the play's basic subject matter. Subtitled "The Three Trials of Oscar Wilde," *Gross Indecency* manages to turn relatively familiar material—the trials and imprisonment of Wilde on charges of sodomy and pederasty (the judicial British euphemism is "gross indecency")—into a damning indictment of the way in which government tries to regulate our private lives.

Under Kaufman's dynamic direction, a strong energy drives this play, from the moment Wilde decides to arraign the Marquess of Queensbury ("the most infamous brute in London") for calling him a "posing Somdomite [sic!]," to the day of his death after serving two years in Reading Gaol. Wilde's relationship with Queensbury's son, Lord Alfred Douglas ("Bosie"), had enraged the marquess, and

Wilde, on the crest of his fame as a popular dramatist, conceived the bad idea, encouraged by Bosie, of bringing the marquess to trial for libel.

Ultimately, of course, this strategy was bound to backfire, and Wilde found himself in the dock—indicted not only for his relations with Bosie but with a number of young working men in London. Wilde never regarded these encounters as acts of unlawful behavior but rather as extensions of a special sensibility shared by Socrates, Plato, and many Renaissance artists. As a modern commentator points out during a break in the action, the trial was the first to treat the modern homosexual as a social subject, even though Wilde (anticipating Roy Cohn in *Angels in America*) didn't consider himself a homosexual, just a man who loved sex with other men. Wilde didn't believe in isolating the erotic from the aesthetic components of life. But that was the source of his tragedy—that he tried to turn morality into art during an age that preferred art to be an expression of morality.

One of the powerful things about this play is the way it subtly suggests that such constraints are not confined to the Victorian age. The continuing conflict between artistic expression and family values is, of course, at the heart of the congressional unpleasantness over Mapplethorpe, Serrano, Karen Finley, and the NEA. At his trial Wilde predicted that "the world is growing more tolerant. One day you will be ashamed of your treatment of me." He was only half right. The press today may display more sympathy for homosexuals than did the hysterical jackals of Fleet Street, but not much has really changed. Even in our more permissive time, when what Bosie called "the love that dare not speak its name" has grown a little hoarse from shouting it, the prohibitionist Puritan impulse to impose its narrow will on the private lives of citizens remains as insistent as ever. The hysteria over adultery among army officers is only the latest example.

Wilde, as depicted in this play—and as poignantly interpreted by Michael Emerson in a performance that perfectly catches his arrogance and innocence—represents a flawed but inspired artist brought to his knees by people who refuse to recognize the rights of privacy or respect the twists of idiosyncratic behavior. The depressing thing is that, almost a hundred years later, the same winds are chilling individual freedom, not just from the direction of the benighted conservative Establishment, but from that of its enlightened opponents on the liberal left as well.

1997

Funding Audiences

Piercing the media din after the Town Hall debate between August Wilson and me was a shriek of pain from the Lila Wallace–Reader's Digest Foundation. It was not hard to understand why. About the only thing the two of us had managed to agree upon was that the foundation's $26 million initiative for developing culturally diverse audiences was proving a monstrous waste of cash. Wilson had complained that instead of funding needy black institutions, the Wallace money was going to so-called white theatres to help stage plays by black writers. I had bemoaned the fact that coercive philanthropy of this kind (and Wallace is not alone in using economic resources to influence the direction of the arts) was forcing resident theatres to comply with external foundation agendas rather than internal artistic needs.

A letter circulated to all the resident artistic directors by Holly Sidford, currently program director of the foundation, protested our brusque dismissal of its audience-building initiative and enclosed a statement by Christine DeVita, president of the Lila Wallace–Reader's Digest Foundation. There Ms. DeVita wrote that of the forty-two grant awards in 1996, twelve went to "minority organizations run by people of color and based on African American, Latino, or Asian American artistic traditions." It was the foundation's mission, she went on, "to enhance the cultural life of communities and to make the arts a more active part of people's everyday lives. . . . Our grants enable a wide variety of cultural groups to actively engage people from all walks of life in outstanding artistic programs."

These are noble-sounding democratic goals, and the statistics do show that, contrary to August Wilson's belief that only "white" theatres are beneficiaries, a reasonable number of minority theatres, some of them black-directed, are indeed receiving significant grants. The problem is that the Wallace Foundation's concept of audience-building has more to do with social work than it does with art. They distribute works of the imagination among the hungry and disfranchised as if these were loaves of bread.

There are, however, obvious differences between a hunger for food and an appetite for culture. The first is an instinctual need, the other has to be cultivated. Once you make quality ("outstanding artistic programs") synonymous with quantity ("people from all walks of life"), you invariably begin to degrade the product. The initial purpose of the nonprofit theatre, and its major justification, was to provide a creative alternative to the audience-driven manufactures of Broadway. To support the nonprofit arts from the point of view of the audience rather than the artist is effectively to dump these theatres back into the marketplace.

The Wallace Foundation furnishes its own proof in a semi-annual report it publishes called "Building Audiences." The text of these pamphlets would be dynamite material for stand-up comedy if it weren't so depressing. Here are a few of the more uproarious routines. The August 1996 issue records that Philadelphia's Freedom Theatre "listened carefully to what its audiences said it wanted and gave them a season they couldn't resist." Freedom's marketing director had discovered that the theatre's audience, 90 percent black and 70 percent female, "were quite specific about what they like. They said that when they go to the theatre they want to see plays that are about them, and they want to be entertained and have fun." As a result, she proposed a schedule that "offered all the right ingredients— lots of music, humor, some star talent, shows about women and some family entertainment." The marketing director might have been planning the next season for ABC. A five-year Wallace grant was arranged to help Freedom "achieve its primary goal of broadening its African American audiences." How does a theatre "broaden" an audience that's already 90 percent black? I suspect the correct word is "enlarge." Freedom is obviously being encouraged to enlarge the size of its audience by cheapening its season offerings.

As for the Repertorio Español, the Wallace Foundation has helped this distinguished Latino theatre understand how "nationality-specific productions are the key to attracting Hispanic audiences and introducing them to theatre." Eureka! I hope the Repertorio Español has expressed sufficient gratitude to Wallace for learning how to "broaden" its Hispanic audiences. But wait, there's more wisdom. "Once the initial barrier has broken down, new audiences are more likely to return and try something else—maybe even a play from another part of the Latino world." I think what Wallace is trying to say is that a "nationality-specific" audience, having dined sufficiently on the cultural fare of its own country, might some day be ready to digest some European fare in the Spanish language, possibly works by Lope de Vega or Garcia Lorca, which the Repertorio Español has routinely produced for years. This reminds me of David Susskind's oft-expressed conviction, in the early days of television, that couch potatoes watching middlebrow "Golden Age" teledramas were being prepared to embrace Shakespeare. We're still waiting.

The Wallace Foundation is now engaged in a very costly "major evaluation" of its impact on resident theatres. Advance reports are already turning up startling conclusions. One incredibly deep insight is that "members of culturally specific groups, such as African Americans and Latinos, are particularly sensitive to how they are portrayed on stage . . . they want to see positive, more balanced images of themselves in the theatre . . . the kind of piece they can bring their children to and feel proud about." In short, precisely the sort of fare already being consumed on "the Chitlin Circuit" (as described by Henry Louis Gates in his *New Yorker* article). Will such ambitious black theatres as Crossroads and Penumbra also be forced to join this circuit so as to "broaden" their audiences? The Wallace Foundation offers similar advice to what it calls "white theatres." For example, it has helped the Victory Gardens Theater in Chicago to understand that in order to attract more African-American and Latino audiences "it needed to make a long-term commitment to develop and produce new work by African American and Hispanic playwrights." The workings of the human brain are sometimes simply dazzling.

As for the Goodman Theatre in the same city, "most black ticket buyers . . . still consider the Goodman a white theatre occasionally doing black plays," despite its nontraditional casting policy and its programming of at least one African-American play each season, How does Goodman use Wallace money to change this racial perception? The theatre hosts events where new subscribers have a chance to meet the director. The Mark Taper Forum in Los Angeles has increased its Latino audiences from 2 to 5.3 percent. How? Why, by doing more Latino plays. Similarly, the Alabama Shakespeare Festival increased its black subscribers by offering four plays likely to appeal to African-American audiences (only one—*Othello*—by Shakespeare). Perhaps this may be the key to attracting more black subscribers to the Shaw Festival.

Using a phrase we haven't heard much since the sixties, Wallace calls this "relevant programming." And in an "evaluation update" the foundation establishes the following conditions for earning this meritorious sobriquet (and Wallace money): "The work is written by a member of the targeted audience group; it is directed by a member of that group; it features a story depicting their lives; and the majority of cast members are from the target group. From its preliminary analysis, the evaluation team judged a play relevant if it met two or more of these criteria. A season was considered relevant if 25 percent or more of the works met the necessary criteria." This, of course, is only a "preliminary analysis." But, we are assured, the Wallace Foundation is sparing no expense to support and advance the research of this "evaluation team." Imagine what such a brains trust might turn up about the greenness of grass or the wetness of water.

There is, of course, no way of knowing whether the recipients of Wallace largesse would have devised their "relevant programming" without the requisite grants. There are certainly a number of good minority plays available to theatres without foundation bribes. But the reports leave no doubt that this well-meaning liberal funding agency is profoundly altering the selection process at a number of nonprofit institutions, and hardly for the better. I'm not sure it is a proper function of philanthropy to advise theatres about what kind of works to choose for a season. Isn't it more appropriate for artistic directors to produce plays because they believe in them, and not because they attract audience-development grants or make minorities feel good about themselves? Isn't it the artist's function to create his own "relevance" by leading rather than following public taste? The populist alternative is what Eric Bentley once called "democrateering" (my name for it is "dumbocracy")—another example of how Americans analyze a problem correctly and then come up with the wrong solution.

It is wrong because it is shortsighted. The long-term way to develop audiences of any race or ethnicity is through expert arts education in the schools, a task which (despite some recent efforts by the Annenberg Foundation) remains woefully underfunded. If the public and private sectors persist in ignoring the training of young audiences, the only sensible alternative is to keep challenging adults through powerful new visions, stretching their imaginations with experiences that are penetrating and unexpected. To offer some personal history, when I was young neither of my parents had the slightest interest in music or literature. But at the age of ten I was taken to see a benefit production of a musical called *Swinging the Dream*. It was my first experience with Shakespeare, an all-black treatment of *A Midsummer Night's Dream*, starring Bill Robinson and Ella Fitzgerald as Oberon and Titania, and Louis Armstrong as Bottom the Weaver (the Benny Goodman Quintet was one of the pit bands). A budding swing musician myself, I was totally enchanted by the show, though the reviews were bad and it closed in a week. *Swinging the Dream* was not "about" me, nor did it provide any "positive images" of my racial, ethnic, or sexual background. Yet this musical was partly responsible for developing my lifelong love of Shakespeare, particularly in fresh irreverent approaches, not to mention a healthy skepticism about the opinions of theatre critics (including my own).

Audience development, in short, is a process best left not to foundation officials but to artists. There is no substitute for exposure, whether early in life or late, to the finest work available to all races, sexes, and ethnicities.

1997

In 1998 the Lila Wallace–Reader's Digest Foundation discontinued its program of specific grants to theatres. Some theatres cut back their commitment to culturally diverse work.

The Decline of
Serious Culture

Over 150 years ago, Alexis de Tocqueville wrote in his study of *Democracy in America*: "I do not believe that it is a necessary effect of a democratic social condition and of democratic institutions to diminish the number of those who cultivate the fine arts, but these causes exert a powerful influence on the manner in which these arts are cultivated. . . . The productions of artists are more numerous, but the merit of each production is diminished. . . . In aristocracies, a few great pictures are produced; in democratic countries a vast number of insignificant ones."

These Delphic notations, inscribed after a visit to our shores in the early years of the Republic by a foreigner who is still among the most prophetic commentators on American life, in effect defined the problems that serious or high culture would henceforth encounter in an increasingly massified and industrialized society. What Tocqueville prophesied was that among the things a political democracy might have to sacrifice to egalitarian needs would be a civilization of real importance. American culture, in his view, would become flooded with insignificant forms of expression, genuine works of art being rare and often unacknowledged, and artistic standards would be determined not by the intrinsic quality of the art but rather by the extrinsic size of the audience. Put another way, the evolution of American culture would be based on a continuing tension, and later on a state of hostility, between the minority expression called high art—subscribed to by a decreasing number of "fastidious consumers"—and what constituted the culture of the masses.

Tocqueville, though an aristocrat himself, was highly partial to the new political experiment being tested in this country. But he yearned for a system that could join a democratic politics with a meritocratic culture. He correctly saw that, without access to the civilizing influence of great artworks, the voting majority in this country was bound to remain benighted. Only art and education could provide the synthesis needed to evolve a more enlightened and cultivated electorate. There were times when this synthesis looked achievable. In the nineteenth century, certainly, high art and popular culture seemed to coexist in healthy if often separate compartments. Not only were Hawthorne and Emerson traded in the same bookstalls as penny dreadfuls but traveling troupes performed Shakespeare, albeit in bowdlerized form, attracting wildly enthusiastic audiences from the most primitive frontiers (so indeed did Oscar Wilde on his famous lecture tour across America).

Even in our more embattled century, high art and popular culture managed to enjoy a brief honeymoon for a time. Certainly serious American artists in the first half of this century drew great infusions of energy from indigenous American forms. Try to imagine Gershwin without access to the music of the Harlem Renaissance, or Copland without the impact of Mexican and Latin American dance rhythms, or Bernstein without the influence of jazz, cabaret, and rock. T. S. Eliot's metrics, like those of e. e. cummings, owe a lot to vaudeville and the music hall, though the results may not always suit contemporary taste (his dramatic fragment, *Sweeney Agonistes*, climaxes in a minstrel show). And many twentieth-century American novels, beginning with those of John Dos Passos, have been deeply indebted, in their episodic structure and cinematic sweep, to Hollywood movies. It is obvious, furthermore, that Robert Rauschenberg, Jasper Johns, Roy Lichtenstein, indeed virtually everyone associated with the Pop Art movement, have been obliged to such popular visual forms as cartoons, comic strips, newspaper print, and advertising.

Of course the channels of exchange have flowed the other way as well. Neither American advertising nor the world of fashion would have produced many original ideas had they not been able to loot the iconography of high art. No sooner does a new visual artist emerge in this country than his or her advances are instantly appropriated by Madison and Seventh Avenues. Similarly the history of the movies would have been sadly impoverished had studios not been in a position to feed off contemporary literature and theatre. So intimate were the relations between high and popular culture, in fact, that it was sometimes difficult to determine whether an artist like Andy Warhol belonged more to bohemia or surburbia, whether his true home was the Factory or the creative department of a fashionable advertising firm. Similarly such respected figures as F. Scott Fitzgerald, William Faulkner, Nathanael West, among many other American writers—not to mention expatriate Europeans such as Bertolt Brecht and Aldous Huxley—spent almost as much time huddling in script conferences in Hollywood as bending over their writing desks.

The interdependence of popular and high art in our country had both positive and negative effects. One obvious advantage was economic. The commercial system subsidized a lot of needy artists whose customary royalties would have been too meager to pay for their typewriter ribbons. It is true that the same system often distracted these artists from their legitimate work, though not so much as commonly assumed. Fitzgerald wasted his time writing third-rate movies like *Winter Carnival*, but his motion picture studio experience also inspired a fine if unfinished Hollywood novel, *The Last Tycoon*. It can be argued that working with such popular forms as the detective novel, science fiction, and film noir screenplays provided a stream of energy that kept high culture hard-boiled, vigorous, and vital. Still, the relationship between the artist and the commodity culture was always uneasy. And it soon began to curdle, partly through the efforts of a number of highbrow intellectuals who regarded the participating artist as a sellout or, worse, a collaborator in a mass art that was leaving a brutalizing imprint on American minds.

The fear that popular culture would absorb high art had always worried social commentators, from Tocqueville on. But that fear intensified during the culture wars of the fifties. Then, such crusading highbrows as Dwight Macdonald began protesting the power of "Masscult" and "Midcult" to debase and overshadow "High Cult" (note how even Macdonald's terms were infected by the mass media, reflecting the glib clipped style of *Time* magazine where, along with other intellectuals like James Agee, he made his living). Particularly incensed by the way James Gould Cozzens's novel *By Love Possessed* had been overestimated by the middlebrow press, Macdonald was typical of those irascible critics who not only identified and analyzed high art but also elected themselves to expose pretense and sham. At the same time the increasingly vocal opponents of the highbrows, usually representatives of the value-free social sciences, were defending middle and mass culture as the more democratic art. And more democratic it was if you measured culture by statistical instead of qualitative criteria—namely, the incidence and popularity of the commodities consumed by the mass public.

To be sure, a democratic art was always the dream of great poets like Walt Whitman. But it was somehow easier for a nineteenth-century artist to imagine "Democratic Vistas" without relinquishing his belief in artistic standards. That balance is more difficult today. The culture wars of the fifties, raging in such periodicals as *Partisan Review* and *Commentary*, not only planted wedges between high, middle, and popular culture, it also resulted in a hostile backlash against serious art and the critical intellect.

This eventually spread to include the whole construct of Eurocentric civilization and its "dead white male" artists and intellectuals, as they are now scornfully identified. We had entered a time when competing special-interest groups were beginning to clamor for recognition of their own forms of cultural expression, often identifying both traditional and avant-garde art as "elitist" (the populist epithet that was henceforth to control the terms of this debate). The charge of "elitism" was hurled not only against the wealthy consumers of art but also against its often penniless creators, thus confusing patronage with talent, class with taste, economic status with artistic vision. You were "elitist" if you created works of art and you were "elitist" if you bought them. No wonder so few people were willing to come to the defense of elitism (a significant exception being the late William Henry III, the drama critic for *Time* magazine). Love of art was perceived in some quarters as equivalent to being indifferent to suffering, inequality, and injustice. These implications of callousness (and, more specifically, of racism) caused a major retreat—the surrender of many of the standards and values that make a serious culture possible. I do not mean to suggest that inspired artists are no longer able to function in America, but rather that what was once a hospitable climate for their work has turned mean and indifferent. Native talent may be as abundant as ever, but never in memory has it been so inadequately evaluated, published, produced, disseminated, and supported.

Although the ongoing war on culture originally had economic

causes related to the recession, its thrust has now become mainly political. Forces opposing the high arts advance by means of a three-pronged incursion—from the right, left, and center of the political spectrum, all claiming endorsement from the majority. One of the homes for these incursions is the National Endowment for the Arts— and that is sad, since in its early years this agency did a lot to maintain and encourage creative achievement. Under the Johnson and Nixon administrations, when the NEA was led first by Roger Stevens, then by Nancy Hanks, and the total budget never rose above $100 million, the agency was not yet conspicuous enough to become a political football. After the Carter administration appointed the populist Livingston Biddle as chairman, however, the emphasis of the Endowment changed from the support and encouragement of serious American art to its "dissemination," which is to say it shifted from the artist to the public. Simultaneous with this change, after the NEA budget began to inch toward its high of $176 million in 1980 (from which dizzying height it has now taken such a serious nosedive), Congress began to make serious inroads into the decisions of the Endowment. Biddle explained his populist stance by announcing that "the voice of the constituent is the one most clearly heard by Congress," which was his way of saying that instead of supporting the artist, the NEA was now courting the voter and those who represented him.

In short, the National Endowment for the Arts, in company with its sister agency the National Endowment for the Humanities, was in process of being "democratized." But this process went deeper than the intervention of pressure groups, vested interests, and political pork barrelers. It was the very politics of consensus American democracy that was now influencing the policies and appointments of these federal agencies. Once fully professional and oriented toward the artist, the Endowments were beginning to spread their relatively meager moneys among educationalists, audiences, and amateurs as well. This change was inspired by the essentially political assumption that any resources generated by the people should directly benefit the people—as if there were not enough precedents, in medical, space, and scientific research, for identifying and supporting those best qualified to make advances in specialized fields. The concept of excellence and expertise—Tocqueville's meritocratic achievement within a democratic society—was perfectly in harmony with our founding ideals. Indeed, it informed the constitutional concept of an Electoral College—originally planned as a group of qualified and informed people chosen by the voting majority to select the chief executive. Nevertheless, this concept was now being abandoned in favor of such extra-artistic concerns as advocacy, arts appreciation, geographical distribution, dissemination through the media, and, later, multiculturalism and cultural diversity.

The democratization—more accurately *politicization*—of the Endowment exploded with full force after President Bush appointed John E. Frohnmayer as chairman of the NEA. It was then that controversial grants to Robert Mapplethorpe and Andres Serrano, among others, aroused the fiery wrath of such conservative bullies as North Carolina senator Jesse Helms, who took the position that the government should not fund any artistic work offensive to the majority. Such was Helms's power that he even persuaded Congress to impose content restrictions on grantees in the form of a new obscenity clause that all applicants were obliged to sign, though a successful class-action suit by Bella Lewitzky temporarily resulted in the provision being struck down as unconstitutional.

Frohnmayer not only punished those institutions responsible for the Mapplethorpe and Serrano shows. He canceled a grant for a New York art exhibit because he found the *brochure* too political (it blistered such homophobic legislators as Helms). Acting Chairwoman Anne-Imelda Radice, was, if anything, even more responsive to right-wing pressures on the arts. But despite her need to placate the conservatives, it was under her brief regime that populist policies gained the greatest purchase at the Endowment—an inheritance the next chairman, Jane Alexander, was in no position to reverse. First Radice declared that the agency would henceforth be more responsive to majoritarian or popular demands when handing out money, thus tainting the originally countermarket strategy of the NEA with marketplace values. Then she made it official policy to fund every species of ethnic and racial expression, regardless of its intrinsic value as art.

The attack on the arts from the politically correct left proved just as disturbing in its way as that from right-wing minions of moral correctness. And it is significant that both sides claimed the endorsement of the democratic majority. For the right, this usually meant those clean-cut Americans who celebrate Thanksgiving in Norman Rockwell paintings and sip vanilla sodas in Thornton Wilder plays. For the left, the majority was represented not by churchgoing Anglo-Saxon patriots but rather by those previously excluded from the cultural banquet, a diverse mixture of racial, sexual, and ethnic constituencies summed up in the catchwords "multiculturalism" and "cultural diversity."

Now there is no question that intercultural exchange has been a source of great artistic refreshment. Cultural diversity is responsible for much that is vital and original in our culture. Multicultural grants have also helped to increase the visibility of deserving minority artists, especially in artistic institutions, which is a highly welcome move. But frequently awards have been made on other than artistic grounds, as if there were different standards for people of different colors, sexes, and ethnicities. Such awards are less a form of patronage than of patronization, reflecting not so much a love of art as a passion for social engineering. As H. L. Mencken has written, "Every third American devotes himself to improving and lifting up his fellow citizens, usually by force; the messianic delusion is our national disease." Trying to compensate for the failures of society in an area least prepared to be an avenue of social change, namely the arts, the cultural bureaucrats began to threaten hard-won achievements for the sake of evangelical gestures.

Finally there is the threat to the high arts from the middle spectrum, more accurately the middlebrow arbiters of culture, those vigilant watchdogs who bark at anything not immediately accessible to the middle-class public. With artistic standards being controlled by media critics, many of them incompetent, and publication and production controlled by publishers and producers hypnotized by the bottom line, the possibility of sustaining high culture in our time is becoming increasingly problematical. Serious bookstores are losing their franchise; small publishing houses are closing shop; little magazines are going out of business; nonprofit theatres are surviving primarily by commercializing their repertories; symphony orchestras are diluting their programs; classical radio stations are dwindling; museums are resorting to blockbuster shows; dance is dying. Only opera is increasing its audience. And the academy, once the last refuge of the highbrow intellectual, is becoming captive to agenda-driven departments more and more dedicated not to teaching works of intellect and appreciating works of art but rather to forcing political ideas on them, like stuffing a healthy goose in order to enlarge its liver.

This incorrigible tendency by right, left, and center to muddle culture and politics has had the result of altering the terms of the cultural debate. Certainly the traditional arguments between "High Cult" and "Masscult" could not be heard today; serious and popular culture no longer coexist in their separate compartments. The once proud and confident highbrow has fled the field, pursued by a hail of arrows shaped in the form of epithets, while the serious artist finds it harder and harder to resist the pressures of popular taste. Is Tocqueville once again confirmed in his belief that a meritocratic art is not indigenous to a democratic society? He is certainly right that the relationship will always cause tensions. Each age chooses different weapons for its war on the serious arts, but the nature of the war remains the same. What should really worry us is the resolution of that war in the total collapse of high culture. It is not the proper way to celebrate American pluralism. It is not what our Founding Fathers envisioned when they conceived the American Republic. It is not a healthy sign for American democracy.

1997

PART 2

PRODUCTIONS: AT HOME

Aspects of Arthur Miller
(Broken Glass; The Ride Down Mount Morgan)

Now that so many American dramatists (David Mamet, Richard Nelson, Arthur Miller, and others) have started premiering their plays in London, you would think that New York has become less a venue for new work than another stop on the road, like Philadelphia or Boston. Most of the more impressive New York productions in recent weeks have been English imports—the powerful *Medea* of Diana Rigg, Nicholas Hytner's exquisite rendering of *Carousel*, Stephen Daldry's imaginative resuscitation of *An Inspector Calls*, Adrian Noble's stunning *The Winter's Tale*. I feel a little foolish about having made the trip to London to review them. With a little patience I could have stayed home, saved myself the flight fares and hotel bills, and just covered the tours.

Arthur Miller didn't open *Broken Glass* abroad, but I'll bet he wishes he had. He may not be able to rouse much admiration for his new plays in this country, but he's a living monument in England. Indeed, he has virtually become that country's playwright laureate. Miller's collected works (including his adaptation of *An Enemy of the People*) are periodically revived to great acclaim, and all the youth of England are on fire to imitate him. If the United States and Great Britain have sometimes been identified as two nations separated by a common tongue, we are now two countries separated by a common playwright. *Broken Glass* may very well dazzle the critics and delight the public when it is eventually produced in London. Here it seems like just another spiral in a stumbling career.

I'm happy for Miller that he has an artistic home, and it is regrettable that, along with Williams and (till recently) Albee, he has not been locally appreciated in his later years. There was a time when Miller was regarded as America's greatest playwright, indeed the culminating figure in the Western dramatic tradition (one anthology was called *From Aeschylus to Arthur Miller*). Today he's lucky to be published by Samuel French. My regret about Miller's declining reputation, however, doesn't change my opinion of his style, which often seems plodding, pedestrian, predictable, and a little pompous. It continues to baffle me how moral preachments in lumbering prose could once have passed for major modern tragedies, and I have a suspicion that if his early reputation had been less inflated, he might have enjoyed more respect today. Still, an Old Vic version of *The Crucible* some years back (directed by Laurence Olivier) gave that play the kind of loftiness and magnitude it never enjoyed in its American incarnations. And it may well be that the reason the English so admire Miller is that they are able to produce him with the grandeur of Shakespearean tragedy rather than (as here) with the prosaic flatness of a sociological primer.

Perhaps the English will manage to streamline the creaky machinery of *Broken Glass*, but at present it looks to me very old-fashioned and clunky. The time is 1938, the year of Kristallnacht. The heroine, a Brooklyn housewife named Sylvia Gellburg, is paralyzed from the waist down because, as we later learn, she's been obsessing on the looming Holocaust. She needs others to sympathize with her fears, and her husband is a man who suppresses his Jewish identity (also, apparently, his sexual drive, since he hasn't slept with her in twenty years). A dour conservative who forecloses on properties for a Gentile firm, Gellburg pretends his family name is Finnish and takes pride in a West Point son who gives lectures on artillery and twice spoke to General MacArthur. Harry Hyman, the doctor they consult, explains (and *explains*), with all the gravity of Paul Muni discovering a serum for smallpox, that Gellburg's wife is possessed not with a virus (as she suspects) or a dybbuk (as Gellburg suspects) but with hysterical symptoms. Eureka! The cure he suggests is sexual, that Gellburg sleep with his own wife. The doctor has apparently been thinking of applying that treatment himself because at one point he advises Sylvia to "imagine we've made love and you're telling me secret things."

I know it's hard to believe, but I think we're being told that all Sylvia needs to walk again is a little poke from someone who really hates the Nazis. Although Gellburg pretends to have made love to her and she didn't remember, neither he nor Hyman succeed in applying the proposed therapy. Instead this self-hating Jew is forced to confront his own Jewishness after concluding that his Gentile employer may be anti-Semitic. The boss suspects him of collusion in a property deal with a pushy *landsman* named Alan Gershowitz (Alan Dershowitz should sue). This revelation leads to a heart attack and Gellburg's eventual death. I'm told that Miller wrote a number of different endings for the play. The one he chose is borrowed from old MGM movies. The instant Gellburg dies, his wife rises unsteadily from her wheelchair as the curtain descends. I imagined I heard Peter Sellers in the background shouting: "*Mein Führer*, I can walk."

I'm sorry to be so beastly about *Broken Glass*, but it really is a shaky piece of stage architecture. Located at the corner of Cliché Avenue and Banal Boulevard, the play is riddled with such rhetorical self-parodies as "This will all pass" and "This is a whole life we're talking about" and (more inscrutably) "How can there be Jews if there's no God?" Clearly Miller has been furrowing his brow a lot lately over what it means to be a Jew, and once again seems to be saying (as he did in *Incident at Vichy*), "I don't want your guilt, I want your responsibility." It is hard to give him either when his own Jewish identity has not been all that strong. It certainly hasn't been strong enough to make him create many Jewish characters (*cf.* the ethnic vagueness of Willy Loman), except for a comic peddler in *The Price* and the hero of an early novel called *Focus*, a Gentile *mistaken* for a Jew. Miller comes to the subject of Jewish self-hatred quite a few years after everyone else has exhausted it, which may explain why his plot seems inspired by fifties movies like *Gentleman's Agreement*, and why the dramaturgical technique is worthy of the Golden Age of Television.

As for the production, it might have won Emmys for the Philco Playhouse. John Tillinger has tried to match Miller's moral earnestness by substituting momentum for depth, staging *Broken Glass* as if it were a lay lecture on Freud's *Studies in Hysteria*. This may explain why such a normally sensitive designer as Santo Loquasto has created such an antiseptic space, including a doctor's office that features the book-lined decor of a law firm. It may also explain why such usually dependable American actors seem stuck in generalized performances. Ron Rifkin's Gellburg is something of an exception. Looking like a younger Hume Cronyn in a black three-piece suit, Rifkin throws all his force into this sour, mean, insensitive Brooklynite (his death scene, resembling an apoplectic fit, made me fear for his blood pressure). But he's stuck in two dimensions. Once having established the character, he fails to surprise us with it. Amy Irving is an actress I've always admired as an ingenue, but as the aging Brooklyn-accented Sylvia, she seems miscast, flat and static in her wheelchair. The part would have been better played by someone like Anne Bancroft (whom she's beginning to resemble). David Dukes as Harry Hyman endeavors to do something that made Ron Silver confess failure and quit, namely impersonate Arthur Miller ventriloquizing through the mouth of a Jewish doctor (a character combination, I admit, that might appeal to a number of marriageable Jewish girls). Frances Conroy brings her customary warmth to a small part and George N. Martin is properly repressed as Gellburg's Gentile boss. But the climactic office scene struck me as a replay of the climax in *Death of a Salesman* in which Willy gets the boot from his boss. In fact, much of *Broken Glass* is made up of fragments from a more shatterproof phase of Miller's career.

1994

Arthur Miller's *The Ride Down Mount Morgan* was first produced in London a few years ago. It enjoyed a somewhat mixed reception, despite the playwright's unassailable reputation among the English. The same play received its belated American premier recently at the Williamstown (Massachusetts) Theatre Festival in a new production directed by Scott Elliott. It was performed for only two weeks under summer-stock conditions. It deserves further rehearsal and a longer life.

The Ride Down Mount Morgan is very loosely structured for a Miller work. Even more unusual, it is very engaging. I'm not surprised that this octogenarian author could have dreamed up such subject matter. I am agreeably surprised to find him writing about it with such a singular lack of earnestness. Considering the dignity and solemnity of his public persona, Miller has often seemed to be posing for a place on Mount Rushmore. The title of his new play may be un-intentionally symbolic. It is the work of a much more lively, supple, and mischievous man.

In the past, it is true, these craggy Miller features were occasion-ally capable of relaxing into a sly, impish smile. What was needed to break the stoneworks was an appropriate character and the right oc-casion (in *The Price*, Miller found it in the character of Solomon, the Jewish furniture dealer, the occasion being his shrewd wheeling and dealing). In *The Ride Down Mount Morgan* the playwright has again found an opportunity for exercising his comic muscles, though in a most unlikely arena.

The subject of the work is bigamy, and the central character is a sensualist. A number of Miller's previous characters (Willy Loman, for example, and John Proctor) have been guilty of philandering. Yet for once Miller doesn't treat the issue of sexual infidelity with his pre-dictable self-flagellating moralism. Consider the plot. During a diffi-cult winter in the 1980s, Lyman Feld has been badly injured driving in a blizzard down a treacherous mountain in upper New York. Most of the action takes place in his hospital room, where among his bed-side visitors are his Gentile New York wife, Theodora, accompanied by their grown-up daughter—and his Jewish wife from Elmira, Leah, who has borne him a son. Thanks to geography, neither wife knows he has a relationship with the other. The first meeting of these two women at the foot of his bed provides the crisis of the play.

That crisis has a potential for stiff theatrics. But the fact that both wives show up in identical mink coats suggests that Miller is mining the situation for something other than melodrama. Moreover, Lyman's delusionary condition—the result of his head injuries—al-lows for a more fantastical style than one usually finds in Miller's es-sentially social-realistic drama. It also permits some visits by a long-dead character (reminiscent of Uncle Ben in *Death of a Sales-man*)—notably his cranky immigrant father, who badgers him over his womanizing.

Moving between reality and dream, Lyman searches through his past for meaning like a derelict foraging in trash cans. He loves and needs both wives, though he loses them both. "A man can be faithful to himself or other people," he muses, "but not to both—the first law of life is betrayal." Starting his career as a poet and short story writer (once praised by James Baldwin), Lyman has ended up in his fifties as an insurance salesman. His sense of failed purpose, and his pain over aging, lead him to seek emotional fulfillment in an affair with Leah, his upstate insurance partner. When the affair turns serious, he lies about having divorced his first wife and marries the second.

Without absolving Lyman of spiritual emptiness ("He's an endless string attached to nothing," remarks his lawyer-friend Tom), Miller digs beneath the moral imperatives of the situation to examine deeper motives. If Lyman resembles the hero of *The Captain's Paradise*, shuttling blithely between two domestic households, he also reminds us of the anguished hero of Graham Greene's *The Heart of the Matter*— not because he suffers from a sense of sin (his conscience is virtually free of guilt) but because of his genuine concern for the well-being of both women. "I just couldn't bear to destroy your happiness," he says to one of them. "I am a bad man who loves you all," he tells them both. Later he affirms that he cannot "stand still for death," though it is always sitting on his shoulder. "Life, life," he moans, "fuck death and dying."

The romantic escapades of this aging Lothario, therefore, are actually his defense against old age and oblivion. They are also his way of defying boredom. Both wives believe in fidelity, largely because it strengthens the social system. Theodora reflects: "The stronger the family, the weaker the police, and that is why monogamy is a high art." But Theodora's banal domesticity, not to mention her "incredibly Protestant cooking," have made him hunger for more passionate alternatives. He claims he rode down Mount Morgan in order to persuade Leah how much he needed her, and also to reinvigorate his life. But this foolhardy ride may have been an unconscious effort to punish himself through suicide. By the end of the play he has lost everybody he loves. His nurse, a black woman, sits by his side and gives the lonely man a quick kiss on the forehead. Why? "No reason."

Scott Elliott's production evoked some finely tuned performances. But in Williamstown they seemed modulated more for the camera than for the stage. Though intimate and relaxed, the actors were not always audible, as if they had been asked to sacrifice theatricality for reality. In the theatre the balance between projection and truth is usually the hardest to achieve. It was not always achieved in Williamstown. Still, F. Murray Abraham seemed to be having a really fine time as Lyman, and his infectious warmth and high spirits communicated well to the audience. Michael Learned's Theo alternated between understanding and outrage, occasionally breaking into a wonderfully goofy hysteria. Patricia Clarkson as Leah etched an attractive portrait of a good-natured, forgiving woman, slowly turning sour. Derek McLane's setting was an abstract space, framed by walls fallen out of the perpendicular and backed by a huge impressionistic mountain, which proved both serviceable and haunting. More work has to be done, both by playwright and director, on heightening the contrast between the real and fantasy life of the play. When it's ready for prime time, *The Ride Down Mount Morgan* promises to be an exhilarating journey as well as an exciting debut for its youthful author.

1996

P.C. Whipped

(*Twilight: Los Angeles 1992; Politically* Incorrect)

The most cogent commentators on our stormy times have unquestionably been not the columnists but the cartoonists, which is another way of noting that representational satire has more capacity than political or social commentary to relieve the pressures of a fractious age. On stage, two inspired performers have recently been offering their own perspectives on the issues that divide us, and while the African-American Anna Deavere Smith and the Jewish-American Jackie Mason seem worlds apart in tone, attitude, focus, and ethnicity, they each provide more insight into the nature of our discords than an army of op-ed pundits.

It is true that Anna Deavere Smith might be more accurately described as a sociologist than as a satirist. Both in her previous *Fires in the Mirror*, which covered the Crown Heights affair, and in her current piece at the Joseph Papp Public Theater, *Twilight: Los Angeles 1992*, which deals with the riots in South Central L.A., she has drawn her material from interviews with the actual participants in those events. Still, Smith is not only an objective ear but a characterizing voice, and just as she shapes her text through editing and selection, so she achieves her emphasis through gesture and intonation. In the course of the evening, the actress impersonates forty-six different people, capturing the essence of each character less through mimetic transformation, like an actor, than through the caricaturist's body English and vocal embellishments. Just look at her photographs— you'd never guess from any of those contorted head shots that she's an extremely handsome young woman.

Smith's subjects divide essentially into victims, victimizers, and viewers, though it is sometimes difficult to determine which is which. If former Police Chief Daryl Gates (defending himself against charges that he permitted the riots to rage while attending a fund-raiser) and Sergeant Charles Duke (complaining that Officer Powell was "weak and inefficient with the baton" because he wasn't allowed to use the "choke hold") are clearly the patsies of the piece, the riot-ers, looters, gang members, and assailants often appear more sinned against than sinning. A white juror in the first Rodney King trial, asked by a reporter, "Why are you hiding your head in shame," is ap-palled to receive approving calls from the KKK. Keith Watson, one of those acquitted of beating the innocent trucker, Reginald Denny, justifies his rage and the burnt-out vacant lots by saying "justice didn't work," while Paul Parker, chairperson of the "Free the L.A. Four Defense Committee," charges "You kidnapped us, you raped our women . . . you expect us to feel something for the white boy?" One gringo-hating Latino, ranting against the "peckerwoods" and "rednecks" who have persecuted his family, expresses pleasure in the way Mexicans are able to terrify whites. Another Latino is encour-aged by a policeman to "go for it, it's your neighborhood." A black woman "touring" in the white suburbs loots I. Magnin's because she finds it "very offensive" that rich stars should feel protected from rioting.

Then there are the other victims—the Asian shopkeepers who, in those tumultuous days, lost 90 percent of their stores and a number of their family members. At the same time that a spokesperson for a young black girl shot by a Korean shopkeeper (she was later acquit-ted) is raging against Asians, Mrs. Young-Soon Han, a former liquor store owner, speaks of her disenchantment with blacks. There were none in the Hollywood movies she saw in Korea; she thought this country was the best. Now "they" have destroyed the shops of innocent merchants simply because "we have a car and a house. . . . Where do I find justice? What about victims' rights?" Another store owner, inveighing against shoplifting and looting, remarks, "After that, I really hate this country, I really hate—we are not like customer and owner but more like *enemy*."

"Enemy" and "hate" are the operative words of *Twilight*. With each ethnic group bristling at the other, one might think "cultural diversity" had become a euphemism for race war. A Mexican woman reporter, told her life is in danger, replies: "How could they think I was white?" The African-American Paul Parker boasts how "we burnt down the Koreans—they are like the Jews in this neighborhood." And this is countered not by appeals for tolerance but by counsels of caution, like those of Elaine Brown, former Black Panther, reminding the gun-brandishing, swashbuckling looters about America's willingness to use its power: "Ask Saddam Hussein."

To judge by the interviews in *Twilight*, however, the Los Angeles riots caused a lot of soul-searching, and considerable guilt, among a number of white Americans. The experience certainly stimulated considerable generosity from Reginald Denny, who, pleading for recognition as a person rather than a color, expresses profound gratitude to the black people who risked their lives to save him. By contrast, others, like a reporter named Judith Tur, wonder why South Central blacks can't be more like Magic Johnson or Arthur Ashe, adding that "white people are getting so angry, they're going back fifty years." A suburban real estate agent named Elaine Young, who has had thirty-six silicone surgeries on her face, whines that "we don't have the Freeway, we can't eat anywhere, everything's closed," meanwhile defending her decision to hole up in the Beverly Hills Hotel.

These are easy targets, and it is true that *Twilight* sometimes lacks the dialectical thickness as well as the surprise and unpredictability of *Fires in the Mirror*. Lasting over two hours, it seems at the same time too long and too short for its subject. The L.A. riots were a response to violence and injustice through acts of violence and injustice. And the paradox still to be explored is why looting and burning Korean stores and destroying your own neighborhood, not to mention racial assaults on innocent people, could be considered acceptable means of protest against inequity and racism. With most of them still in shock, few of Smith's respondents are in a position to examine the irrationality of such acts unless, like Shelby Coffey, they cite "a vast even Shakespearean range of motives."

Smith makes some effort to penetrate these motives by ending her piece with a poetic reflection by a gang member on the "limbo" twilight of crack addicts. But the metaphor somehow seems inadequate. Still, if she has not always gone beyond the events of this tragedy, she has powerfully dramatized a world of almost universal tension and hatred. George C. Wolfe's elaborate production, with its videos of Rodney King's beating and films of Los Angeles burning, is probably more appropriate for the coming Broadway move than for the stage of the Public. But it leaves us with a shocking sense of how America's hopes for racial harmony were left burning in the ashes of South Central L.A..

Jackie Mason's *Politically* In*correct* is bound to fan these fires further. It is totally inflammatory, offensive in the extreme, brazen, cheeky, reckless, unapologetic. It is also painfully funny in that rude, unbuttoned manner first patented by Lenny Bruce, then developed by Richard Pryor and Eddie Murphy (though, unlike them, Mason uses no obscenities). Still smarting from the abuse he suffered— mostly from white liberals—for using the word *schvartze* in the first Giuliani campaign, Mason is now delivering a ferocious assault on all the PC fortresses, not only black power but feminism, gay pride, affirmative action, Hillary and Bill, a sensation-hungry press, and anyone stupid enough to blame the media for crime and violence ("The Three Stooges poke out each other's eyes—do you do it to your brother Irving?").

Mason is tempting fate and knows it. The real purpose of his show, he says, is to tell the truth as he sees it, and for that "I can get killed"—or at least clubbed in the knees for ridiculing Tonya Harding. I was reminded of Lenny Bruce who, after questioning Jackie Kennedy's motives for climbing out of the presidential limo in Dallas, pointed at the chandelier and predicted it was going to explode. Like Bruce, Mason has turned himself into a sacrificial object. At the preview I saw, he was roundly heckled by a woman in the balcony who he referred to throughout as "that sick stupid yenta." Once self-identified as the "hit of the building," he now half-expects to be hit *by* the building.

This may account for the slightly nervous manner of his delivery. His dyed red hair topping his half-closed eyes and masklike face, a guided missile in a double-breasted suit, Mason seems terrified of silence. Even when he dries, he still keeps spritzing. The perfect embodiment of the Jewish anxiety which is his subject, he's confident only when he stays on Jewish themes. Entering the stage announcing that "this is one of the great thrills of all time to be able to see me in person," he immediately begins badgering the few Gentiles in the audience ("Do you understand this, mister?" "Who am I talking to?"). His safety zone is Jewish-Gentile contrasts. Jews always have the biggest doctors in the world—the head of the hospital. Rising from his chair, he kvetches and moans: "Did you ever see a healthy Jew?" Jews have no desire to be in rodeos, while Gentiles love to fly off broncos ("I say, schmuck, use the other hand"). Jews won't become jockeys because they could never weigh eighty-five pounds ("A Jew is not going to give up coffee and Coke just to sit on a horse").

This is familiar stuff from an entertaining insult comedian, but, for most of *Politically* In*correct*, Mason has considerably less engaging things on his mind. One of them is to defend the Jewish civil rights record against anti-Semites like Farrakhan. He rejects the charge that Jews were slave traders. They came from Kiev, not plantations, carrying matzoh balls, not cotton balls. Mason is enraged by the whole notion of what constitutes a "minority" in America. Jews, who are lumped with the majority, are "the most persecuted minority in the world." He therefore would like affirmative action for Jews, starting with a lower basketball net. Whites get fired for saying that blacks make better athletes, but blacks are allowed to make movies called *White Men Can't Jump*.

Indeed, it is reverse discrimination that really shivers his kishkes: "Only the majority is allowed to be persecuted." Because of rules barring previous knowledge of a case, the judicial system is a total fraud—you have to be mentally retarded to get on a jury. The proof: the Menendez brothers "admitted that they killed their parents and the jury said: They didn't." To be charged with sexual harassment, all you have to do is show up: "You're not looking, you're leering; you're not walking, you're stalking." And no matter how lazy or incompetent she is, you can't fire a woman from a job—employ a black homosexual female and "you'd better close your business in a second." As for homosexuals, they're always parading. "Not only that, they demand to be in *your* parade. At the Mafia party, do you invite women from the Hadassah? Never!"

As if this were not enough to alienate him from the Broadway audience, Mason spends most of the second half of his show attacking President Clinton, largely because of what Mason considers his wayward treatment of the truth. "Washington couldn't tell a lie; Nixon couldn't tell the truth; Clinton can't tell the difference." Nixon used to schvitz when he lied; Clinton only schvitzes when he tells the truth. "He says he smoked marijuana but didn't inhale. Would you put a pastrami sandwich in your mouth if you didn't want to eat it?" Whether on the subject of Bosnia, Haiti, Whitewater, or his own health plan, Clinton can do nothing right. The only thing, in fact, that Mason will defend about Clinton is his alleged adultery, a subject on which he finds the press to be totally hypocritical. Still, Mason can't resist his own digs at Clinton's sex life. The president is always in shorts because he doesn't have time to put on his pants, and Hillary selects the women he appoints on the basis of their unattractiveness (Ruth Bader Ginsburg was chosen because she was so skinny Clarence Thomas wouldn't bother her).

I may be wrong, but as a commercial venture I think the new Mason show may be a serious miscalculation. Certainly the tepid applause at the conclusion of the evening did not augur well for future ticket sales. The liberal Jewish spectators that Mason usually attracts are hardly the likeliest audience for satire on minority groups, and *Politically* In*correct* will undoubtedly be charged with sexual and racial intolerance. Still, what we need in a time when free speech is being muzzled is not more restraint—let's leave that to Catharine MacKinnon and the professional sensitivity trainers. It is the freedom to hear the unmentionable, even when it hurts. Mason may be wrongheaded at times, but he's brave, fearless, and funny, and that makes for an exhilarating, if disturbing, evening in the theatre.

1994

The American Mouth

(Sally Marr . . . and her escorts; SubUrbia)

Sally Marr . . . and her escorts, which features five actors and a four-piece band, is actually a one-woman show. If that strikes you as an anomaly, you've never watched Joan Rivers. Endowed with the thrust of a jackhammer and the insistence of a dentist's drill, she gives new meaning to the American tradition of self-reliance. People are allowed on stage with her, but except for a few recorded voice-overs no one else is allowed to speak (the Rivers signature "Can we talk?" obviously contains an inaccurate plural subject). In *Sally Marr*, Rivers monopolizes the play for more than two hours, permitting her "escorts" only to smile or dance or scowl or lip sync like a chorus of the mute. There should be a new Equity category for this kind of passive acting. She even drowns out the band. Yeats dreamed of Shaw as a relentless sewing machine. How would he have dreamed of Joan Rivers? As a perpetual-motion mouth?

We've seen performers before who are always on. Joan Rivers is on and on and on. One has to admire the boundless vitality that drives such an engine, but it's exhausting to watch. We may laugh a lot, but we feel depleted at the end, as if she were filling her reserve tank with the audience's energy. Since Rivers's idea of speech is a soliloquy, listening to her amplified hoarse voice braying at us like a yammering yenta is equivalent to Chinese water torture. She must have been born not like Richard III with a full set of teeth but with a full set of monologues.

Sally Marr, the mother of Lenny Bruce and a stand-up comic herself, is clearly a character with whom Rivers closely identifies. She has based her new play (written with Erin Sanders and Lonny Price) on the emotional history of the woman—unfortunately not recollected in tranquility. On her first appearance she is shlepping a movie screen up the aisle of the theatre, sporting a mink coat and huge black horn-rimmed glasses, complaining about her aging body and how nobody is helping with the screen ("fucking liberation, we did this to ourselves!"). The screen is a visual aid for her comedy class, conducted in a gymnasium otherwise used for basketball by the "Our Lady of Esperanza All Stars." Not long after, she is rolled into a hospital on a gurney, having been raped by a robber when he learned she was Bruce's mother.

She narrates the story of her life while watching herself lying unconscious being worked over by doctors and ignored by a callous nurse. Sally has her own Yiddish-inspired routines, usually performed in transvestite burlesque theatres, and some of the jokes are funny—a miscreant told to "Sin no more and say twenty Hail Murrays," a gay rabbi who "doesn't blow the shofar, he blows the cantor." She also manages a few laughs over her failure to keep a clean home ("People would wipe their feet when they left"). But if Sally Marr is no balabusta, she is no ballbuster either. Her abiding good nature is the source of her difficulties. On the other hand, the various details of her unhappy childhood, mistaken married life, and perfunctory love affairs (including an unsuccessful effort to seduce the rabbi in exchange for a free bar mitzvah for Lenny) would engage us more if they were accounts of a significant historical figure. But Sally, for all her color, has interest mainly as the mother and mentor of a celebrated son.

No doubt because of Rivers's compulsion to dominate the evening, there is far too much Sally Marr and far too little Lenny Bruce. We learn of his exposure, at an early age, to the kind of raw language that would later inform his routines, his tour of duty as a gunner's mate in the navy, his change of name from Schneider to Bruce, and his "skyrocketing to fame" as an underground comic. But there are only a few snatches from his great nightclub spritzing, and virtually nothing about his groundbreaking struggle with the legal system over the use of obscene material. Bruce's death from an overdose is treated primarily as an opportunity for Rivers to exercise her tear ducts.

By the end, when Sally's nurse, who hasn't once cracked her sour features, begins giggling uncontrollably, a theme begins to emerge, which is that people like Sally Marr (and Joan Rivers) serve a crucial human function—to make people laugh. But if others on stage are allowed to respond only with laughter, and not with language, then dramatic relationships are virtually impossible. It may be that *Sally Marr . . . and her escorts* has been inspired by the current mythology that the person responsible for the achievements of every talented, celebrated man is an even more talented, uncelebrated woman (Hélène Cixous's new novel *Manna*, according to a recent ad, is about how wives like Winnie Mandela "disclose and restore their partners' lives"). I have no doubt that Sally Marr was gifted. So is Joan Rivers. But on this occasion those gifts are eclipsed by the solipsism of a totally self-infatuated performer.

Eric Bogosian is another American mouth, another monologuist who has written a play, but since Bogosian has usually been less interested in displaying personal ego than in delineating observed characters, *SubUrbia* is a lot more engrossing than *Sally Marr*. The third in the Festival of New American plays at Lincoln Center, the work is not entirely realized, partly, I suspect, because the author, who normally writes and acts his characters, isn't performing any of the roles. But *SubUrbia* shows a real if developing dramatist at work, with an impeccable ear, who needs only to extend his control of dialogue and character into a command of plot and action.

Recalling Bogosian's birthplace in Woburn, Massachusetts, the play takes place in a working-class suburb called Bernfield, "the pizza and puke capital of the world." In a manner similar to such genre pieces as Fellini's early film *I Vitelloni* and George Lucas's *American Graffiti*, it concerns a group of wayward, listless youths. They spend their endless leisure hours lounging in the parking lot of a 7-Eleven, quarreling, cursing, eating 'shrooms and smoking pot and trying to make out with girls when they are not munching pizza takeout or swilling Budweisers (by the end of the play the stage is strewn with crunched beer cans and potato chips). Without purpose or ambition, they are virtually imprisoned in their squalid environment and personal anomie. Only one of their number has escaped to the outside world—a second-class rock star named Pony—and they await the arrival of his black stretch limo during the early scenes of the play as if it were the coming of some pop-culture Godot.

In short, *SubUrbia* is about Bogosian's perennial themes of sex, drugs, and rock and roll, and about the testosterone-clogged people from his past who enacted those themes. Each seems to be competing over who can sound most alienated ("the end of the world, man," says one, "no hope, no ideas, fucking apocalypse"). The nicest, and perhaps the author's surrogate, is Jeff, a would-be writer and comparative liberal among a band of bigots. Jeff is hopeless about his future and his inability to hold on to Sooze, a girl with ambitions to go to New York, become an artist, and "make people think for a change." Then there is Buff, "the postmodern idiot savant," a hyperactive long-haired scuzzball pothead and alcoholic, who makes his entrance on roller blades wearing a tie-dyed shirt, and spends the rest of the play getting shit-faced. There is also Bee-Bee, a depressed ex-alcoholic fresh from rehab, where the other girls got convulsions from shooting up on cough medicine. And there is Tim, the mercurial air force vet who won himself an honorable discharge by cutting off the end of his finger and now seems to be virtually eaten up with self-hatred, fury, and prejudice against other races, particularly the Indian proprietor of the 7-Eleven where they hang out.

The coming of Pony with Erica, his gorgeous booking agent, initiates a number of sexual encounters which all end badly, and all at one time. Pony goes off with Sooze, Tim fails to get it up with Erica and tells Jeff that he killed her. Though this proves untrue, he comes very close to killing the Indian proprietor. In a tense climax, the two men face each other with drawn guns until Tim, escaping onto the roof, discovers Bee-Bee up there dead from an overdose.

With so little happening throughout the play, the accumulation of events in the last few minutes seems somewhat forced and melodramatic. It only emphasizes the absence of a significant plot line in *Sub-Urbia*, for all its intriguing characterizations. As if to compensate for this lack of action, the gifted Robert Falls of the Goodman Theatre has directed a production that sometimes displays the virtues of Chicago Realism but more often seems overpunctuated, with some of the cast behaving as if they're auditioning for a sitcom. I admired Tim Guinee's performance as Tim, however, a charge of compacted plastique ready to detonate at the sight or even the thought of any minority member. And Derek McLane's construction of the 7-Eleven store, a floating island of products multiplied by clever mirror reflections, not only serves as a flexible acting space but also as an impressive example of American pop art.

If *SubUrbia* is less concentrated than *Talk Radio*, Bogosian's previous play, or less diverse than his previous one-man shows, that may be because it is a considerably more ambitious effort, involving nine mouths rather than one. He has always shown a remarkable capacity to encapsulate cultural moments through single character portraits in assorted places. He is now attempting to stretch his canvas by focusing on numerous figures in a single landscape. That is an important and necessary development for his art. And his vision of the depressed suburban circumstances that foster violence and racism is often searching and true. There is a potentially strong gritty playwright here, another David Mamet or David Rabe, who deserves a salute despite the structural imperfections of his play.

1994

Shakespeare in Our Time
(All's Well That Ends Well; The Tempest)

After a spirited *Measure for Measure* in July, the New York Shakespeare Festival has produced a haunting *All's Well That Ends Well* in August. Much of the credit for this double triumph, surely among the best productions yet seen in Central Park, must go to JoAnne Akalaitis, who first conceived of pairing two of Shakespeare's most difficult problem plays with directors imported from England. Akalaitis was not allowed to enjoy the fruits of her planning, having been removed from her job last spring, but she deserves a posthumous salute for helping to bring the Shakespeare Marathon to its maturity.

All's Well is the third American production directed by Richard Jones, who staged *La Bête* on Broadway in 1991 and a less successful production of Bulgakov's *Black Snow* with my own company last December. From his previous work in theatre and opera, Jones was known as a stylist with a special flair for farce. Recently he has been applying more tenebrous tones to his palette, and *All's Well*, though not without its giddy moments, emerges as an unusually somber experience even by the standards of dark comedy. Always a strong visual director, Jones has provoked a stunning design from the English artist Stewart Laing, whose costumes and setting create an atmosphere of surreal disorientation.

Wide-screen movies broadcast on cable TV are often provided with a "letterbox" format, which elongates the width of the screen and narrows the height. This is a letterbox version of *All's Well That*

Ends Well. The set sits in a horizontal opening spreading across the entire expanse of the stage, with huge doors on either side, madly skewed and raked. This allows for continuous lateral motion and, with the aid of a traveler, uninterrupted scene changes. It also provides room for a few spectators to look down on the action from upstage above, sometimes joining the scene by waving green flags.

The design is essentially an abstraction. On a sea-green backing, marked by an aqua blue strip, hangs a white Rothko-like panel with a Donald Judd–like sculpture in the center which doubles as a mirror. When the action moves to Italy, the panel divides to reveal a lovely Tuscan countryside, decked with burnt-umber fields and a tiny medieval town reminiscent of Robert Wilson's miniature future cities. Washed by Mimi Jordan Sherin's sea-change lighting, the visual impact is ravishing. With this design Mr. Laing takes his place alongside such brilliant young English designers as Bob Crowley and Antony Macdonald.

When the audience enters, a row of candles are flickering on stage, in front of a long table bearing the shrouded body of a man. The body seems to be laid out on a bier and is guarded by a diminutive figure in black (played by a child) wearing a death's-head and carrying a scythe. But death is just waiting, not stinging, and this is no corpse. It is the king of France, languishing from a fistula, and when he is carried off stage by black-clad courtiers to the accompaniment of vibrating chimes and tinkling triangles, the miniature death's-head ominously follows. This figure will appear and reappear throughout the action. Jones has made disease and death the central metaphors of the play.

The decision seems entirely appropriate since not only is the king ailing but the play culminates in the resurrection of a "dead" woman, much like *The Winter's Tale* and *Pericles*. Helena will return from the dead to claim her recalcitrant husband. Before dealing with her own life-and-death problems, however, Helena must resurrect or resuscitate the king with a remedy she has inherited from her father, a famous physician. As shrewdly played by the Irish actress Miriam Healy-Louie, Helena is a shy, passionate, redheaded scholar in spectacles, lonely and abandoned, befriended only by the maternal Countess Rousillon (endowed by Joan Macintosh with magisterial elegance).

Contrasting with images of death and disease, embodied in emblematic black, are images of innocence, embodied in white. In the cure scene it is innocence that medicates disease. Helena, first seen wearing a white robe covered with a black cardigan, is a virgin in the shadow of death. If she fails to heal the king, her life will be forfeited. As she describes the secret remedy while the countess braids her hair, the king is carried in on his long table by uniformed officers who turn his body to prevent bed sores and hover over him like figures in Rembrandt's "The Anatomy Lesson." She climbs on the king's table, facing him on her knees; he sits up, head bowed. When the lights come up after a blackout, the two are merrily dancing while the courtiers applaud and stars sprinkle from the sky.

The reward she elects for curing the king is to choose her own husband. All the court bachelors (including a ten-year-old child) appear before her, but she demands the hand of the Countess Rousillon's son, Bertram. It is Bertram's mean rejection of her (he finds her "base") that poses the major problem of the play, for why would this accomplished woman set her cap for such a soulless snob? Despite his contemptuous treatment, she persists in her chase, only too eager to cast off chastity, which makes Parolles's rebuke to her virginity ("it is too cold a companion . . . away with it. . . . Virginity breeds mites, much like a cheese") seem superfluous. By order of the king, Bertram is married in the Elizabethan equivalent of a shotgun wedding. (Bernard Shaw, praising Helena's aggressive pursuit, made her a model for the "unwomanly woman" Ann Whitefield in *Man and Superman*.) The wedding takes place in a slow march, just before everyone's departure for war. Helena poignantly expresses regret that she chased Bertram from his native land (he can't wait to leave). She nevertheless undertakes to follow him to Italy, a pilgrim with a crook and a backpack.

Much of the second part is dominated by the antics of Parolles, a "notorious liar" and braggart soldier on the pattern of Pistol and Falstaff. As played by a goateed Michael Cumpsty, Parolles spends much of his time in front of a mirror, admiring his bright blue beribboned uniform. As the courtier Lafeu remarks, "The soul of this man is his clothes." By the end, this sartorial fop will be reduced to filthy long johns. Captured and blindfolded by his own soldiers speaking gibberish and pretending to be the enemy, Parolles instantly spills his guts about all the secrets of his camp. It is a scene that reminds us of Falstaff peaching on Prince Hal, but Parolles does not have the wit to extricate himself from charges of cowardice.

Bertram's lusty passion for Diana Capilet provides the means by which Helena can meet the conditions he has made for continuing their marriage—possession of his wedding ring and evidence of marital consummation. For like the companion piece of the summer, *Measure for Measure, All's Well* accomplishes its climatic reconciliation through sexual deception (the Park's 1993 season might be called "The Bed Trick Repertory"). Waiting for Bertram, having substituted herself for Diana in the dark (Helena brings her own pillow and sheets), she lies on the same table that bore the body of the king, observed by the same diminutive figure of death.

And death is an attendant when the victorious army returns to France. Jones interpolates a scene in which the Countess Rousillon has become sick and languishes on the table; instead of ending well, the play concludes in melancholy. Diana comes to accuse Bertram of seducing her, as Isabella accused Angelo in *Measure for Measure*, but discovers that Bertram is equally disposed to libel a decent woman (he calls her "a common gamester to the camp"). The "dead" Helena appears, rising through a trap, not only alive but quick with child. The entire stage turns blue. She and Bertram vow to love each other "ever ever dearly." But even this admittedly unconvincing hymeneal is dampened by the dying countess, who is borne off stage in a slow-motion, Robert Wilson–like procession, trailed by the figure of death.

Most of the acting, in addition to the standout performances of Healy-Louie and Macintosh, is strong and deep. Herb Foster is commanding as the king of France, Graham Winston properly sulky as Bertram, Patrice Johnson appealing as Diana Capilet, Patricia Kilgarrif decisive as her mother, Bette Henritze poignant as the countess's companion, and Henry Stram authoritative as the elderly courtier Lafeu. Michael Cumpsty's Parolles, though well spoken, is more of an egotist than a braggart, a musical comedy star on the order of Robert Goulet. And Rocco Sisto's Lavatch, played as a bourgeois in a white-feathered fedora, lacks true eccentricity. The only genuine comedy is provided by the chorus—courtiers, waiting women, and soldiers drilled within an inch of their lives—whether simultaneously lighting clay pipes during the interrogation scene, or returning from Italy with identical suitcases. Still, comedy is not the point of Jones's production. His approach is more akin to Beaumont and Fletcher's tragicomedy, a style that skirts perilously close to disaster without falling off the edge.

Let me say a word, too, in praise of Jonathan Dove's original music, as performed by some fine instrumentalists under the direction of Alan Johnson. The continuous underscoring of mostly mournful melodies enhances the funereal proceedings at every point (except during the unmasking of Parolles, where it seems inappropriate). The doleful music accomplishes the same function as the surreal set and the ethereal acting style, which is to shut out both the bucolic splendor of the Park and the urban grit of the city while planting the audience in a wholly invented atmosphere. Even with jets and helicopters roaring over our heads, we are persuaded of worlds we never imagined.

1993

George C. Wolfe's dynamic production of *The Tempest*, which played last season in Central Park and has now moved to the Broadhurst, proves once again that Joe Papp's latest successor is a brilliant showman. There is hardly a moment in this New York Shakespeare production that is not alive with dazzling and spectacular effects: Bunraku puppets, Indonesian shadow play, Caribbean carnivals, Macy Day floats, Asian stiltwalkers, death masks, stick dancing, magical transformations effected through a haze of smoke pots. Don't look to spend any quiet time here. The stage is in constant motion. This may be the busiest *Tempest* in history.

It has the advantage of a confident central performance by Patrick Stewart in the role of Prospero, the wronged Duke of "Melon" (Stewart's way of pronouncing "Milan"). Best known to American audiences as Jean-Luc Picard in *Star Trek: The Next Generation*, Stewart comes to the part with considerable stage experience, particularly in England (perhaps this explains why his bio is seven times the length of any other actor's). Although Stewart is clearly better trained for Shakespeare than William Shatner or Leonard Nimoy, his star (trek) presence nevertheless tilts the production. It's hard to believe that this cool, self-possessed Englishman could be father to Carrie

Preston's hyperactive Miranda or brother to Nestor Serrano's hot-blooded Antonio. Stewart represents a calm island of Royal Shakespeare Company acting in a confused sea of American multiculturalism. Usually two worlds are represented in *The Tempest*; here I counted at least eight.

Alas, none of them is very deeply probed. Aside from Serrano's Antonio, a darkly brooding misanthrope with considerable emotional resources, few of the other characters display an internal life. Even Stewart left me relatively unmoved, though he certainly enjoys moments of transcendence, particularly during his renunciation speech, spoken with great suffering at the pace of snails making love. I would guess that Wolfe lavished more time on devising theatrical effects than on deepening character or clarifying action. This is understandable, given his need to hold a distracted spectator's attention in big spaces like the noisy Delacorte and the cavernous Broadhurst. But I left the theatre thinking that, rather than being a transplant, this *Tempest* truly belonged on Broadway, in company with such other stage spectaculars as *Phantom of the Opera* and *Sunset Boulevard*.

In the tradition of current historical revisionism, Wolfe has interpreted the play as a critique of European imperialism. Not only Caliban but also Ariel behave with overt hostility toward their slaveholding colonial master. Because these black islanders treat Prospero more like a malignant Simon Legree than a benign Robinson Crusoe, lines like "So, slave, hence!" and "this thing of darkness I acknowledge mine" ring with new racial meaning. Something is gained in this interpretation. Something is also lost. Played by Aunjanue Ellis in what looks like a decaying Balmain gown, Ariel always seem to be scowling and threatening other characters when she is not on point, hopping, dancing, and twirling as if performing at a Martha Graham concert.

As for Caliban, Wolfe's casting and directing of Teagle F. Bougere in the role strikes me as a major miscalculation. His head shaven and painted red (he looks like he's wearing a colorful bathing cap), Bougere is a slender actor with a winning quality, given to broad smiles, worldly winks, and graceful bows. He'd make a fine Puck. I'd even like to see him play Ariel. But a smiling, worldly, winning, graceful Caliban? In his effort to redeem the natives, Wolfe seriously underplays Caliban's brutal, lecherous quality. This "monster," after all, represents man in a state of nature (his very name is almost an anagram for "cannibal"). Wolfe also chooses to forget the fact that, rather than being allies, Caliban and Ariel fear and loathe each other, and that he almost raped Miranda.

And what a Miranda! Behaving as if she trained for the part by flipping between network sitcoms, Carrie Preston indulges in such goofy glandular mannerisms that she manages to persuade us the girl is not only ignorant but simpleminded. Preston is mismatched with Paul Whitthorne's lyrical Ferdinand. Trinculo and Stefano are simply tiresome vaudevillians. And the courtiers, with the exception of Serrano and McIntyre Dixon's gentle Gonzalo, seem to be as stranded in their characters as in the Bermoothes.

What I did admire were the elements of physical production: Riccardo Hernandez's setting—a circular ramp, miraculously covered with sand after the opening storm at sea; Paul Gallo's shafts of pinpoint lighting; the thunderous sound design of Dan Moses Schreier; Barbara Pollitt's mask and puppet designs; Hope Clarke's lively choreography; and the usually unendurable masque of Juno, Ceres, and Iris (played on stilts). All of Wolfe's design collaborators, in fact, have united to provide a visual and aural feast. And the epilogue constitutes a breathtaking piece of stagecraft, as Prospero, with no art left to enchant, speaks his lines in front of a disappearing set, revealing a naked stage wall illuminated by bare stage lights. But because of Wolfe's emphasis on racial divisions, a play about forgiveness is not sufficiently allowed to enjoy its reconciliations. Near the end of the show Antonio refuses Prospero's hand, and Caliban almost clubs him. Shakespeare's isle "is full of noises / Sounds and sweet airs, that give delight and hurt not." Wolfe's enchanted island is certainly full of delight. But lacking sufficient human dimension, it offers little depth or warmth.

1995

The Roots of Love
(Passion)

The original score of *Passion*, the latest Stephen Sondheim–James Lapine musical, is a mid-nineteenth-century Italian novel by I. U. Tarchetti called *Fosca*, which also inspired an Italian film called *Passione d'Amore*. The similarity between the name of Tarchetti's heroine and Puccini's Tosca is no doubt accidental. The two women are of an entirely different order, having little in common but their nationality and that odd syllabic assonance. After witnessing this work, however, I couldn't get Puccini out of my head, partly because *Passion* left me drenched with the same overpowering emotion I felt after seeing *La Bohème* at the New York Public Theater some years back. I know it is not seemly for a drama critic to admit to experiencing excessive feeling, especially over a work that, despite its (grudgingly given) Tony awards, is drawing a lot of scorn in sophisticated theatre circles. But I am compelled to tell you that, like the similarly derided *Bohème* at the Public, *Passion* held me in its grip from the opening chords and had me sobbing uncontrollably at the end.

I believe *Passion* to be Sondheim's deepest, most powerful work, and I've been trying to figure out why it's not been more appreciated by the profession. Of course it's possible that I'm wrong, that I'm suffering a lapse in taste, that I'm a sucker for plots in which women die (my friend, the Broadway producer Rocco Landesman, has advised me to have my head examined). I prefer to think there's another explanation for our differing opinions, namely that *Passion* has been misidentified as a musical and mislocated in a Broadway house. The work is clearly an opera, and were it sitting where it belongs, on the stage of the Houston Grand Opera or the Chicago Lyric, I'm convinced it would have elicited the kind of respect it truly deserves. Aside from being largely sung, *Passion* differs from a conventional musical in the way it strengthens inferior texts instead of cheapening good source material. Although Verdi made successful use of Shakespeare in *Falstaff* and *Otello*, that is an exception. More often, good operas are inspired by hacks like Sardou and Belasco, while, with the exception, say, of the Lerner–Loewe *My Fair Lady*, which improved on Shaw's *Pygmalion*, musicals usually debase and vulgarize their books. Sondheim and Lapine have previously been concerned with sophisticating, urbanizing, and intellectualizing their source material. Now they are engaged in a musical exploration of the irrational and mysterious roots of love. The results are refreshingly wholehearted and unpretentious. The time is 1863, and the action begins with a nude couple in bed, extolling their sexual pleasure in one another ("so much happiness, so much love"). Giorgio is a dashing officer in the Italian army, Clara is a redheaded actress with an alabaster body. Though they are ideally suited, there are two obstacles to the fulfillment of their passion—she is married, and he is about to be transferred from Milan to a regiment in Parma. Following this transfer, their love becomes largely epistolary. They exchange letters in song, remembering their pleasurable nights together and anticipating their reunion.

Quickly the musical mood shifts. The moment Giorgio joins the Parma regiment and takes his place at the regimental table, the male camaraderie at dinner is broken by an anguished female cry. The colonel's cousin, Fosca, is "a medical phenomenon," suffering from a mysterious ailment that causes convulsions and leaves her nerves exposed. The doctor can do nothing, and on her first appearance we see that Fosca suffers not only from physical pain but from considerable ugliness. Pale and pinched, brooding and forlorn, her forehead punctuated with heavy eyebrows, her nose decorated with a huge wart, her coarse black hair pulled into a homely bun, she is a portrait of gloom and melancholy, in charmless contrast with the sunny and wholesome Clara.

Fosca's only consolation is literature, particularly Rousseau novels, but literature for her is largely an escape from wretchedness: "I do not read to think, I read to dream." Staggering and swaying, bent into a question mark of pain, she essentializes the doomed, self-pitying invalid. But although too fragile to be a lover, she immediately conceives an uncontrollable passion for Giorgio. We expect to learn, at this point, that, like the Elephant Man's, Fosca's hideous exterior conceals a beautiful soul and a great heart. But this is far from a conventional story; the woman soon proves as repellent inside as out. Giorgio, kindly to a fault, counsels Fosca to dwell not on pain but rather on beauty and on life. She willfully misinterprets his offer of friendship as a protestation of love. Her own passion soon turns into an annoying obsession. She grabs his hand, hugs him against his will, falls to her knees, crying "What can I do to get you to love me?" though Giorgio has hidden nothing from her, least of all his feeling for Clara, whom Fosca declares her rival.

Fosca falls ill and takes to her bed, prepared to die because "You rejected my love." When he visits her bedside, she exploits his guilt and sympathy, demanding that he compose a love letter to her which she dictates. Giorgio's pity for her deepens when her cousin tells of how deeply she was wounded by a fortune hunter, a fake Austrian count, a bigamist who stole her dowry and gambled it away. But Giorgio's compassion only makes him more vulnerable to Fosca's persistent advances. Recovering from her illness, she continues to plague him wherever he goes, with her "endless and insatiable smothering." Although the other officers suspect that he is toying with Fosca in order to advance himself, Giorgio is physically deteriorating from her obsession, feverishly dreaming that she is dragging him down to the grave.

Departing for Milan on sick leave, Giorgio still finds himself hounded by Fosca. She joins him on the train, burrowing like an earwig into his skull, like a mole into his heart. Exasperated beyond endurance, he cancels his leave and berates her for her selfish behavior, to which she replies, "I feel too much—I often don't know what to do with my feelings." Her passion is selfish, but it is also selfless. She would sacrifice herself for love: "Would Clara give her life for you?" Giorgio soon learns that Clara's healthier love is not capable of sacrifice. She will not leave her marriage, lest she lose her child. The two break up after Clara sends him a letter suggesting that he wait until her son is grown: "Just another love story—no one is to blame."

But the colonel has discovered the dictated love letter and, believing that Giorgio has taken advantage of his cousin's affections, challenges him. The evening before the duel, Giorgio tells Fosca that his affair with Clara is over. And in a stunning reversal, wracked with sobs at the thought that she would die for him, he confesses that her stubborn and fretful passion has replaced Clara's wholesome affection in his heart: "No one has ever loved me as deeply as you. . . . Love within reason, that isn't love—and I've learned this from you." They kiss awkwardly and, even more awkwardly, make love. The colonel is wounded in the duel, Giorgio is hospitalized with a nervous disorder, Fosca dies from her disease. And that is the end of this bizarre story about the inexplicable and unpredictable sources of romantic passion.

Sondheim's music and lyrics are as ferocious and tremulous as Fosca's love, whether driving the ecstatic exchanges of Giorgio and Clara or the gloomy declarations of the heroine. And aside from fashioning a powerful book, James Lapine has staged a truly elegant production, with a precision worthy of the military environment. The physical setting is gorgeous. Jane Greenwood's costumes—particularly attractive on Clara, whose gowns change color with each exchange of letters—are not only exquisite in themselves but help to characterize the players, whether the officers in their crisp uniforms or the severe black clothes of Fosca. And Adrienne Lobel's brown and mauve setting—essentially made up of sliding panels, a scrim, and, on one occasion, a huge swath of red velvet curtain—conjure up the perspectives of Canaletto and the harbors of Caravaggio, as well as the ominous moors of a Brontë landscape.

The performances are superb, not only the three leads but even minor roles like Tom Aldredge's sympathetic though baffled regimental doctor. Jere Shea brings a tender manliness and baritone appeal to the role of Giorgio which makes him a fitting object for the love of two entirely different women. The moment, right before he declares himself to Fosca, when his jaw starts to shake and his body trembles, is an expression of such deep grief it transfigures the spectator. (I was reminded of Rudolfo's breakdown over Mimi's body at the Public.) Marin Mazzie's Clara is a woman of great attractiveness and worldliness, capable of warm feeling but not at the cost of survival. And Donna Murphy, both ferocious and lyrical as Fosca, is giving a truly powerful performance. Her capacity to attract pity for this woman, and to make her worthy of Giorgio's love, without ever once underplaying the sour and repulsive aspects of the character, is a sign of very special histrionic control.

At the performance I attended the audience responded with subdued and tepid applause in contrast to the customary hysteria and pandemonium one hears at Broadway musicals, including those of Sondheim. But *Passion* is a triumph of rare and complex sensibility, fully imagined, fully realized. As a fairly consistent critic of Stephen

Sondheim's recent work, I am grateful for the opportunity to reverse myself. He and his collaborators are to be congratulated for bringing dignity, profundity, and passion to the impoverished commercial stage.

1994

The Merchant of Venice Beach
(The Merchant of Venice)

Peter Sellars's production of *The Merchant of Venice* at the Goodman Theatre in Chicago is a four-hour media-soaked event that loses half its patrons after the first curtain. Don't be surprised. Sellars has been dividing audiences at least since his Harvard undergraduate days, when he performed the entire *Ring* cycle with marionettes and staged *Antony and Cleopatra* in the Adams House swimming pool. He is an artist endowed with great whimsy and considerable imagination, but not, in my opinion, with a commensurate conceptual mind. This imbalance tends to make his productions appear both daring and predictable at the same time. Sellars approaches classical operas and plays with a lot of dazzle but usually the same overall concept, which is to substitute for the original historical setting a modish contemporary equivalent. He seems most comfortable, in other words, in the role of transcultural travel agent, booking rooms for *The Marriage of Figaro* in the Trump Tower, making reservations for *Julius Caesar* in the Nile Hilton. However he may annoy people with this kind of fashionable time-tripping, Sellars is rarely boring. His *Merchant of Venice* is designed to irritate the bejesus out of you, which explains why so many skipped out on the second part. But it is never dull and, to be honest, I think it deserves a certain grudging respect.

Merely to describe the production concept is to be complicit in its self-consciousness and preciosity, so I wouldn't be surprised if readers decide to walk out on my review as well. Visually Sellars has abandoned his customary scenic display (not to mention his favorite set designer, Adrienne Lobel), settling for a bare stage festooned with television monitors. When the lights come up, Antonio is explaining to Salarino and Salanio why he feels so sad ("It wearies me, you say it wearies you"). His lines are from the text, except that his companions are now pushing video and sound equipment into his face. Obviously Antonio's depression is an item for the evening news. So is virtually everything else that happens in this prime-time world. Privacy no longer exists. Every major speech is miked, every major action televised. Shylock's poignant "Hath not a Jew eyes?" is an occasion for a celebrity interview. Salarino and Salanio feed us exposition like two sports announcers commenting on a game at halftime. The trial scene is played out on Court TV. This *Merchant of Venice* is channel surfing for couch potatoes. If you get bored by the text, you can always switch to Warhol-like videos (surf scenes, pool scenes, garden scenes) projected by Sellars on the alternate monitors.

When Antonio begins fondling Bassanio's thigh (also on camera), we learn the source of his blues—his gay partner has conceived a heterosexual passion for Portia. I'm puzzled why the melancholy Antonio would be willing to risk his fortune (and his life) to help Bassanio court another lover, and a woman at that. But since this merchant conducts his business not in Venice, Italy, but rather in Venice Beach, California, perhaps Sellars is trying to tell us something pertinent about West Coast polymorphous perversity.

Racially mixed Southern California certainly accounts for the culturally diverse makeup of the cast. Antonio, Bassanio, Gratiano, and all their friends are played by Latinos, sometimes in zoot suits, fresh from the barrio. Portia, Nerissa, and another servant are Asians. Launcelot Gobbo and Old Gobbo are Caucasians. Shylock, Tubal, and Jessica are black. Only the Prince of Morocco is of the color Shakespeare intended, though hardly of the class, since he is conceived as a street dude sporting gold chains and a woolen cap. It goes without saying that this is hardly conventional nontraditional casting, which is typically color-blind. Rather, it is determinedly color-conscious, even color-perverse. To cast blacks as Jews, for example, may strike one as pure accessorizing—multicultural chic. Yet occasionally the choice begins to make some vague subterranean sense.

I suspect Sellars would like us to see the play as an essay on the subject of race and sex. For example, not only have Antonio and Bassanio been having an extra-textual love affair. So have black Jessica and white Launcelot Gobbo, creating in them a state of separation anxiety, even (following her abduction) sullenness and anger. When

Lorenzo, Jessica's Latino lover, says of the letter written by his African-American mistress that "whiter than the paper it is writ on is the fair hand that writ," we experience an unexpected shock that startles the scene into irony (the same thing happens after Portia's racist remark about the Moroccan prince, "Let all of his complexion choose me so").

Additionally, the sequence where Portia and Nerissa disguise themselves as lawyers Sellars uses as an extended commentary on feminist cross-dressing. Portia, attired in a double-breasted Melrose Avenue suit, grabs her crotch and launches into a satirical rap on macho males ("We are accomplished with that we lack"), strutting like a stud and pretending her shoe is a penis. Similarly, the harmless trick which she and Nerissa play on Bassanio and Gratiano—demanding the men's rings as a reward for freeing Antonio—later becomes an occasion for spats about their relationships that may impair them permanently, while Jessica, always sulky with Lorenzo, walks out on him after learning she is Shylock's heir. These recriminations make the conclusion of the show extremely bleak, hardly the stuff of romantic comedy. But the dark ending is typical of how the entire production has been tilted. Sellars changes the meaning of every single line of Shakespeare's play, which makes his refusal to cut a single line seem more like loyalty to his own clever ideas than to the playwright.

And he has certainly managed to skirt the central problem of the work for modern audiences. There is nothing here to stir the feathers of the Anti-Defamation League. To cast Shylock as an African-American businessman instead of a usurious Jew not only blurs the anti-Semitic overtones of the play. It changes it from a satire on a menacing outsider into an indictment of American racism. Phoning Tubal about the loss of his daughter and his ducats, Shylock begins sobbing so hard over his dead wife and the precious jewel she gave him that he can't continue the call. As Paul Butler plays the part, with hooded hauteur, towering dignity, and gathering rage, this Shylock is seeking vengeance for every humiliation suffered by black people since the days of slavery.

In the climactic trial scene, as Shylock sharpens his knife on the sole of his shoe preparing to cut his pound of flesh, the video monitors are dominated by scenes of the L.A. riots. This is a typically suggestive and typically inexact analogy, since Butler's Shylock looks more like Clarence Thomas than Rodney King, and since it is Antonio rather than Shylock who is being tried. Nevertheless, the scene is highly charged, its ominousness underscored by sound designer Bruce Odland's moody piano arpeggios. Shylock waves away Portia's mercy speech as if it's nothing but racist cant. But when he takes the stand to testify about his daughter, he is once again racked with grief.

The duke (Del Close)—unlike Judge Ito he encourages cameras in the courtroom—permits Portia to humiliate, debase, and disinherit Shylock, leaving the audience with the sense not that a vengeful scapegoat has been ejected from a just society, but rather that a black man can never obtain justice either from whites or Latinos. Following the anticlimactic hassle over the rings, the play ends in darkness and gloom. Lorenzo and Jessica are Splitsville. Gratiano throws his ring at Nerissa's feet. Only Bassanio and Portia are allowed a moment of reconciliation, as he puts his coat over her shoulders and she strokes his hand.

It is important to add that the cast provides the most confident acting I have yet seen under Sellars's direction. In addition to the superb Shylock of Paul Butler and the fatigued duke of Del Close, Elaine Tse makes a volatile Portia, Rene Rivera an appealing Lorenzo, Geno Silva a suave Antonio, and John Ortiz an engaging Bassanio. Dunya Ramicova's costumes and James F. Ingalls's lighting are tailor-made for postmodern deconstruction, and the audiovisual technology is handled with efficiency. That very efficiency, however, makes the evening, in the end, more a media event than a work of theatre. Some vital spark of humanity is buried under the stockpile of bright ideas, just as the intrinsic quality of the play is submerged beneath the extrinsic impact of the interpretation. When a little human feeling is allowed to escape from all the high-tech ostentation, as in the shaking shoulders of Shylock, this *Merchant of Venice* bursts momentarily into life. Whatever my caveats about the interpretation, whatever the audience reception, the Goodman Theatre deserves congratulations for mounting the production. It is an important (I won't say a healthy) antidote to the recurrent realism of the Chicago School.

1994

Plays for the Parch

(Simpatico; The Waiting Room; Death Defying Acts)

Sam Shepard's new play, *Simpatico*, which he also directed, has taken as many critical lumps as his last play, *States of Shock*. Viewed as an overarching dramatic work, *Simpatico* probably deserves a few knocks, but I found it an absorbing evening nevertheless. It is Shepard's best since *Buried Child*—not because of the cryptic writing, which is strong in individual scenes but ultimately too swamped by its own mysteries. I admired it largely for its acting values. Shepard's directorial technique has advanced considerably in confidence and precision since his last staging assignment (*A Lie of the Mind*). He's a whiz now with scene work; there isn't a slack moment in the play. But, as in *Lie of the Mind*, the director is too reluctant to edit the playwright; some fat could have been profitably cut; at three hours, *Simpatico* is simply too long for its subject matter. Even supplied with ample detail to distract you from the anorexic dramatic purpose, you tend to leave the theatre feeling a little underfed. Still, the evening is wonderfully conceived and performed, and riveting moment by moment. *Simpatico* is a sustained piece of virtuosity that makes you happy Sam Shepard has returned to the stage.

At some point in the proceedings, a character says, "Who is it decided to do away with all the plots?" Well, whoever it was, all the plots ended up in *Simpatico*, which has enough for a dozen such plays. It is true that Shepard has already written some of these plots, and often written them better. He's looted *True West* for the symbiotic tension between his once "simpatico" central male characters, *Geography of a Horse Dreamer* for reflections on the corruptions of the racetrack, and *Fool for Love* for some sultry love scenes. He's also borrowed some sexual teasing from Tennessee Williams's *Baby Doll*, some film noir atmosphere from James M. Cain's *The Postman Always Rings Twice* and *Double Indemnity*, and a whole character (a drifter masquerading as a detective) from the movie *Miami Blues*. This is larceny on a grand creative scale, but *Simpatico* still bears the characteristic stamp of its author. Like Brecht, Shepard knows how to convert others' private property into his own idiosyncratic real estate.

The trouble is that a coherent dramatic purpose tends to get lost in the underbrush. *Simpatico* is tantalizing enough in its narrative twists and turns to hold your interest, but what it finally delivers is not substantial enough to reward your patience. As the action drifts from Cucamonga, California, to blue-grass Kentucky, and back again, *Simpatico* begins to revolve around a racetrack scam that is now causing Carter, the central character, to come apart at the seams. Fifteen years before the action begins, Carter switched a couple of thoroughbreds in order to make a quick bundle, and when the racing commissioner detected the swindle, arranged to have him discredited. In the manner of a private eye collecting evidence for a divorce, he had photos taken of the commissioner in a motel encounter with a young woman, and blackmailed him into silence.

The commissioner (Simms) agreed to hold his tongue and go to another town under an assumed name. But Vinnie Webb, the accomplice who took the photographs (his ex-wife, Rosie, was the woman in the motel room), now wants to expose the truth, partly to come out from under his long exile, partly to pay Carter back for stealing Rosie and his '58 Buick. As in most Shepard plays, the sibling rivalry between these longtime companions is the nub of the action. The playwright draws a familiar contrast between a slick successful achiever (Carter) who is nevertheless riddled with guilt, and a disheveled, disreputable loner (Vinnie) who maintains the moral high ground.

Carter and Vinnie are played by Ed Harris and Fred Ward, both of them (along with Shepard) alumni of *The Right Stuff,* so the casting is like a class reunion. Harris, wearing a tan double-breasted suit in danger of being shredded by his muscles, does a subtle take on a rigid man without a center, an ex-ex-alcoholic with quivering shoulders, an eggshell in process of being shattered. Ward, sporting a two-day growth of beard and a mischievous glint as Vinnie, fully inhabits the role of a derelict masquerading as a private dick and only dicking himself.

Vinnie takes a tour of Kentucky, carrying a shoebox full of the incriminating photographs, eager to find "the man who fell from grace," the mysterious Simms. Simms (another strong raspy performance by James Gammon), while denying his identity, nevertheless admits that he once heard of a man who had been vilified and railroaded out of town, losing his entire family (though, Simms adds, "loss can be a powerful elixir"). When Simms spurns the photos, Vinnie goes to Lexington to offer them to Rosie, his ex-wife (Beverly D'Angelo in a steamy, gin-soaked performance). First she refuses to recognize him, then she also refuses the negatives.

In the meantime, Carter has been making time with Vinnie's girlfriend, Cecilia (Marcia Gay Harden). He eventually persuades her to visit Simms by hypnotizing her with sagas of the Kentucky Derby. She believes Simms has bought Vinnie's negatives and now wants to buy them back for Carter. But Simms's ironic manner, his insinuating stories of such great thoroughbreds as Secretariat, work on her like an aphrodisiac, making her short of breath. Simms tells her he was betrayed by two snakes: "Some of us get caught with our pants down and some of us don't—I was one of the lucky ones."

When Vinnie rejoins Carter, holed up in Vinnie's bed, he finds a shivering wreck of man who can't put on his own pants and believes his number is up. Carter now wants to swap lives, just as he once swapped horses. He offers Vinnie his fortune, his estate, and Rosie in return for Vinnie's purity of conscience. Vinnie, "working on a new case," ignores him and leaves. Cecilia returns to pour Carter's blood money over him on the bed, just as Tilden in *Buried Child* once poured vegetables over his father's sleeping body. The phone rings. Carter is too paralyzed to answer it.

Aside from its impressionist portrait of treachery, betrayal, and failed redemption, this doesn't add up to much more than manipulated suspense, but it is a wonder how Shepard can keep us traveling with him on this long day's journey into blight. *Simpatico* is a treasure hunt that never yields much treasure, except as a demonstration of fine ensemble acting and powerful directing (along with sharp minimalist designing by Loy Arcenas, who can even make a dirty kitchen sink look like a sinister symbol). If it doesn't entirely deliver as a play, *Simpatico* certainly satisfies as a rich theatrical effluvium, and that's no small thing in a time of drought.

Another antidote to drought has been playing at the Trinity Repertory Company in Providence, a play called *The Waiting Room* by a young, extremely gifted West Coast writer named Lisa Loomer. The title refers to a waiting room in a doctor's office, occupied by three sickly women of different nationalities, periods, and temperaments: Forgiveness from Heaven, an eighteenth-century Chinese wife whose bound feet (size three) have caused her toes to fall off; Victoria, a Victorian lady with a sixteen-inch cinched waist, whose "hysteria" is treated as a gynecological disease (she had tried everything, including leeches on the vagina, and now must have her ovaries removed); and the modern Wanda whose mountainous silicone breasts, surgically implanted along with nose, cheekbone, thigh, and tummy tucks, have resulted in a fatal case of breast cancer ("How did you get cancer?" asks a nurse. "You don't have a single body part that's real").

Each is a victim of idiotic male ideals of beauty, but instead of angry indictments, Loomer provides an evening of black comedy in the corruscating manner of Caryl Churchill, lacing it with wit, grace, and insight. Douglas, who provides primary care for all these suffering ladies, is an overworked doctor with a head cold, hawking and spitting and offering minimal comfort ("It's perfectly normal . . . call me if it turns green"). Victoria's husband, Oliver, is an uptight British fop who stammers when he utters the word "Mother" (Victoria involuntarily hits him in the chest whenever she says the word "husband"). Forgiveness from Heaven agrees to bind the feet of her husband's fifth wife, an eleven-year-old, as long as she gets to pull on her opium pipe. Wanda, who has no husband despite her surgical sacrifices, has come to believe that "the odds of my getting married by forty are not quite as good as my getting shot by a terrorist."

The keen clinical satire would be enough to carry this play, but it eventually veers off into something more important—a lacerating examination of the limitations of modern medicine (symbolized by the goddess Hygeia, a triple amputee) and the venal reasons why cancer has not yet been cured. Everyone seems to have the disease, including Dr. Douglas, but the only promising treatment has been blocked by the FDA through the machinations of a greedy drug company. By the end, all three women are on gurneys performing a hospital bed ballet—Forgiveness has lost four toes to gangrene, Victoria has had her uterus removed, and Wanda has said goodbye to her breasts. The future of all three is dim. "But we'll see each other in the waiting room, won't we, and it's always such a long wait."

It is a very moving play, all the more remarkable for being so hilariously cross-cultural (Victoria tells a noisy rapper to shut the hell up—"There's no melody"). And under David Schweitzer's crisp and effortless direction, it is extremely well acted by the entire cast, especially the three central women, June Kyoko Lu, Anne Scurria, and Janice Duclos, and by William Damkoehler as the sniffling po-faced physician, Dr. Douglas.

The Waiting Room arrives in the first season supervised by Trinity's new artistic director, Oskar Eustis, who was responsible for the play's debut at the Mark Taper in Los Angeles. If Eustis can continue to attract work of this high quality, then Trinity will soon be an important oasis for plays that relieve the parch.

1994

Death Defying Acts, in a crisp elegant production directed by Michael Blakemore, is a trio of one-act plays by David Mamet, Elaine May, and Woody Allen. It is superbly acted (by a cast of seven) and designed (by Robin Wagner) in a manner that evokes the heyday of great sixties comedy.

Mamet's "An Interview" is perhaps the slightest of the three but also the most contemporary, a colloquy between an attorney and his interrogator which turns out to be his entrance exam for hell. In a small room illuminated by shafts of light on grey walls, the lawyer is continually pressed to admit what he continues to deny: that he once buried a lawnmower. It is a metaphor for a life of legal deception. His crime is that he "passed the bar and neglected to live forever." "Are you saying there are no honest lawyers?" asks the attorney. The interviewer only smiles. Strongly acted by Paul Guilfoyle and Gerry Becker, the skit continues Mamet's vendetta against the legal profession that he began in his earlier one-act play "Oh Hell."

Elaine May's "Hotline" is about a middle-aged hooker who swallows some pills, then changes her mind and attempts to seek help from a suicide counselor. It is simply hilarious, distinguished by Elaine May's deft control of character and the funniest performance I have seen in years by Linda Lavin. Playing Dorothy the call girl with a broad Long Island accent, redheaded bangs, and uncontrollable fury, Lavin provides a classic demonstration of how the best comic acting proceeds from an interior of pain. Trying to get through to the suicide hot line before she gobbles the pills, she can't even reach 911 until she announces that a bomb has been planted at Police Emergency. Dorothy has epic encounters with a telephone system populated by non-English speaking operators ("I didn't say she was an asshole because she's Puerto Rican, I said she was an asshole *and* Puerto Rican—just like you're an asshole and not a Puerto Rican! See?"). Isolated and alone, her life is one loud bark of despair: "I don't have any friends. Why? Because I'm *unpleasant*! Haven't you noticed?" Sliding into narcosis from her overdose, she falls asleep, wakes up, then crawls toward her phone—to inquire after her messages! Her desperation is matched by that of her hot-line contact (played by Gerry Becker), who makes it his mission to save her: "Tell me where you live. . . . You owe me another twenty fucking years of your life." Finally he discovers her address—"I found you, I found you, I found you!"—in a climax which establishes the most intimate relationship between two people who never manage to meet. I suspect "Hot Line" began as a telephone monologue, in which form it might have been more potent, but even extended into dialogue it is a powerful piece of comic theatre.

Woody Allen's "Central Park West" is another relationship play which showcases Linda Lavin's superb acting talents. Visiting her friend Phyllis (played by Debra Monk) in her West Side apartment—a decorated living room festooned with the obligatory African sculpture—she appears as a bourgeois matron named Carol in a blonde wig and yellow Bloomingdale's cloth coat, looking like a cross between Barbara Walters and Kitty Carlisle. Someone has been sleeping with Phyllis's husband Sam (Paul Guilfoyle), and Phyllis is ready for divorce (Sam has agreed to keep paying for her Sunday *Times*, though that was not part of the nuptial agreement).

Inevitably it is revealed that Sam's lover is Carol, which Phyllis knew all along ("You're the all-American whore—they should put your diaphragm in the Smithsonian"). Carol protests that "It's sensual, yes, but it's more—we share feelings and dreams." But after Carol has confessed to her nerdy husband Harry (Gerry Becker) her plan to marry Sam, Sam himself reveals that he has fallen in love with a young actress and abandons Carol ("Sometimes there's God so quickly," says the vengeful Phyllis).

"Central Park West" is loaded with (very funny) one-liners as well as heavy autobiographical baggage. It never transcends its form to become the promised satire on the vacuous and bored wife-swapping classes, possibly because the dramatist is a member of that class, instead of on the outside watching. But as its best the play evokes the sharp wit we associate with Nichols and May, Lenny Bruce, and *Doctor Strangelove*, as well as an occasion for superb ensemble work.

1995

Boat Show
(Show Boat)

Hal Prince has brought *Show Boat* into home port after a maiden cruise in Canadian waters (it was first commissioned in Toronto). You won't immediately recognize this streamlined ocean liner as the Mississippi paddleboat that first dropped anchor on Broadway in 1927, sailed to London's Drury Lane in 1928, made a Hollywood cruise in 1936 skippered by Charles Winninger as Cap'n Andy (Joe E. Brown in the 1951 Technicolor version), and later returned to a Broadway harbor in 1946, refitted for brief voyages to open-air amphitheatres, light-opera houses, summer-stock stages, and other second-rate tour stops. Instead of leaving this overworked old tub in drydock, Prince has totally refurbished it with jet engines and a brand new coat of paint. But if the decks look spanking clean and the hull knifes through the water like a destroyer, the hold still carries the same cargo of treacle and molasses.

Prince is one of those directors—so are Des MacAnuff (*Tommy*), Nicholas Hytner (*Carousel*), and Stephen Daldry (*An Inspector Calls*), among others—who now lavish considerable creative gifts on inferior matter. In the past Prince brought Brechtian staging techniques to a number of innovative musicals (*Pacific Overtures, Evita, Sweeney Todd*). Recently he has fit less in the tradition of Bertolt Brecht than that of David Belasco, supervising big bludgeoning stage spectaculars (*Phantom of the Opera, Kiss of the Spider Woman, Show Boat*) instead of works of substance. Prince no longer has to prove he is a remarkable showman. There is no doubt he is brilliant at enlivening recalcitrant material with sensational stage effects (*vide* the falling chandelier in *Phantom of the Opera*). But how does he justify spending so many millions simply to make over a leaky old scow like *Show Boat* into the prize feature of a Broadway boat show?

Prince's program note provides the answer—social conscience. This is not, he believes, just another American musical but "the first to merge the traditional, happy-go-lucky naiveté of B'way musical comedy with serious themes." It was *Show Boat*'s lyricist and book writer, Oscar Hammerstein II, Prince reminds us, "who time and time again (the subject of miscegenation was central to *South Pacific* 22 years later) took fierce aim at prejudice in our society. 'You've Got to Be Carefully Taught' are *his* words."

Indeed they are his words, and they mark a moment when the light entertainment known as musical comedy became weighted with leaden social messages—the time, that is, when Broadway became the happy hunting grounds of people who managed to feel liberal while making a lot of money. Since this production of *Show Boat* is very much in that pious tradition, there is irony in the fact that it became the object of racial protest in Toronto before rehearsals had even begun (some black Canadians declared the work insulting). Prince responded to those protests by eliminating "any inadvertent stereotype" and "Uncle Tom" dialogue from the original material. A Southern river rat is still permitted to utter the word "nigger" as evidence of his bigotry, but the black cast members working on the Mississippi have stopped referring to themselves as "darkies," and they no longer get a little drunk and land in jail.

Prince boasts that the racial protests stopped when the allegations proved to be unfounded. But I wouldn't be surprised if his production encountered renewed objections from the African-American community. *Show Boat* may take a bold stand on behalf of "miscegenation" (somewhat less provocatively known as "interracial marriage"), but for all the laundering of offensive language, black people may still feel somewhat insulted at their treatment in the production. Both Oscar Hammerstein's operetta and the Edna Ferber novel on which it was based drew heavily on such tremulous nineteenth-century melodramas as Dion Boucicault's *The Octoroon* in devising the subplot of the mulatto Julie, persecuted by Southern bigots for her illegal marriage to a white man. To save her from prison, her husband cuts his wrist and mingles her tainted blood with his own. That stirring moment of nobility aside, there is little in this lightweight plot to suggest any "fierce aim at prejudice," and most of the black actors in the huge cast of seventy-three serve primarily as background decoration. The basso Joe wanders over the stage singing Jerome Kern's classic "Ol' Man River" even when the action moves to Chicago (the Chicago River?), and his wife Queenie (Butterfly McQueen?) does a job birthing Magnolia's baby. But the others function mostly as local color, not to mention cheap labor. When not toting barges and lifting bales, they are pulling winches, hoisting anchors, dusting paintings, and cleaning floors. I know that Prince is trying to emphasize that the work assigned to blacks under post–Civil War segregation was exhausting and demeaning. But after making his black supernumeraries moonlight as stagehands and techies, sweeping the stage and changing the sets, he could very well be accused of having established his own plantation.

Actually the production draws its energy not from social issues but from visual effects. It is most effective when most theatrical, and it is most confident treating the characters whom show-people know best—namely other show-people. The first, and by far the better, of the two acts begins with the docking of the Cotton Blossom, all flags waving, on a Natchez levee, nudged into berth by a full-size tugboat. The stock company of this "Floating Palace Theatre" is thereupon introduced, both as characters in its current attraction, a creaking melodrama called *The Parson's Bride*, and as characters in the equally corny attraction known as *Show Boat*. These include Cap'n Andy (John McMartin) and his starchy wife, Parthy (Elaine Stritch); their daughter Magnolia (Rebecca Luker), who becomes a leading lady when Julie (Lonette McKee) is forced to flee town with her husband Steve (Doug LaBrecque); the comic dancing duo, Frank (Joel Blum) and Ellie (Dorothy Stanley); and, finally, Gaylord Ravenal (Mark Jacoby), the gambler turned leading man, who joins the troupe after falling in love with Magnolia.

As long as *Show Boat* is involved with show business, making gentle fun of old-fashioned theatre conventions and egoistic theatre people, it remains on an even keel. There is considerable affection in the way Prince treats arthritic stage traditions, and considerable authenticity in the way he renders them. Then, of course, there are the remarkable tunes of Jerome Kern, which constitute the major reason for reviving *Show Boat*. In a fever of inspiration, he created a medley of some of the most enchanting songs ever written, among them "Make Believe," "Can't Help Lovin' Dat Man," "Misery's Comin' Aroun'," "Life Upon the Wicked Stage," "You Are Love," "Why Do I Love You," "Bill" (borrowed from another show written by P. G. Wodehouse), and, of course, the classic "Ol' Man River."

The latter is sung by Michael Bell, an actor with a voice that seems to come from a deep region in some remote basement of the earth (is he the spectator mentioned in *The Seagull*, who chanted "Bravo Silva" a whole octave lower than the basso?). The song is reprised at least three times, while the actor visibly greys. This repetition represents an effort to impose some unity on the increasingly disordered action which moves from South to North and back to the South again over a period of forty years (1887 to 1927). Most of these years flash by in the second act after Gaylord Ravenal and Magnolia (don't you love those names?) have traveled to Chicago with baby Kim. Unable to provide for his family, Ravenal abandons it, and Magnolia is forced to go back upon the wicked stage.

Prince handles the passage of time in cinematic fashion—not by riffling calendar pages but rather by riffling historic headlines ("Teddy Roosevelt Elected," "Lusitania Sunk") while the door of the Palmer House giddily revolves. But however clever his devices, he cannot disguise the contrived nature of the meandering plot where coincidental meetings between the leading characters become almost an organizing principle of the action. The second half of *Show Boat* would seem to be about the breakup of families: not only does Ravenal abandon Magnolia but Steve runs out on Julie, giving her the opportunity for a drunken rendering of "Bill." Since Cap'n Andy doesn't have much use for his grouchy wife either, about the only adhesive relationship in this show, aside from Joe and Queenie, is between Parthy and her granddaughter. Prince underlines this intragenerational love affair by having Parthy sing "Why Do I Love You" to the newborn baby. And at the end of the show, the flapper Kim, now a Broadway star, sings the same song to her grandmother.

By the time this happens, the show boat is back in its Southern berth, and virtually everyone but Julie and Steve is having a happy reunion. The floating theatre is now "cooled by electricity" and presents motion pictures in addition to its stage attractions. The whole show ends with a rousing Charleston (choreographed by Susan Stroman). Kim is freeze-framed standing triumphantly in a roadster. And of course we get the inevitable reprise of "Ol' Man River."

The entire cast performs with authority and credibility, especially Elaine Stritch who turns Parthy into an oddly appealing grump, with a singing voice that doesn't deliver a song so much as scratch it. Prince's brilliant collaborator, Eugene Lee, has designed a handsome wrap-around set decorated with sepia photographs of life on the Mississippi, along with a completely equipped nightclub, the Palmer House façade (including the Chicago El), bars and theatres, and at least five different interior and exterior views of the show boat. The costume designer, Florence Klotz, generally scorning primary colors, has used muted tones for her linen, cotton, and calico gowns that help authenticate the period. If you're impressed by engineering, you'll find this show an instrument of precision; even the slamming of a door is synchronized with the music. But Kern's score remains the major reason to revisit *Show Boat*, particularly if you need an occasion to listen to great music, and you like to look at expensive boats.

1994

Intellect into Passion
(Slavs; Hapgood)

This is the year of Tony Kushner in the United States and Tom Stoppard in England, and both currently have new plays. Kushner's *Slavs* is more modestly conceived than his epic *Angels in America* and perhaps for that reason has not been greeted with the same riotous abandon. Still, despite its disorderly plot and random structure, I found *Slavs* at once more weighty, more moving, and more intelligent than the flashier, better-constructed, more warmly received *Hapgood*. I'll try to stifle my temptation to generalize from this opinion about the comparative state of playwriting in the two countries.

Slavs has been described as a work built on outtakes from *Angels in America*. It is true that the play borrows one character (and portions of his opening speech) from Kushner's *Perestroika*—namely the world's oldest and most garrulous Bolshevik, Aleksii Antedilluvianovich Prelapsarianov. But while Kushner admits that the entire first act of *Slavs* was cut from the earlier work, it nevertheless seems like a genuinely new play, even something of a new direction for this young artist. If Tennessee Williams was Kushner's model for the anguished personal relationships of *Angels* (discounting the underplot involving the historical Roy Cohn), here Kushner seems to be more indebted to Bernard Shaw. Instead of an investigation of sexual transactions, *Slavs* looks more like a Shavian play of ideas. Considering its nimble mental dancing and rhetorical virtuosity, it looks even more like a Shavian preface. But as in Shaw at his best, the intellectual pirouettes in *Slavs* build to a genuine emotional climax.

The painful question asked throughout the play is the same one Lenin, glancing at the title of a Chernyshevsky novel, asked throughout his revolutionary career: "What is to be done?" After the failure of communism and the discrediting of Marx—as dramatized by Stalin's crimes and conceded by Gorbachev's reforms—neither social injustice nor economic inequity disappeared from the earth. But for the first time in this century there was no left-wing ideology, however misguided, to inspire hope for change—not even through the agency of benevolent political movements like democratic socialism, the New Deal, or the welfare state. Progressive theory was now being abandoned, "and how," as Prelapsarianov moans, "are we to proceed without *theory?*" Blindly and pragmatically, that's how, into the heartless individualism and unregulated greed of Newt Gingrich's Contract with America.

Kushner regards this sorry situation with the inexpressibly mournful eyes of a disillusioned yet deeply engaged radical thinker whose red diaper has left him with a permanent rash. Like many former socialists, he is still committed to action but robbed of any means to effectuate it. And like many of the best modern playwrights, he dramatizes this problem without offering any answer, confirming that the artist's role is to ask the questions, not suggest the solutions.

The most moving formulation of the dilemma is made in the play by an eight-year-old "nuclear mutation" named Vodya Domik, a little mute girl who died as a result of the Chernobyl accident. Having recovered her voice along with preternatural vision in heaven, she reflects, "Perhaps it is true that social justice, economic justice, equality, community, an end to master and slave, the withering away of the state: these are desirable but not realizable on earth . . . and to the ravages of Capitalism there will be no conceivable alternative," to which Prelapsarianov, also in heaven contemplating a hopeless future, replies, "It is bitter."

It *is* bitter, and most of the play is devoted to dramatizing how such a tragic situation could have evolved out of a system nominally devoted to resolving those inequities. The action begins in ice-cold Moscow in the year 1985 where two "babushkas" are sweeping the streets of snow (a "Sisyphean" enterprise) while discussing the failures of Marxism. Before long, five long-winded commissars are engaging in further discussion of their disintegrating system. They bewail a future dominated by American commercial interests, a future of Burger Kings and Pizza Huts. During their interminable debates ("logorrhea, not revolution"), they become persuaded that the reason evil always triumphs is because progressive people are the political enemies of a Menshevik God.

When two of these old Bolshies, starting with Prelapsarianov, expire on stage from too much theorizing, the discussion proceeds over their dead bodies. This provides some frantic farcical interludes, but in the next scene the vaudeville ingredients of the plot begin to sour as a young female security guard, curator for the stored brains of dead Soviet functionaries, is propositioned by one of the commissars. A lesbian and an anarchist, she refused to respond to his amorous advances, and following a hilarious drunken debauch, he retaliates by sending her and her woman lover, the oncologist Bonfila Bonch-Bruevich, to Siberia.

It is in a desolate Siberian medical facility in 1992, where Bonfila is vainly trying to treat the cancer victims of Chernobyl, that the play begins to find its true form, evolving from intellectual farce into political tragedy. The same fatheaded bureaucrats have survived into the new Russia, no less indifferent to the suffering of the masses, whose despair is read in the blank eyes of the voiceless little girl and the irrepressible fury of her mother.

The cumulative power of the final scene in heaven comes as a surprise considering how the play has wandered in its disunified journey through so many variations of style and purpose. But it is in this poignant episode that Kushner realizes Pirandello's ambition "to convert the intellect into passion"—not only through the exercise of a fervent intelligence but through his capacity to write really meaty roles for actors. These roles are performed with vigor and penetration, though perhaps with excessive Russian accents, under the otherwise expert direction of Lisa Peterson. I particularly liked Joseph Wiseman as Prelapsarianov, a doddering skeleton afflicted with verbal diarrhea, as well as Gerald Hiken, John Christopher Jones, Ben Hammer, and David Chandler as the Gogolian apparatchiks Serge Esmereldovich Upgobkin, Ippolite Ippopolitovich Popolitipov, Vassily Vorovilich Smukov, and Yegor Tremens Rodent. On the distaff side, I was strongly impressed by Marisa Tomei as the galvanic Katherina, Mary Schultz as the harassed Bonafila, and Barbara Eda-Young as the furious mother of the contaminated child ("Fuck this century! Fuck your leader! Fuck the state!"). Praise must also go to Neil Patel for set design, Gabriel Berry for costumes, and Christopher Akerlind for lighting. But we should especially praise Tony Kushner for being able to create a deteriorating social and political universe so far away and yet so near. *Slavs* is proof that he is capable of imagining reality through something other than a sexual prism.

Tom Stoppard's *Hapgood* is another intellectual exercise, but only intermittently does it manage to convert intellect into passion. Stoppard's research into his subject—the intricacies of state espionage—is no doubt as rigorous as Kushner's into Marxism. But whereas Kushner uses his intelligence to advance his theme, Stoppard wears his brilliance on his sleeve. After seeing *Rosencrantz and Guildenstern*, I called this playwright a "university wit." He remains the cleverest conversationalist in the common room, but he is still behaving more like a ventriloquist than an artist. I think I'd rather listen to him be brilliant without the intervention of stuffed characters.

Nevertheless *Hapgood* is graced with a stunning performance by Stockard Channing, who has now become one of the finest leading ladies on the American stage (apart from Cherry Jones, she may be the only leading lady on the American stage). Whatever interior life the play possesses is her contribution, though the rest of the cast (particularly David Straitharn as a Russian physicist who is either a double, triple, or quadruple agent and Josef Sommer as his laconic control) offers strong support. Jack O'Brien's direction is liquid and graceful, and Bob Crowley's setting—an abstract surround which effortlessly transforms, with the aid of Wendell K. Harrington's imaginative projections, into a variety of specific locations—maintains this Irish artist's eminent place in the world of stage design.

Indeed, the evening possesses everything except a coherent dramatic purpose. Partially conceived as a rather condescending satire on the spy novels of John Le Carré, *Hapgood* is such an intricate series of pyrotechnics, such a dazzling display of plot maneuvers illuminated by artificial light, that your interest in the outcome grows anesthetized. Beginning with a dizzying chase in a Saint Paul swimming pool (the year is 1989) after an undisclosed double agent deposits purloined though useless secrets in a locker, the play grows more concerned with the convolutions of spydom than with the identity of the spy. Nothing is really at stake in this impossibly dense charade except the complexity of the plotting. Everyone is a suspect but, lost in the maze of the opaque action, we lose interest in its resolution. Stoppard's attempts to intellectualize this cryptic procedure through references to quantum mechanics and Heisenberg's uncertainty theory only manage to distance us further.

Through an analogy between a double agent and twins, Stoppard eventually exposes the identity of the real Russian spy in a melodramatic climax, but by this time he's lost the audience. "Frankly I don't know which side I'm supposed to be working," remarks one of the agents, and frankly we don't care. None of these characters has much emotional life, aside from Stockard Channing's Hapgood—a vaguely neurotic but elegant Mayfair matron in the style of Maggie Smith (watch the way she says goodbye to her lover, first awkwardly, then passionately, before rearranging her features to cheer on her soccer-playing son). Stoppard is confident in his knowledge of particle physics, but his grasp of human behavior is less sure. Everybody's motives are entirely clear. Only the plot is cloudy.

I'm going to break my resolution to avoid comparative generalizations with the following observation. American drama, with some notable exceptions, is often crude, untidy, undisciplined, overwritten, but pulsing with subterranean power, on the model of Eugene O'Neill. British drama, with some notable exceptions, is often polished, civilized, witty, technically ingenious, but rather undernourished emotionally, on the model of Noel Coward. Harold Pinter and the late John Osborne, especially in their early plays, fed an infusion of new working-class energy into English theatre without losing the

Coward connection. David Mamet and Tony Kushner introduced a supply of wit and intelligence into American theatre without losing the O'Neill connection. The better playwrights of both countries narrow the ocean that divides us. The lesser ones keep us insular and disengaged.

1996

The Rehabilitation of Edward Albee
(Three Tall Women)

A number of years ago, while praising Edward Albee's much-reviled stage adaptation of *Lolita*, I commented on the startling reverses in the fortunes of this once-lionized American dramatist: "The crunching noises the press pack makes while savaging his recent plays are in startling contrast to the slavering sounds they once made in licking his earlier ones. . . . If each man kills the thing he loves, then each critic kills the thing he hypes . . . brutalizing the very celebrity he has created."

I was generalizing not only from Albee's career but from that of Miller, Williams, and Inge, for although I had often depreciated works by these playwrights myself, it struck me as unseemly that mainstream reviewers were displaying such fickleness toward their favorite Broadway icons. This may sound territorial, but it's not. Readers expect highbrow critics to express dissent about an overinflated dramatic work, but it is an entirely different matter when those with the power to close a show become so savage and dismissive in their judgments. If it is a function of the weekly critic to try to correct taste, it is the function of the daily critic to guide theatregoers, not to trash careers or demolish reputations.

Fortunately Albee's stubborn streak has kept him writing in the face of continual disappointment, a persistence he shares with a number of other artists battered by the New York press (Arthur Miller, David Rabe, Arthur Kopit, Christopher Durang, Philip Glass, etc.). I call this fortunate because Albee has a vein of genuine talent buried in the fool's gold, and, as I wrote then, there was always a hope, provided he was not discouraged from playwriting, that this would ap-

pear again in a work of some consequence. That work has now arrived in *Three Tall Women*, and I am happy to join his other former
detractors in saluting Albee's accomplishment.

Three Tall Women is a mature piece of writing, clearly autobiographical, in which Albee seems to be coming to terms not only with
a socialite foster parent he once satirized in past plays but with his
own advancing age. Three women are discovered in a sumptuously
appointed bedroom decorated with Louis Quatorze furniture, a rare
carpet, and a parquet floor. They are called A, B, and C, which suggests a Beckett influence, though on the surface the play appears to
be a drawing-room comedy in the style of A. R. Gurney. The oldest
of the women is an imperious rich invalid (A) who appears hobbling
on a cane, her left arm in a sling. She is attended by a middle-aged
companion (B), an angular woman with a caustic tongue and a
humped back, and a young, politically correct lawyer (C) who has
come to discuss A's business affairs.

The first of the two acts examines some scratchy transactions
among this symbiotic trio, consisting of A's recollections (clearly not
in tranquility) and the shocked reactions of her companions. A has
turned sour and abrupt in old age, and there are traces of Albee's celebrated talent for invective in her rage against life. Her spine has col-
lapsed, she has broken her arm in a fall, and now the bone has
disintegrated around the pins. Likely to wet herself when she rises
from a chair ("A sort of greeting to the day—the cortex out of sync
with the sphincter"), she is inordinately preoccupied with the aging
process—"downhill from sixteen on for all of us." She even wants to
indoctrinate children with the awareness that they're dying from the
moment they're born, and anyone who thinks herself healthy, as C
does, had better just wait.

In short, A is an entirely vicious old wretch, with a volatile tongue
and a narrow mind, but it is a tribute to the writing and the acting
that she gradually wins our affections. Although prejudiced against
"kikes," "niggers," "wops," and "fairies" (among them her own son),
she is a model of vitality and directness when compared with the
humor-impaired liberal democrat C, who protests against her intolerance. A remembers a past of supreme emptiness, of horse shows,
dances, and loveless affairs, and particularly of the time her husband
once advanced upon her with a bracelet dangling from his erect penis

("I can't do that," she said, "and his peepee got soft, and the bracelet fell into my lap"). That arid marriage, and the son who brings her chocolates but doesn't love her ("He loves his boys"), represent memories that can bring her to tears. They also bring A to a stroke at the end of the first act, as she freezes in mid-sentence describing her deepest family secrets.

Act Two begins with A lying in bed under an oxygen mask. By this time B has been transformed from a sardonic hunchbacked factotum, like Igor in *Frankenstein*, into a stately middle-aged matron in pearls, while C has become an elegant debutante in pink chiffon. Before long they are surprisingly joined by A, newly rejuvenated (the figure in the bed is a dummy), and the play shifts gears into a story of one woman at three different moments in time (A at ninety, B at fifty-two, and C at twenty-six). Just as B has shed her hump and C her primness, A has lost her feebleness. All three share the same history, the same child, the same sexual experiences, but A and B are united against C in their hatred of illusions. They warn C that her future will be one of deception and infidelity: "Men cheat a lot. We cheat less, but we cheat because we're lonely. Men cheat because they're men."

The prodigal child, now a young man carrying flowers, returns to sit by the bedside of his dying mother ("his dry lips on my dry cheeks"), silent and forlorn. None of the women will forgive him, nor will they forgive each other. A dislikes C, and C refuses to become A, while B bursts out bitterly against "parents, teachers, all of you, you lie, you never tell us things change." The inevitability of change is responsible for the obscenities of sickness, pain, old age, and death, but A, having accepted her fate, affirms that "the happiest moment is coming to the end of it." Taking a deep breath, she allows the action and her life to stop.

Beckett was the first dramatist to condense the past and present lives of a character into a single dramatic action, and *Krapp's Last Tape* is a play to which *Three Tall Women* owes a deep spiritual debt (it was also the companion piece to Albee's first New York production, *The Zoo Story*, in 1960). Beckett compressed youth and age through the device of a tape recorder; Albee uses doppelgangers; but both plays evoke the same kind of existential poignance. Lawrence Sacharow's direction reinforces this mood with a performance of considerable grace. Myra Carter as the aged A combines the classic calm of Gladys Cooper with the snappish temper of Bette Davis. She can move from meanness to winsomeness and back again in nothing flat. (When C, coolly played by Jordan Baker, accidentally hurt A's shoulder, Carter threw her a look of such ferocity I expected the younger actress to shatter.) Marian Seldes, angular and inscrutable as B, her hands thrust deeply into her cardigan, plays the part as if she is continually tasting something bitter, screaming "Bad girl!" when A breaks a glass in the sink. Most of us have encountered horrible old women like A, fuming over their pain and helplessness. It is Albee's personal and professional triumph to have made such a woman fully human. His late career is beginning to resemble O'Neill's, another dramatist who wrote his greatest plays after having been rejected and abandoned by the culture. Happily, unlike O'Neill, he may not have to wait for death to rehabilitate him.

1994

On a Cold Planet
(Roberto Zucco; Mathew in the School of Life)

A remarkable dramatic work has just ended a brief run at the Cu-caracha Theatre in New York. *Roberto Zucco* is the last play of Bernard-Marie Koltes, published in 1989 and produced posthumously after the author died of AIDS at the age of forty-one. His premature death represents another loss to postmodern drama. Although Koltes was a Frenchman, *Roberto Zucco* is composed (as Richard Eoin Nash-Siedlecki correctly notes in a recent article in *American Theatre*) in a style that approximates the spirit of German theatre. It clearly belongs to that idiosyncratic neo-romantic tradition that erupted in the early nineteenth century with Buechner's *Woyzeck*, reemerged a century later in Wedekind's *Lulu* series, flowered in early Brecht plays, expressed itself through art with the drawings of George Grosz and the paintings of Max Ernst (not to mention such movies as Fritz Lang's *M the Murderer* and von Sternberg's *Blue Angel*), and then reached its postwar culmination in the mordant minimalistic naturalism of Franz Xavier Kroetz.

Like all those feverish works, *Roberto Zucco* constitutes a rebuke to the heroic idealism of the early romantics. It is riddled with the same sadomasochistic dread, permeated with the same elliptical style we associate with the drama of existential revolt. And it is similarly designed to disorder the senses by merging the real and the hallucinatory, thereby making the familiar strange. Just as many of Brecht's works are located in a highly subjective geography (the hero of *In the Jungle of Cities* sets out for Tahiti by sailing across Lake Michigan), so *Roberto Zucco* undermines our confidence in a seated sense of place. One scene is set in the Paris Metro, another in a French police station, but the whorehouse district is a shadowy underworld neighborhood known as "Little Chicago."

That mysterious locus of deception, betrayal, and aberrant eroticism is vaguely reminiscent of Roman Polanski's Chinatown, and there is no question that American movies represent another strong influence on Koltes. Nash-Siedlecki tells us that plastered on the walls of Koltes's studio were posters of James Dean and the young Marlon Brando, those simmering, inarticulate archetypes of fifties angst. Roberto Zucco differs from them in being a serial killer, but he displays the same free-floating rebelliousness, the same irresistible appeal to women and men, the same capacity to initiate fashions in dress and behavior. With his Spanish name and his capacity for casual violence, Zucco has the credentials of an outsider and an outlaw—in fact, he has everything necessary to achieve the obscure glory of the criminal saint. Add to Koltes's German and American influences one French one—the thief and martyr Jean Genet, whose degenerate glamor glows fitfully through this dark work.

Travis Preston's meticulously controlled production is set in a large warehouse whose back wall features photos of Zucco's face and private parts. The photographs are significant because, we are told, the police could not make a composite picture of the character on whom Zucco was based (a killer named Succo)—every shot of him was different. Just as he eludes capture, so Zucco eludes definition. He exists only in his impact on other people; in himself he is nothing. The very beginning of the play shows him escaping from prison while two guards watch in wonder—a wonder we share since the character is walking along a vertical wall on a perpendicular journey. Zucco has spent time in jail for tossing his father out of a window. He returns home to kill his mother as well, holding her in a deadly embrace that exerts just a little more pressure than a filial hug.

Before the play is over, Zucco has also murdered a melancholy police inspector, an old pensioner on the Metro, and an innocent boy. Yet he never loses his capacity to attract sympathy and love from other characters, even those he kills. A young girl who has been physically abused by her brother is totally fascinated with him. In a telegraphic exchange he claims to be "a secret agent," which somehow is an apt description. She asks his name. "I'll die if I tell you." "I don't care," she replies. When Zucco discloses himself, she tells him, "I'm yours—you've taken my innocence." Two pair of boots remain on stage to symbolize their union.

Having lost her virginity, the girl is sold into sexual slavery by her irate and brutal brother, joining a brothel in Little Chicago run by a tattooed madam. It is not long before she betrays Zucco by revealing his name. By this time Zucco is contemplating his own death. He wants to be a street dog in his next life. "Words don't work any more," he says. "We have to stop teaching words. . . . Sooner or later, everybody dies. That's what makes the birds sing."

Zucco takes a woman hostage, kills her teenage son, and appropriates her Mercedes. Yet this woman also falls in love with him: "You're like a switchblade. As soon as you finish, you close up and go away" (Buechner's Woyzeck also "runs through the world like an open razor blade"). Following a final reunion with the girl, Zucco is apprehended. And once again he escapes from prison—this time in the striking imagery of director Preston and designers Christopher Barreca and Zhanna Gurvich, climbing up a huge illuminated train station clock like a demented Harold Lloyd. By this time Zucco has entered legend—a Samson brought low by women, an emblematic image of patricide and matricide in a world where "every child kills his parents."

The production features some Robert Wilsonesque choreography and a sound score (by David Van Tieghem) that adds a mesmerizing and sometimes shocking undercurrent to the events. Among the actors, Kirk Acevedo brings a dark catatonic solitariness to Zucco, and the Rumanian actress Elina Lowensohn, decked out in striped red stockings, has appealing ferocity as the girl. They are ably supported by Rebecca Nelson, Marylouise Burke, Alison White, and John Gould Rubin, among others.

The power of the play is obviously not to be found in depth of character or breadth of action. It is in its style and atmosphere, in the Artaudian cruelty and carnage it embodies, and also in the way it depicts ruthlessness and murder without psychology or moralizing. Except for this lack of commentary, Koltes mirrors our modern obsession with cold-blooded killers, those mesmerizing antiheroes who currently dominate our movies, our literature, our media, our dreams. Every day a new figure takes his place in the nomenclature of bloody assassins alongside the murderers depicted in *In Cold Blood*, *The Executioner's Song*, and *The Silence of the Lambs*. *Roberto Zucco* chronicles the spiritual life of the serial killer and the breakdown of the social order that creates him. It also suggests those feelings of ostracism and isolation that we secretly share with him as our planet grows progressively colder and colder.

I had the privilege of witnessing another work with considerable humanity, though its hero is an android. *Mathew in the School of Life* is the product of two stage wizards, John Moran (composer) and Bob McGrath (director), who work as a single-cell unit with a company called Ridge Theater. McGrath trained at Carnegie Mellon; Moran is a homespun product of Lincoln, Nebraska. Although both men are barely into their thirties, their collaboration may be potentially as important for American performing arts as that of Philip Glass and Robert Wilson. Moran actually happens to be a Glass protégé, though he seems equally influenced by the electronic experiments of Laurie Anderson (like her, he uses technology to indict technology). Moran composes on synthesizers and computers and calls his pieces "operas." But they are more like digital collages than musical compositions, mixing acoustical sound effects with recorded voices which are then lip synched by the actors. As for McGrath, he serves as stage director, actors' coach, drill sergeant, and visual magician on behalf of the most intricately technical presentation I have seen since Wilson's *Black Rider*.

Although *Mathew* is my first experience of their work, Moran and McGrath have already fashioned four previous pieces together, *Jack Benny!*, *The Death Train of Baron von Frankenstein*, *Every Day Newt Berman (The Trilogy of Cyclic Existence)*, and *The Manson Family*. Such titles suggest how deeply these two men have been influenced by popular culture and yesterday's news—so does *Mathew*. Yet, like the best of modern artists, they use these images to inform a higher vision. *Mathew* is set on some future planet in outer space, totally mechanized and dehumanized—in short, a planet very much like our own. Featuring "an android built to absorb human suffering," it proceeds as a kind of nightmarish Christian allegory cum Passion Play. Stretching over a period of four days, from Maundy Thursday to Easter Sunday, and concluding with the death of the hero (the opera begins and ends with a black-robed woman mourning over a coffin), *Mathew* audaciously parallels the life and death of Jesus were he to return to life as an alien humanoid.

The progress of Mathew, a holographic unit in a fiberglass white armored suit that gives him the appearance of a medieval knight, takes him from lobotomized infancy to agonized adulthood through a process of enforced education. Everyone and everything contributes to his painful discovery of what it means to be human, especially a tutor named Justinius (the voice of Allen Ginsberg). What he learns is the message of the Gospels and of Ecclesiastes—and also of Strindberg's *Dream Play*—that humankind is pitiable. He learns how to cross a street—and gets hit by a car. He learns about clock time. He learns how to shop in a supermarket. And he learns to feel rage. Over and over again Mathew witnesses the beating of a fleeing perpetrator, much like Rodney King. Over and over again he is taught to "draw" a gun and say "freeze." Finally he is shot by the same forces that instructed him, his last question being, "Is death as long as life?"

Mathew is played by three different actors (one of them Moran), which allows McGrath to use such cinematic conventions as jump cuts and close-ups. He also employs actual filmed sequences and projections, scattered between scenes on two-dimensional cutout sets with three-dimensional elements. With the aid of an excellent design team—Laurie Olinder and Fred Tietz (sets), Elizabeth Evers (costumes), and Howard S. Thies (lights)—he has created an ever-changing physical environment which a large cast navigates with the efficiency of robots. You will find echoes in this work of George Lucas's *THX 1138*, Ridley Scott's *Blade Runner*, Steven Spielberg's *Star Wars*, Stanley Kubrick's *2001*, and just about every other sci-fi film you've ever seen. But *Mathew* is, for all these influences, a completely original achievement. Although the second act seemed to me unfinished (it involves a pirate sequence the relevance of which escaped me), *Mathew* commanded my continuous respect as an electrifying and compassionate work of art.

1995

Alice in Wilsonland

(Alice; Four Saints in Three Acts)

In his *New Yorker* article on Charles Dodgson, Adam Gopnik seeks to revise the popular view that the author of the most cherished books of children's literature, the avuncular cleric who called himself Lewis Carroll, was a man driven by dark abnormal impulses, particularly a passion for pre-pubescent girls. Reviewing Morton Cohen's new biography, Gopnik prefers to see Dodgson less as a stammering neurotic, one grope shy of being a child molester, than as a well-adjusted Oxford rationalist whose interest in such Victorian Lolitas as the eleven-year-old Alice Liddell would have been considered relatively normal in its time. He makes this case even while acknowledging telling evidence to the contrary: Dodgson's banishment from the Liddell household (for reasons never disclosed) and Cohen's recent discovery of the Oxford clergyman's suggestive sepia snapshots of nude and semiclad little girls—the kind of thing that would land a contemporary photographer in jail for child abuse (or else, as Gopnik notes, commissioned to do "a Calvin Klein campaign").

Though Gopnik lays too much stress on the sunniness of Dodgson's disposition, his effort to judge the man by the conventions of his time rather than our own is probably a healthy corrective to historical myopia. But it is understandable why modern artists, who live off the unconscious as their inspiration and material, have nevertheless been more attracted to the tenebrous side of the Dodgson mind. His revolutionary use of language in the "Jabberwocky" poem famously inspired Joyce's invention of portmanteau words in that great dreambook *Finnegans Wake*. (It also influenced the whole range of Absurdist theatre, especially the verbal disarrangements found in Ionesco.) As for Alice in the theatre, the André Gregory and Jonathan Miller stagings of these books in the seventies and eighties also tended to emphasize the irrational side of Dodgson's imagination, which is probably why Gopnik is so ready to write off Robert Wilson's version. "Wilson's piece," he sniffs, before even having seen it, "threatens to be an updated compendium of all these clichés."

As a matter of fact, it is completely original. While it is true that the Dodgson of *Alice* is hardly a happy Victorian logician, the pop opera Wilson has concocted with Tom Waits (music) and Paul Schmidt (book), rather than being a revisionist character study, is a reverie on the nature of dreaming and the human desire to stop time in its tracks. It is a theatrical examination, in other words, much like Calderon's *Life Is a Dream* and Strindberg's *Ghost Sonata* and *A Dream Play*, of the links between dreaming and death. And like them it constitutes a haunting work of theatre. A companion piece to *Black Rider*, which Wilson also created in collaboration with Germany's Thalia Theater and Tom Waits (only William Burroughs is absent this time), *Alice* is a genuine contribution to a new form—the avant-garde musical spectacular—which makes *Miss Saigon* and *Phantom of the Opera* look like children's pantomimes. It is true that *Alice* seems to have been more hastily assembled than *Black Rider*. In his crammed schedule of production abroad (now more than eight big pieces a year), Wilson is beginning to depend a lot more on striking lighting effects than on his scenic imagination, and his choreography, normally metrically precise, occasionally looked a bit jagged as executed by the Thalia chorus.

Still, the performances are admirable, and despite a few technical glitches, the American premier at the Brooklyn Academy of Music was something of a triumph. Like *Black Rider*, *Alice* shows Wilson in a highly playful, whimsical mood, working with the conventions of vaudeville comedy (he once confessed that the greatest influence on his sense of timing was Jack Benny). In the opening moments, before the houselights dim, eleven Dodgson-like figures, made up with dark goatees and starched hair, gradually multiply on stage (much like the replicated Einsteins in *Einstein on the Beach*) to perform a charming choreographic exercise in absolute silence. After the house darkens, the true Charles Dodgson materializes (played by Stefan Kurt, who triples as the White Rabbit and the White Knight), hidden inside the folds of an enormous camera, from which he emerges singing one of

Waits's seriocomic percussive songs ("Raindrops on the window and the ice in my drink. Baby, all I can think of is—Alice"). The photo he takes of his adored subject (Annette Paulmann in an Alice blue gown) is accompanied by a loud magnesium explosion. It is this sound, and the accompanying smoke, that sends her into the fog of fable. Encouraged by Dodgson (now transformed into the White Rabbit) to "Drink Me," she downs the magic potion. And with the aid of shrinking scrims, expanding props, and trick lighting, Alice diminishes to the size required to enter the rabbit hole.

Wilson has essentially translated Lewis Carroll's anecdotes into his own visual vocabulary, a language enhanced by Frida Parmegianni's eloquent *couturier* costumes. The Caterpillar sits atop a toadstool, his body gradually inflated into the proportions of a Macy Day float until the tail snaps sharply into a stinger's point. The Mad Hatter's Tea Party is performed around a long metallic Wilson table to the accompaniment of shattering dishware. Humpty Dumpty squats on the wall, the actor's face protruding through the eggshell, as he advises Alice, "You cannot have a door in a wall—you lose the wallness of it." Paul Schmidt's scenario (performed alternately in charmingly accented English and supertitled German) essentially correlates the fictional episodes of *Alice in Wonderland* and *Through the Looking-Glass* with the actual yearning of Dodgson for his unattainable love. Dodgson composes a series of letters to Alice which he crumples up and throws away (the Cheshire Cat, pouncing on each one in turn, paws them around the stage like balls of yarn). Later he burns them, realizing that "nothing in my life has ever been as real as the silence she brought me," thus reminding us how, after his death, Dodgson's niece burned pages from his diary dating from the period just before his exile from the Liddell home.

But more touching than the unrequited love story is the overpowering sense of loss and desolation caused by the passage of time. "I took a photo, made time stand still. Now it marches on," says Dodgson, in the act of admitting his guilt to the Black Queen (she responds by shouting, "Off with his head"). Near the end, Alice thanks him for the fact that "the story has an end." But he has written one last poignant letter about mortality, a declaration that "neither of us is real and anything can happen and we only wake up when we die." The play ends with birds chirping and Alice, now an old woman, singing a final melancholy love song ("I remember you with leaves in your hair—but I'm still here. . . . You dreamed me up and left me here").

Alice is full of charming dreamscapes and vaudeville turns: the White Knight, in his pointed slitted helmet, doing dance steps and tripping on his feet, then making an exit with a woman's face on the back of his head; the White Sheep (an actress in a flowing platinum wig) endlessly crocheting from her own wool with long metallic needles; Alice crashing through the mirror to the sound of breaking glass; eight bald, pasty-faced Victorian vicars in a chorus line, singing, "He corrected me in the rectory, that's why I'm feeling so blue"; a quiz show, conducted by Dodgson for Alice, in which she is required to solve a number of word puzzles printed on cards. The only episode that seemed obtrusive, though it was visually stunning, represented Alice as a woman in her forties, in a bright red gown, drinking whiskey and remembering her childhood photo session with Dodgson ("No matter how I moved, it wasn't enough . . . I felt the tears coming and the screams coming, but I never blinked")—and of her dream life ("I dreamt of burnt bodies, of rusted pavilions")—as a dressmaker's dummy moves slowly off stage and the entire set turns crimson. It was one of the few moments when the infinite sadness of the piece became explicit, rather than being filtered through a screen of absurdity.

Wilson's *Alice* manages to enter that fabulous country where dreams, farce, and madness exist in perfect unity, which is the land of the unconscious as imagined by an artist. Tom Waits's music and lyrics (with Kathleen Brenna), like his songs for *Black Rider*, employ brass, woodwinds, percussion, and keyboards as a smoky, earthy contrast to the more ethereal quality of the staging. And the twelve members of the Thalia cast, led by Annette Paulmann's charming, slightly oafish Alice and Stefan Kurt's mournful Dodgson-Rabbit-Knight, display once again the supreme advantages of a well-subsidized permanent ensemble. What a disgrace it is that Europe alone can regularly employ one of America's foremost theatre artists, and that works such as *Alice* and *Black Rider* can be seen here only on brief visits to Brooklyn. But that is the kind of handicap we suffer living in an artistic third world.

1995

The centerpiece of John Rockwell's enterprising first season as producer of the Lincoln Center Festival was obviously the Robert Wilson production of the Gertrude Stein / Virgil Thomson *Four Saints in Three Acts*, the first professional staging of the opera in sixty years. Summer programs at this cultural complex have traditionally been considerably more adventurous than its winter seasons, and the summer of 1996 was no exception. Yet for all the visual beauties of the Houston Grand Opera production, it contained fewer surprises than we have come to expect from Wilson.

Clearly Robert Wilson has found another kindred spirit in Gertrude Stein, as he last proved in 1992 with his Hebbel-Theater production of *Doctor Faustus Lights the Lights*. The way in which Stein deconstructs language resembles Wilson's early experimentation with the language of deaf and autistic children, and her postmodernist imagery obviously stimulates Wilson's visual imagination. "I felt a creative dialogue with her," writes Wilson in his program note, "especially with her notion of seeing a play as a landscape." Still, some creative dialogues can be too agreeable, just as some artistic marriages can be too comfortable. If Wilson's *Four Saints in Three Acts* seems like a minor work, it may be because this prolific artist was not sufficiently challenged by his material to move into territory not yet explored.

As usual, Wilson is painting in motion. The setting, costumes, props, and lighting (all his creations) are splendid. Liberated from consecutive plot—and what he calls "ping-pong dialogue"—Wilson can concentrate his imagination on stage pictures. And at the same time that he fills the void with exquisite imagery—crescent moons, two-dimensional sheep, disembodied hands, transparent eggs, six white giraffes—he arranges the large cast of singers into continually changing groupings that create a sense of strangely amorphous humanity.

The title of the opera is essentially its primary subject. But even the title is whimsical. There are not four saints on stage but twenty. There are not three acts but four. "Four saints are never three," chants the unisex chorus, "three saints are never four." Stein makes continuous references to the number of acts and scenes in the opera ("How many acts are there in it? Four acts") and continually announces the place we have reached ("Third act, which is a fact"), as if amusing herself with the paraphernalia of play structure. And she occasionally throws us a humorous bone with one of her now familiar nonsense rhymes ("Pigeons on the grass alas") along with a number of pointless puns ("As loud as that and as allowed as that"). At times her playful way with words evokes the kind of language Joyce invented in *Finnegans Wake*. Usually it just seems precious, a tiresome form of repetitive absurdity.

Aside from Wilson's stage magic, it is Virgil Thomson's score, elegantly conducted by Dennis Russell Davies with the New York City Opera Orchestra, that rescues the evening from monotony. It is not great music, but at least its ironies are coherent, and its control of Americana evokes a kind of lyrical nostalgia. Thompson combines echoes of Samuel Barber, pastoral strains, quotations from patriotic hymns like *America*, and familiar movie music, suggestive of covered wagons breaking the West. The rousing Houston Grand Opera Chorus and the gifted cast of soloists are in fine voice, especially the grinning Compere of Wilbur Pauley, with his half-fur-covered tuxedo, slicked-down black hair, and slithering gait, and the Saint Ignatius of baritone Sanford Sylvan, who maintains his quiet dignity regardless of what nonsense he is required to sing (or wear). In short, I'm glad I saw Wilson's *Four Saints in Three Acts*. There will never be a more definitive version of this opera. Now that he's gotten that out of his system, I hope Wilson will go on to more challenging projects.

1996

The New Bohemia
(Rent; The Green Bird)

The American theatre chases after a new musical sensation with all the messianic fervor of a religious sect pursuing redemption. And when the composer/librettist dies the day before his show begins previews, we have all the conditions required for cultural mythmaking— a martyred redeemer, a new gospel, hordes of passionate young believers, and canonization by the *New York Times*, which devoted virtually all the theatre columns of a recent Arts and Leisure section to *Rent*, the "rock opera for our time."

Jonathan Larson's premature death at the age of thirty-five from an aortic aneurism was a misfortune from many points of view. He was a young man on the brink of a strong career who did not live to enjoy the early fruits of his talents, a promising artist who would undoubtedly have gone on to write much more finished works. I hope it will not be construed as coldhearted when I say that his death was also a misfortune for contemporary criticism, being another example of how it can be hobbled by extra-artistic considerations.

Rent (which I saw at the New York Theatre Workshop before it moved to Broadway) is an updated version of *La Bohème*, substituting the multicultural denizens of New York's East Village for Puccini's Latin Quarter bohemians. It is good-natured, fully energized, theatrically knowing, and occasionally witty. It is also badly manufactured, vaguely manipulative, drenched in self-pity, and sentimental in a way that makes Puccini and his librettists (Illica and Giacosa) almost look like cynics.

Rent is being advertised as "*Hair* for the '90s," and there are indeed certain similarities between the two musicals. Both idealize their socially marginal characters, both are poorly constructed, and both fail to penetrate very deeply beneath a colorful and exotic surface. Larson was a sophisticated librettist, if a somewhat sloppy play architect (there is twice as much incident in his brief second act as in the much longer section that precedes it). But his score for *Rent* struck me as the musical equivalent of wallpaper, the rock version of elevator music ("tame and second hand," as Bernard Holland wrote in the only *Times* dissent). Compared to Galt McDermott's exhilarating compositions for *Hair*, Larson's songs—except for the moving "Another Day"—show little lyric genius. Their impact derives less from intrinsic inspiration than from extrinsic amplification. Whenever the show begins to flag, the appealing cast lines up down stage to holler into microphones.

The cast, in fact, is highly amplified throughout the entire evening, often leaving us in bewilderment over whose lips are issuing the sounds. All the principals wear head mikes, which not only leaves them looking like telephone operators but makes any physical contact between them (such as a hug or a kiss) sound more like a scrape.

Rent has a lot to say about the need for human communication, but nothing very human is allowed to emerge from all this acoustical racket. "You're living in America where it's like the Twilight Zone," notes one character, while another (cribbing from Philip Roth) asks, "How do you document real life when real life is getting more like fiction every day?" What isn't being probed is how these people also contribute to a sense of the American unreality, especially when they are being so superficially examined.

Although its heart is in the right place, Larson's book is basically superficial and unconvincing too. In this piggyback *Bohème*, the painter Marcello becomes Mark, a documentary filmmaker; Rudolfo the poet turns into Roger, a rock composer; Colline the philosopher emerges as Tom Collins, a black anarchist expelled from MIT for his work on "actual reality"; and Schaunard, the musician, metamorphoses into Angel, a black sculptor by profession and transvestite by disposition. As for the women, Musetta evolves into a bisexual rock singer named Maureen who has left Mark for Joanne (Puccini's Alcindoro transformed into a black woman lawyer from Harvard), while Mimi, the mignonette, has turned into Mimi Marquez, a Latina strip dancer and heroin user (when she enters Roger's apartment with frozen hands, carrying a candle, she's looking for her stash).

The background for all this interracial, intersexual character grunge is a rent strike. Blacks, Latinos, and whites alike, whether gay, bisexual, or straight, all stand in common opposition to the uptight Benjamin Coffin III, who, though also black, is, like his Puccini prototype Benoit, a grasping landlord and rent gouger. What they protest is his hardheartedness toward the homeless ("Do you really want a neighborhood where people piss on your stoop every night?") and his desire to gentrify the surroundings ("This is Calcutta. Bohemia's dead").

Aside from this easy mark, and similar simplistic oppositions, what virtually all these people have in common is AIDS (an analogy for Mimi's tuberculosis in *La Bohème*). Some have contracted the disease from sexual activity, some from drug use, but in *Rent* it seems to be an East Village epidemic. During an AZT break, the entire cast pops pills. Most of them are dying. Angel, minus his wig and connected to an IV, is provided with a protracted death scene, after which Mimi memorializes him as "so much more original than any of us." (Following Kushner's *Angels in America*, Phyllis Nagy's *Weldon Rising*, the PBS documentary *The Time of Our Dying*, and other such theatrical examples, one wonders how "original" black drag queens really are in American culture.)

The death of Angel (the angel of death?) sets the stage for Mimi's demise. She and Roger have finally consummated their love after discovering they are both HIV-positive and therefore can't contaminate the other. Nevertheless Roger decides to leave for Santa Fe to write one great song before he dies. Upon his return he learns that Mimi has been living on the street, in deteriorating health. Maureen carries the dying girl into Roger's apartment, and all the comrades gather round for the obligatory death scene. Roger declares his love in song ("Who do you think you are, leaving me alone with my guitar"), Mimi falls back on the couch, and the concluding strains of *La Bohème*—the most powerful music of the evening—swell up over the sobs and groans.

Fear not. Unlike bel canto opera, American musicals allow resurrections and require happy endings. Mimi awakes. Her "fever has broken." Love has triumphed over immune deficiency. And the show concludes with the lovers in each other's arms as movie memories are projected onto an upstage screen.

We don't ask our musicals to be like real life unless they pretend to be: *Rent* is offered to us as an authentic East Village *tranche de vie*. This pretense makes the final Puccini musical quotation seem cheap and the ending sentimental. George Meredith once defined the sentimentalist as "He who would enjoy without incurring the immense debtorship for the thing done." He accurately describes the emotions forced upon the audience in *Rent*, where a ghastly disease is exploited for mawkish purposes.

Michael Greif's highly charged production employs a host of gifted young performers: Daphne Rubin-Vega as a dejected Mimi in skin-tight spandex pants; Adam Pascal as the rock-and-rolling Roger; Anthony Rapp as the camera-toting Mark; Wilson Jermaine Heredia as the transvestite sculptor Angel; Idina Menzell (a Sandra Bernhard look-alike) as the sexually ambivalent Maureen; and Taye Diggs, Fredi Walker, and Jesse L. Martin in other roles. The energy of the entire cast is prodigious (no *gravitas* in this particular youth culture).

I hope that energy can be sustained over what promises to be a long Broadway run.

Larson has been hailed for creating the downtown equivalent of bohemian life. I fear he has only created a fashion. Bohemia used to be characterized not just by flamboyant lifestyles but by artistic breakthroughs. Indeed, many bohemian artists (Ibsen, Manet) dressed like burghers and lived exemplary lives. It was Flaubert who famously said that he was orthodox and conservative in his life in order to be tumultuous and radical in his work. Alas, Larson's New Age bohemians display nothing but their lifestyles. As for their art, it's just a little daunting to note that most of them have no greater ambition than to dominate the rock charts.

I left *Rent* feeling like a Thurber character, the one who feared that electricity was escaping all over the room. I found an antidote in Julie Taymor's exhilarating staging of Carol Gozzi's *The Green Bird* (produced by the Theatre for a New Audience). There the electricity was contained, focused, and channeled. Taymor has invested enough visual imagination in this production to satisfy a dozen such evenings, and her actors have responded with bravura performances of dazzling wit and style. Gozzi mixes Italian *commedia dell'arte* characters with Asian plots. Taymor adds touches of Balinese movement and Indonesian mask work along with American vaudeville and burlesque.

Like most of Gozzi's fairy-tale plots, the story of *The Green Bird* looks silly on the page, revolving as it does around talking stone heads, statues that come to life, and singing apples which (like the citrus fruit in *The Love of Three Oranges*) help to resolve the plot. Here the story serves largely as a scaffolding for low comedy, magical transformations, and unexpected conjunctions. Using half-masks and nose masks, along with fantastic costumes, puppets, and floats, Taymor creates a grand show, partly acted, partly mimed, partly sung, and partly danced (to the accompaniment of Elliot Goldenthal's shimmering music).

Albert Bermel's adaptation has a delightful contemporary ring to it, but the evening's real triumph is the performance. While full of admiration in the past for Ms. Taymor's visual genius, I have not hitherto been impressed much by her work with actors. If *The Green Bird* is her finest achievement to date, it is because she has done remarkable things with the cast. Derek Smith as Tartaglia the King is especially winning. Decked out in a white suit, red shoes, and a pair of protruding ears, he presents a mournful picture of a regent with mood swings, calling for his "king thing" (his crown) and lamenting that "It's as easy to make a true friend as it is to wipe your ass with a rose." Andrew Weems is also highly amusing as Pantalone, the king's adviser, which he plays in a bowler hat with a vaudeville Italian accent. And he is simply brilliant playing a series of beauticians, particularly as a dressmaker advising Barberina on her costumes and accessories ("Trust me, darling, take the gold").

Priscilla Shanks as Tartagliona, the king's mother, is an ancient crone who hates her grandchildren and despises her son ("My only disgrace was giving birth to Dumbo"). With an upward sweep of hair and long hanging breasts with tassels on them, she looks like a bad-tempered centipede on a rampage. Didi Conn and Ned Eisenberg are immensely appealing as Smeraldina and Truffaldino, two sausage vendors who ply their trade off an enormous pig, segmented to display the ham, the bacon, and the pork chops. And Eric Villanueva has a showstopping number as "Dancing Water," adding circus acrobatics to the other popular forms employed in the production.

Although they used the same *commedia* characters, Gozzi was the very antithesis of his contemporary rival Goldoni—aristocratic, fantastical, and imaginative where Goldoni was bourgeois, realistic, and conventional. This conflict between fantasy and realism in the theatre (similar to the conflict between the methods of Meyerhold and Stanislavsky in Russia) established the terms for a theatrical opposition which persists to this day. Julie Taymor—along with her early Gozzi collaborator, Andrei Serban—seems ideally equipped to advance the inventive, theatrical, and fanciful side of the equation.

1996

Revisiting Plays

(Night of the Iguana; A Funny Thing Happened on the Way to the Forum; A Delicate Balance)

One of the more humbling experiences a veteran theatre critic can suffer is to visit revivals of plays he saw when they were originally performed. Nothing exposes more abruptly the ephemeral, arbitrary nature of opinion-making. Having been a reviewer now for almost four decades, I often find myself revising earlier judgments, chastening the arrogance of my youth with the attitudes (no doubt equally arrogant) of my later years. Still, I can't blame these changes of mind entirely on fickleness or mutability. Obviously the theatrical occasion is not just a textual reading, it is a staged event. Often a new production can reveal the virtues of a play that was once too easily dismissed, just as time can unearth the faults of a play that was originally overpraised.

Let me try to support this case with three examples, the first being *The Night of the Iguana*. When I first saw this play in 1962, I called it another of Tennessee Williams's innumerable later exercises in marking time. But my review was mixed. While the writing seemed to me somewhat aimless and self-derivative, I also had to admire its dark humor, febrile warmth, and atmospheric richness. Above all, I found *Night of the Iguana* to be an occasion for ripe characterizations, especially of the crapulous, vaguely demented central character, a spoiled priest named T. Lawrence Shannon. Shannon bears some resemblance to the self-hating alcoholic consul in Malcolm Lowry's *Under the Volcano*. And Patrick O'Neal in the original stage production (as well as Richard Burton in the film version) managed to etch a nagging portrait of self-laceration and self-loathing, while Bette Davis, Margaret Leighton, and Alan Webb powerfully performed the other overwrought characters, exiled in a Mexican resort hotel.

Like one of these—Nonno, "the oldest living and practicing poet in the world"—Williams was showing a lot of fatigue in this play, flapping about like an aged eagle too tired to spread his wings. As a result, the work lacks an organizing principle, though it covers familiar terrain. The defeated heretic Shannon, raging against a "senile delinquent" God, is yet another self-portrait of a sexual miscreant (he sleeps with underage girls) punished for his transgressions. And Williams's compulsion to repeat his litany on the subjects of fleshly corruption and the way life maims the sensitive is so strong that he no longer bothers to provide a substructure of action to support his themes.

Oddly, the play now seems even more an act of desperation, if not of automatic writing, than when it first appeared, largely because of Robert Falls's ineffective production. Loy Arcenas's rendering of the ramshackle Casa Verde hotel near Acapulco drips with lush fecundity, the steaming tropical underbrush closing in on its battered tin roofs. And Cherry Jones gives a sensitive and penetrating, if sometimes overemphatic, performance as the spinster Hannah Jelkes.

But other perfectly competent actors seem to have been seriously miscast or misdirected. Marsha Mason, for example, is an attractive, warmhearted woman, but she looks persuasive only when swatting away mosquitoes. Mason is utterly lost as Maxine Faulk, too bland and suburban, too lacking in animal power, to find the juice of this lusty Patrona—and the German tourists who entrap and torture the symbolic iguana are World War II movie cartoons. As for the usually dependable William Petersen as Shannon, he acts less desperate than jumpy. Instead of having a crack-up, he appears to be suffering a case of coffee nerves. Because of such acting, it becomes even more obvious that these characters share no common necessity. In *A Streetcar Named Desire* the clash between Stella and Stanley was predestined. Shannon, Hannah, Maxine, and Nonno all seem to inhabit different plays.

A Funny Thing Happened on the Way to the Forum was produced in the same year as *Iguana*, starring Zero Mostel as Pseudolus. I blessed it then for reminding us of the musical theatre's roots in farce action and burlesque characters, at a time when the musical stage was being dominated by the sanctimonious overchoreographed "book" shows of Rodgers and Hammerstein. For the same reasons, I bless it now. Burt Shevelove and Larry Gelbart's script is a bracing modern compendium of Plautine farces—notably *Casina, Curculio, Miles Gloriosus*, and *Pseudolus*—one of the few Broadway adaptations that doesn't betray its source material. Although the momentum of the farce action is often interrupted by Stephen Sondheim's (admittedly witty) songs, *Forum* represents the resurgence of a fading but still vigorous slapstick tradition, with sexual pursuit as its animating impulse.

Jerry Zaks's new production is a well-rehearsed, efficiently paced, colorfully enacted evening of theatre. It features Broadway favorite Nathan Lane, who has only to step in front of the curtain to get the patrons clapping. Both director and star are complete professionals. There isn't a shred of stage business that hasn't been carefully worked out. And no expense has been spared. Indeed, about half the production budget is eaten by the opening number, "Comedy Tonight," when the curtain "mistakenly" rises on a fully realized set for *Medea* (never used again) showing figures in tragic masks writhing in agony. Considering all the money and expertise that went into this enterprise, why did I feel so let down?

For one thing, I sorely missed old Zero, and I also missed his ribald cohorts (Jack Gilford, Ruth Kobart, David Burns, Ronald Holgate) from the 1962 production. Nobody owns a lease on a musical role. But the original cast members of *Forum* earned their stripes in vaudeville and burlesque. The revival company seems to have done their training in television sitcoms. No one can reproduce the way Zero Mostel managed to defy gravity with his gross dignity and elephantine grace. But his sense of danger and surprise was generic of all great comics. You never knew what he was going to do on stage, and neither did he. Nathan Lane has the calibrated timing of an actor performing between commercial breaks. He never fails to trigger the laugh meter, especially when, being sent off for mare's sweat for a potion, he whinnies and stamps his foot, or when he tells a eunuch, "Don't you ever lower your voice to me." But why do all his shticks and takes, his passionate love affair with the audience, seem so mannered and predictable?

I have always admired Mark Linn-Baker, my old student and colleague. But except for a few delicious moments in drag he is too laid back to galvanize the manic Hysterium. Perhaps this good actor spent too many years playing straight man on "Perfect Strangers." Lewis Stadlen brings a welcome touch of Groucho to the role of Senex, the lecherous old father. And Ernie Sabella plays Lycus, the brothel-keeper, with refreshing vulgarity. But even the showgirls—courtesans with names like Gymnasia, Tintanabula, and Panacea—who should be animated objects of lust, look more like posed mannequins in a swimsuit issue of *Sports Illustrated*. In 1962 *A Funny Thing Happened on the Way to the Forum* was a wild farce with songs. Now it seems like just another Tony-award-winning Broadway musical.

Edward Albee's *A Delicate Balance* was first performed in 1966 when the Vietnam War was heating up. In Alan Schneider's reverent production it struck me as an entirely superfluous drawing-room drama in solemn imitation of T. S. Eliot's *The Cocktail Party*. To use a favorite word of the time, it was *irrelevant*, so precious that its one contemporary reference (to the Chinese bomb) had a jarring effect. After the redskin ferocities of *Who's Afraid of Virginia Woolf?* the play struck many of us as a paleface mandarin exercise in metaphysics, dispensed in bloated language between generous helpings of strong waters. I opined at the time, rather cruelly, that *A Delicate Balance* was the work of an interior decorator, of someone who was letting his servants do his living for him.

Gerald Gutierrez's recent Lincoln Center production doesn't entirely revise my opinion of the play, which still sounds a bit precious and mannerist. But it vastly increases my respect for it. Gutierrez's casting genius reveals that *A Delicate Balance* is not a metaphysical drama at all but essentially a comedy of manners. Rarely in American theatre do we find such uniformly meticulous performances—and any writing that inspires such brilliant acting must be respected as well. The design team of John Lee Beatty (sets), Jane Greenwood (costumes), and Pat Collins (lighting) has created a haunting world, composed of a diagonal interior with mahogany bookcases, an imposing chandelier, countless bottles of booze, heavily upholstered furniture, and a well-appointed staircase (the setting could work as well for a production of *The Little Foxes*). And director Gutierrez has layered detail upon detail, orchestrating climaxes of genuine power while heightening the brittle wit of the dialogue. His production is at the same time crisp and charged, yet fluid, fresh, and spontaneous.

A Delicate Balance is about a resentful nuclear family, living together in strained if opulent circumstances. They pass the time decanting whiskey, vodka, and cognac laced with bitchy remarks until a neighboring couple invades the household seeking refuge from some nameless dread. Their presence creates a crisis, ambiguously resolved after the family comes to terms with the presence of the intruders. The couple eventually decide to vacant the premises anyway, leaving the family to pick up the shreds of their lives.

The six-member cast performs this like Mozart chamber music. George Grizzard, decked out in a conservative uniform of blue blazer, grey slacks, and open pink shirt, plays the retired Republican stockbroker Tobias with a slight arthritic limp and a subtle hint of upper-middle-class angst. He manages to show both the blocked emotions of this character and the disappointments lying beneath the surface. Agnes, his wife, is a brittle dowager, whose every line of dialogue appears to have been prethought and prefashioned for inclusion in *Bartlett's Quotations*. It is the triumph of Rosemary Harris to make this familiar Albee character seem real and moving. Mary Beth Hurt, as their daughter Julia, is the most neurotic and territorial of the three with her constant demands to repossess her invaded bedroom—but also the most instinctive and alive. And Elizabeth Wilson and John Carter, as the two intruders, subtly suggest the suppressed terror ("We were frightened and there was nothing") that underlies even the most comfortable lives.

It is, however, Elaine Stritch as Claire, the bibulous sister-in-law, who has the lion's share of Albee's acerbic wit. With her ash-blonde hair and great legs, her slightly hunched Texas lope, and the way she clenches her jaws after lobbing a witticism in an effortless whiskey baritone, Stritch creates a portrait of one of the most engaging boozers in modern drama (hitherto Philip Barry had this field pretty much to himself). On the page her lines don't seem half as funny or as barbed as when I heard them on the stage. Albee's dialogue still reads as somewhat literary and strained. But the production as a whole has virtually obliterated my thirty-four-year-old distaste for the play. This splendid revival of *A Delicate Balance* is one of those experiences that reminds a critic of the fallibility of opinion and the changing nature of art.

1996

Resident Theatre Hopes
(The Tempest; Venus; The Dance of Death)

As a result of severe shrinkages in federal, corporate, and foundation support for the arts, the nonprofit resident theatre movement has been increasingly forced to depend on financial sources normally pursued by the commercial theatre—namely box-office income and individual contributions. Apart from being notoriously undependable, reliance on this kind of "privatized" funding represents a growing threat to artistic autonomy and theatrical experiment. It fosters safe program choices designed to appeal either to less discerning audiences or to the idiosyncratic tastes of wealthy donors. I recently visited three institutional theatres in different parts of the country in order to assess how each of them was coping with the new conditions. From what I saw, and on the basis of brief conversations with their artistic directors, it was possible to conclude that all three theatres were still managing to be true to their birthrights, despite the restrictive funding climate.

The American Conservatory Theater in San Francisco, now under the direction of Carey Perloff (former artistic director of the Classic Stage Company), is currently delivering a heady blend of thorny new plays and freshly adapted or rethought classics. Like most institutional theatres, the ACT has been forced to abandon its resident company, though a few of the same actors are occasionally employed from play to play. The cast for Ms. Perloff's production of *The Tempest* was essentially pickup, some of it imported from Hollywood. Still, the play was acted and staged with genuine imagination, if intermittent power. It was performed in the Geary Theatre, beautifully restored from the ruins after a recent earthquake.

Perhaps because of the ACT's experience with disaster, Ms. Perloff was the first director in my experience to make the opening tempest an authentic catastrophe. Usually this difficult scene is rendered incomprehensible by earsplitting noises and screaming actors (the storm scene in *King Lear* is often drowned out by a similar cacophony). Ms. Perloff's solution was so simple I'm surprised nobody ever thought of it before. After a charming interpolated interlude, showing the young Prospero adrift in a boat with the infant Miranda, a single held flute note gave way to crashing tympani, a sailor plummeted head first from the flies, and shadows of shouting figures were dimly perceived through the sails as snatches of Shakespeare's dialogue ("We split, we split") were projected onto the sheets. Thus the spectator could experience the confused terror and tumult of a real shipwreck while visually processing just enough language to understand the event.

Many of Ms. Perloff's other ideas were equally fresh, and her physical production was a striking blend of Edwardian elegance and Caribbean panache. David Straitharn is an excellent domestic actor, stalward and dignified, if not quite majestic enough to realize the heroic size of the character. His Prospero was dark and brooding but lacking in poetic authority.

The scene in which Prospero instructs Miranda about their past, always a bit tedious, was a real snooze here, partly because Miranda was played by an actress closer in age to his wife than his daughter, partly because Straitharn proved unable to relax his trademark solemnity. In some productions, Prospero's magic is in the stage effects, in others in the music. Here it was in the lighting which Straitharn manipulated like a master electrician, at times turning into a shadow himself.

David Patrick Kelly created a melancholy and melodious Ariel while retaining a trace of sneering menace, Graham Beckel was a loutish animalistic Caliban, his snout muzzled so he wouldn't bite, and Gerald Hiken played a warm, rabbinical Gonzalo. Geoff Hoyle, as Stefano, turned this besotted butler into a bibulous Jeeves, while *L.A. Law*'s Michael Tucker as Trinculo, spitting sea water on his first appearance, gave some hint of how W. C. Fields might have played the part. Ms. Perloff provided a generous amount of Balinese shadow play behind sheets, some of it replacing the Masque, which she wisely cut. In a season of *Tempests*, Ms. Perloff's version was not as flashily executed as that of George C. Wolfe, but it was a lot more thoughtfully conceived.

At the Yale Repertory Theatre in New Haven, Stan Wojewodski, its artistic director (and dean of the Yale Drama School), is fashioning adventurous schedules which, though hardly starting box-office stampedes, are reconsolidating Yale's dedication both to fresh visions and to theatre training (along with the usual professional presentations on the Rep's schedule, Wojewodski annually includes one show entirely staffed by students). The production I saw was Suzan-Lori Parks's remarkable *Venus*, produced in association with the New York Shakespeare Festival prior to its appearance at the Joseph Papp Public Theater. It is true that *Venus* played to small audiences, many of whom decamped before the final curtain. But it nevertheless represented a strong endorsement of the resident theatre's risk-taking mandate.

Parks's work has been attracting some very interesting radical directors, among them Liz Diamond and Marcus Stern. *Venus* was staged by the daddy of them all, the redoubtable Richard Foreman, who also provided the splendid production design. Matching Parks's passion for excess scene by scene, he proved an inspired choice. *Venus* is the story—filtered through the playwright's modernist perspective and Joycean language—of an actual historical figure, the Venus Hottentot, abducted from her South African home in the early nineteenth century to become a phenomenon of English freak shows because of her gargantuan breasts and buttocks.

Although the play bears some similarity to *The Elephant Man*, Parks wisely avoided pushing sympathy buttons. Her Venus is hugely exploited, but, whatever her conditions, she always retains an aristocratic dignity and sangfroid, laced with gentle irony. Venus is exhibited, manhandled, seduced, infected with clap, anatomized and finally autopsied by fatuous physicians who think they have found the missing link. Leering customers poke her butt with canes and umbrellas, and ogle her "backie, her bum, her spanker." One cowardly if doting lover makes her his mistress and spirits her away to Paris to avoid social ostracism. Yet the play is not so much an indictment of white oppression as of European smugness and insularity. As with her previous work—notably *The America Play* and *The Death of the Last Black Man in the Whole Entire World*—Parks manages to portray the humiliation of blacks in white society without complaint or indictment. *Venus* is not a victim play but rather a powerful dissent from narrow European concepts of female beauty.

The play needs editing (the play-within-a-play could easily go). And so does Foreman's production, which contains enough rich theatrical ideas for five such extravaganzas. Employing his customary alienation techniques (strings across the stage, blinding lights, continuous acoustical accompaniment), Foreman prodigally expends his brilliant inventiveness, at the same time directing his talented cast with absolute precision. The lovely Adina Porter as the amply bottomed Venus is especially spellbinding, but so are Peter Francis James, Sandra Shipley, and Mel Johnson, Jr. playing a variety of roles, both white and black. This interracial, intersexual, and intercultural pageant represents a major advance for an integrated American theatre.

At the Arena Stage in Washington, things are more corporate and traditional. Still, in an otherwise somewhat conventional season, Douglas C. Wager, the artistic director, has had the nerve to commission JoAnne Akalaitis to stage Strindberg's little-produced *Dance of Death*. The result is a triumph for the Arena and another vindication for Akalaitis, expelled from the New York Shakespeare Festival before she had the opportunity to fulfill her vision.

The Dance of Death brings back the warring couple of Strindberg's *The Father* (now a lot older and renamed Edgar and Alice). The misogyny of the earlier play, though hardly abated, is here leavened with surprising tenderness. Written toward the end of Strindberg's life, it takes place, like many plays by aging men (Sophocles' *Philoctetes*, Shakespeare's *Tempest*), on an island where Edgar runs a military lighthouse. With the aid of a magnificent design team (sets by John Conklin, costumes by Gabriel Berry, lighting by Jennifer Tipton), and using a terse, sensibly abridged adaptation by Bill Coco and Peter Stormare, Akalaitis creates a brooding atmosphere of rocks and sea where time is often suspended and people are ashamed of being human.

As the dark sky turns amber and the tormented characters enact their passion within, uniformed guards in spiked helmets and upraised swords circle the lighthouse at a glacial pace reminiscent of the Cologne section of Robert Wilson's *the CiVil WARS*. One visitor smells poison leeching from the walls: "There's so much hatred in here it's hard to breathe." As in *The Father*, the male character goes into coma. This time he recovers ("Alice, call off the celebration, I'm not dead yet") in time to torture his wife further. Although she makes love to a visitor before his eyes, she cannot leave Edgar: "You're the biggest shit and hypocrite I ever met—but at least you're a man." They prepare to celebrate their silver anniversary. After all, it is their fate to be each other's hell.

Two Arena actors, Henry Strozier and Tana Hicken, make a ferocious pair of sexual gladiators, he rasping and croaking with rage, she furious because he "didn't die before I was born." *The Dance of Death* is not the truth about marriage, but every married couple will recognize it as a bit of the truth, as well as the main source for Albee's similar marriage play, *Who's Afraid of Virginia Woolf?* Strindberg remains the great chronicler of the war between the sexes, a confirmed woman-hater who nevertheless understood women better than Ibsen and wrote them better parts.

Akalaitis's scorching *Dance of Death* is one of the landmarks of recent stage history. Along with what's happening at the ACT and YRT, it suggests that, despite economic woes, the resident theatre movement is not quite ready yet to throw in the towel. While some institutional theatres are attempting to relieve financial stress by relying on revivals of recent New York hits—or trying out shows on their way to New York—these three companies still manage to remind us of why people originally went into nonprofit theatre, and with what hopes.

1996

The Quest of Robert Lepage
(The Seven Streams of the River Ota)

Robert Lepage, a thirty-nine-year-old Quebecois theatre director, is one of the most respected artists in Europe. But except for a few brief appearances in New York sponsored by the Brooklyn Academy of Music, his work, like that of a growing number of the best people working in theatre today (American artists included), is rarely seen in our own country. Once again thanks to BAM's Next Wave Festival and its enterprising leader, Harvey Lichtenstein, *The Seven Streams of the River Ota* was made available to New York audiences for two weeks. A Lepage masterpiece, it confirmed a general belief that this imaginative French-speaking Canadian artist is a theatre visionary of the very first rank.

The River Ota, the product of Lepage's collaboration with Ex Machina (his permanent company operating out of Quebec), was originally created to commemorate the fiftieth anniversary of the Hiroshima bombing. It is in perpetual rehearsal. Much of it is improvised. Indeed, it grows longer with each performance. (Lepage shares the writing honors with the entire acting company as well as with the nonperforming Gerard Bibeau.) The unusual length of *The River Ota* provokes a sidebar. For some reason which I have yet to understand, the most powerful theatre works of our time have usually been either under two hours in duration (like the deconstructions of the Wooster Group and the terse dramas of David Mamet) or more than six hours (like many of Robert Wilson's productions, one of which takes place over a period of four days). *The River Ota* falls into the second category. Separated by a dinner break, it is an epic play in two parts, which requires almost eight hours to perform. Winter traveling problems compelled me to watch the two parts in reverse order, and to skip out on the last few scenes of Part One. But with the aid of the complete printed text, I think I can piece together the gist of Lepage's intentions.

The River Ota fully explores America's responsibility for the horrors inflicted on Hiroshima in 1945. But it is not, as one might think, a device to press the guilt glands of Western spectators. Rather, it attempts to show how suffering, and sensitivity to suffering, are human qualities that somehow manage to unite people. In short, the play probes—and I know this may strike some as a pious cliché—the illusory nature of the various boundaries that divide the nations of the world. I think Lepage makes a more successful case for one-worldism than Peter Brook, another proselyte of intercultural and international harmony. Brook's process (in his work with the International Centre of Theatre Research at the Bouffes du Nord in Paris) is to throw a lot of different nationals together into a single pot and trust the mix will render into a uniform and coherent creative stew. Lepage, on the other hand, takes us on a long journey through time and space in order to demonstrate how actions performed in one country by people of another can eventually result, over the decades, in a startling cultural symbiosis. *The River Ota* leans as heavily on the plot of *Madame Butterfly* as do David Henry Hwang's *M. Butterfly* and the Puccini-influenced musical known as *Miss Saigon*. But instead of treating the story as a paradigm of the seduction of innocent women by insensitive men, or the exploitation of the umblemished East by the impure West, Lepage uses it to expose the artificial nature of all racial, sexual, linguistic, and geographical divisions.

The play begins with a brief love affair between a U.S. Army photographer named Luke, documenting "physical damage" in bombed-out Hiroshima, and Nozomi, a Japanese *hibakusha*, or atom-bomb survivor, who is a living example of this "physical damage." (She has been horribly disfigured by the blast.) That romance accounts for much that happens in the play. The half-Asian, half-American child of the union, known as Jeffrey Yamashita (Jeffrey 2), goes to New York, following his mother's death, to make contact with his father Luke and his half-brother, Jeffrey O'Connor (Jeffrey 1). It is only after his father has died, and after he has helped his drug-addicted brother out of a drug-related financial fix by buying the family camera, that Jeffrey 2 reveals his true identity—by giving his brother a photograph of their common father. When Jeffrey 1 contracts AIDS, Jeffrey 2 participates in his assisted suicide in an Amsterdam clinic. The depositing of his own ashes near the Torii arch in the bay of Miyajima (Hiroshima) completes the expiatory cycle and ends the play.

Other strands of plot weave subtly through the evening. A traveling troupe of French Canadian actors come to perform a Feydeau farce (*The Lady from Maxim's*) in Osaka, and during a one-night stand with a Canadian embassy official, the leading lady is discovered by the official's wife in a scene of adultery and exposure that parallels the Feydeau plot. The Czechoslovakian-born Jew, Jana Capek, who appears in the Prologue as a student of Japanese martial arts brandishing a samurai sword, has pursued the way of Zen after escaping from Theresienstadt with the aid of a magician. (The Holocaust is depicted as another twentieth-century catastrophe whose survivors, at least in this play, are able to find their way to peace and forgiveness.) "I believe Hiroshima chose me," Jana says in tones of supreme serenity. "Ten years ago, I came to visit a friend and I thought I would find devastation here, but instead, I found beauty." Indeed, she found Czechoslovakia when she discovered that the Atomic Bomb Dome in Hiroshima was built in Prague Secession style. That kind of surprise is what initially attracted her to the silence of Buddhism, and that kind of surprise—the reversal of normal expectations—becomes the guiding principle of the play.

Being about the mutual dependence of peoples and cultures, *The River Ota* is inevitably a multilingual project. The text is equally divided between English, French, German, and Japanese, with projected captions providing the translated subtitles. The multinational nature of the work is physicalized in the set by Carl Fillion—a long wooden rectangle with a corrugated roof and sliding rice-paper doors, fronted by a narrow walkway and a terrace filled with stones. Like everything else in Lepage's work, the set transforms. Through the generous use of slide projections and films, Lepage manages to change that neutral structure first into a series of Hiroshima sites (a temple, a dock, a private home) where the action begins, then into a New York tenement, then into a German concentration camp, then into the Japanese stage where the Canadian troupe performs (we see this play from a backstage perspective, as in *Noises Off*). The set also functions as a Tokyo-Osaka bullet-train station, as an airplane runway, even as an American troop ship sailing the Pacific for the West Coast. Perhaps the most stunning use of the scenery is found in the New York episode, where the set is segmented into three parts: the room of Jeffrey 2 on one side, the room of Jeffrey 1 and his father (watching television with his back to us) on the other, and, in the center, a fully equipped bathroom, into which the denizens of the tenement gather (all at once, as in a Marx Brothers farce) to wash their bodies, brush their teeth, and relieve their bowels.

The stagecraft, in short, is magnificent. And so is the acting, alternating between low farce and high solemnity, and performed with the languor and stateliness of Noh plays and Butoh dances. Each scene unfolds to the accompaniment of Gagaku music (composed and performed by Michel F. Coté) with its strange reeds, chimes, cymbals, and percussive sounds. Clearly we are meant to be transported into some kind of dream, and the magic effects—a doll held by a soldier suddenly enlarging into a full-length woman, the doubling of mirrors to reveal a multiperspective suicide, a marionette show in which the puppets become more real than the puppeteers, a woman who levitates after a ferocious fight with her husband, a torrent of rain falling on the corrugated roof after a peal of thunder and dazzling blue lightning—only reinforce the sense of being carried away by illusion into a deeper reality.

The performance is, like everything else about the evening, an act of transformation. Twelve actors play more than forty characters in a flat, elliptical style unhurried by time or passion. The kind of doubling and trebling of parts that this requires is not just a matter of convenience but a theatrical convention subject to the circumstances of the play (for example, the same actor will inevitably play both father and son, or both mother and daughter). I suspect it may be a violation of company unity to single out any one actor for praise, but a particular word must be said about Anne-Marie Cadieux, among whose roles are the *hibakusha* Nozomi Yamashita and the despairing actress Sophie Maltais (who herself plays Mome Crevette in the Feydeau farce). She performs the disfigured Nozomi facing away from us, speaking in the softest of voices, her mournful broken English issuing from a sitting figure of absolute stillness, whose immobile back nevertheless has a remarkable eloquence. It is Nozomi who dominates the most astonishing moment of the entire evening, when six or seven characters, both male and female, magically mutate one into the other by materializing and disappearing inside Nozomi's wedding kimono. Finally we see Nozomi herself wearing this kimono—fifty years earlier—as her lover Luke pauses to take her photograph. This is the very essence of what we mean by symbolic action—the compression of a theme inside a series of physical images which have the power to stop time and conquer space.

The importance of the camera in the play suggests Lepage's obsession with image and reality and, as the commentator Karen Fricker notes, with mirror images—East and West, male and female, theatre and actuality, devastation and rebirth. These are opposites but not oppositions. Indeed, the evening proceeds with an odd absence of conflict. Instead these opposites are abstract entities that eventually combine into what Treplev in *The Seagull* called a "World Soul." By the end of this long day we have entered an atmosphere of quietude and contemplation, paradoxically uplifted by the ordeals and suffering of the various characters, having participated in a ritual that powerfully demonstrates the transfiguring nature of great theatre.

1997

Killer Chorines
(Chicago)

My esteemed colleague John Lahr wrote what may well be the only negative notice of the current production of *Chicago*. And while I love a courageous dissenter, it is one of the few times I have found myself in disagreement with the lively critic of *The New Yorker*. Following the finale of this splendid revival of the 1975 Bob Fosse production—a musical work based on Maurine Dallas Watkins's late-twenties play with book by Fosse and Fred Ebb, music by John Kander, and lyrics by Fred Ebb—I felt the rush that so many people speak of, and I so rarely experience, from America's "native art form."

Perhaps the reason for these unexpected feelings of elation was that *Chicago* exhumed the musical's forgotten roots in our truly native art forms, namely vaudeville and burlesque, at the same time uncovering the musical's neglected affinities with the great music dramas of Bertolt Brecht and Kurt Weill. Lahr protests that *Chicago* has been done on the cheap, that it is a "bare bones" reduction not much more elaborate than the concert version performed last spring as part of the City Center's Encores! series. But although some of the paying customers may complain about not being able to estimate how much was spent on the expensive toys that customarily inflate the price of Broadway spectacles, that is precisely *Chicago*'s strength. John Lee Beatty's setting—an unexpected departure for a designer normally identified with Circle Rep realism—is remarkable for its elegant metaphorical simplicity. It consists of a burnished gold picture frame (beautifully lit by Ken Billington) outlining a stage largely dominated by the orchestra in full view. The visible musicians form a traditional big band predominated by brass and woodwinds, and they are led by Rob Fisher in a variety of ragtime and jazz numbers, beginning with the rousing "All That Jazz" (a title Fosse borrowed for his semi-autobiographical film). The orchestra, in short, becomes virtually another actor in the play.

The old Berliner Ensemble production of *The Threepenny Opera* (directed by Erich Engel) placed the orchestra on stage in much the same way and for much the same reason—to reveal rather than conceal the source of the sound. *Chicago* imitates that production in exposing all the other mechanisms of the theatre as well (lights, pulleys, winches, wings, etc.). Indeed, the spirit of Brecht, who was also fascinated by the anarchic nature and criminal classes of Chicago, hovers over the entire evening. Under Walter Bobbie's propulsive direction, nonillusionistic devices abound. The titles of songs are announced (often by the music director), and the whole cast often sits on stage watching the principals sing and dance. Similarly the narrow playing space, which has been reduced to a rectangle no wider than ten or twelve feet, forces the performers into an extreme presentational style. The direct audience address not only lobs the songs, dances, and wisecracks right into our laps but effectively treats us as members of the cast, as if we were implicated (as we may very well be) in the crimes and double crosses of the characters.

William Ivey Long's costumes, like Beatty's set, are entirely without color—black tuxedos, black derbies and fedoras, black miniskirts, black tights, black T-shirts and slacks, black wigs. The effect is one of crispness and elegance. Even the American flag hanging vertically over the courtroom is a muted shade of gray. The only trace of color, in fact, is a rainbow rain curtain near the end, which signals us that the evening is over.

The traditional weakness of the modern American musical—and for this we have Rodgers and Hammerstein to thank—has been its inspirational book. Audiences in the past have been privileged to hear exquisite music and lyrics, to enjoy spirited choreography, to watch gifted performers. But also invariably we have had to pay for these pleasures with stories of such stupefying triteness and characters of such cardboard nobility that all the joys evaporated. Almost alone among American musicals—I can think only of *Pal Joey*, *Guys and Dolls*, *A Funny Thing Happened on the Way to the Forum*, and perhaps the quasi-Brechtian *Cabaret* (also by Kander and Ebb) that match it in literary quality—*Chicago* has a book equal to its other strengths. Like those musicals, it is both good-natured and hard-boiled. Indeed, there isn't a soft spot or a sour note in its metallic body. Just compare the homicidal revelations of *Chicago*'s characters with the soupy encounter group confessions of *A Chorus Line*, a musical that appeared in the same year as *Chicago*'s first production (and effectively eclipsed it). It is as if the two musicals belonged to two different cultures and epochs.

Chicago not only chronicles but also almost celebrates America's lost innocence. In a town so tough "they shoot the girls right out from under you," where each crime is ballyhooed by a band of ruthless jailhouse journalists straight from *The Front Page*, six women await their trails in a Chicago prison, accused of slaughtering their lovers in a variety of lethal ways. A more ideologically minded book writer might have treated this situation as an instance of minority victimization, a paradigm of the fate of women in a brutalized male society. But *Chicago*'s "story of murder, greed, corruption, violence and treachery—all the things we hold dear" (as the Prologue describes it), doesn't distribute virtues and vices according to gender, ideology, or identity groups. Apart from a falsely accused Hungarian woman who, lacking the language to defend herself, is the only person to be hanged, there isn't an innocent human being on stage, including the matron of the prison, the reporters, the lawyers, and the judge. Should a character claim to have committed her crime "because none of us had enough love in our childhoods," it's an occasion for a horse-laugh. What we have instead of loveless victims with disadvantaged backgrounds is "unrelenting determination and unmitigated ego." And instead of being ground up by a male-dominated judiciary system, the two central characters manage to beat their raps entirely, albeit with the aid of a mercenary silver-tongued lawyer who could have "gotten Jesus off if he had $5000."

Indeed, the women even manage to turn their crimes into celebrity careers, thus proving the prison matron's axiom that "in this town murder is a form of entertainment." *Chicago* recognizes the unacknowledged fact that celebrity is now neck and neck with profit as the animating motive of American life, that show business is just another con game.

Some commentators have observed how Americans have been prepared to accept this kind of cynicism on the commercial stage as a result of such recent travesties of justice as the O. J. Simpson murder trial and the consequent self-promotion of everyone associated with it. That may be. But surely the appeal of *Chicago* has something to do with its remorseless good nature. Not since John Gay's *The Beggar's Opera* (on which *The Threepenny Opera* was based) has a musical work managed to chronicle the weaknesses of humankind with such engaging sangfroid and sardonic shrugs.

Chicago revolves around two "killer chorines"—Velma Kelly (Bebe Neuwirth), who exults in her criminal headlines ("Baby, you can't buy that kind of publicity"), and Roxie Hart (Ann Reinking), who shoots her boyfriend and tries to pin the crime on her wimpy husband Amos. The competition between these two long-legged beauties over who gets the most public attention is the meat of the plot. And when Roxie, sitting on the lap of her oily lawyer Billy Finn, mouthing his words like a jerky ventriloquist's dummy, pretends to be pregnant, Velma protests that she's stealing all her best courtroom bits ("Whatever happened to class?"). Reinking, who also brilliantly recreated the Fosse-style choreography—the spider walk, the tipped derby, the hiked shoulder, the bent knees, the arched back—has been criticized for looking too ripe for the role of Roxie. She even concedes, in what may be a newly interpolated line, that "I'm older than I ever intended to be." But aside from the fact that Reinking gives a wonderfully comic performance—with a hoarse whiskey voice that oozes sentiment, then breaks it with a callow aside—her somewhat ravaged features make for a truly poignant connection with her rival, the dynamic young Neuwirth. That implied mother-and-daughter relationship reaches a powerful crescendo when, having decided at the end to combine their talents as a vaudeville twosome, they join together to sing and dance the "Hot Honey Rag," tipping their derbies, stretching their endless legs, and sashaying into Fosse heaven.

The sustaining element of this musical is surprise, whether in plot, staging, music, or acting. We're told that "things aren't always what they appear to be," and indeed they're not, whether the venal lawyer Billy Finn (James Naughton looking and crooning like a young Dean Martin) is mendaciously singing "I don't care about expensive things (all I care about is love)", or the sob-sister journalist (D. Sabella) is taking off her wig, after performing a series of coloratura arias, and revealing that she is a man, or the hapless Amos (Joel Gray in a very winning understated performance) becomes the only character to be denied exit music. But the biggest surprise of all is how *Chicago* has been able to make such a deep social incision into the flabby flesh of our court system, our newspapers, and our sentimental moral anatomy (Roxie, lying and murdering her way to stardom, is called a "living exemplar of what a wonderful country this is") and still emerge as a successful musical. Could it be that we are finally prepared to accept the truth about some of our motives and values through the medium of mass entertainment? Whatever the case, I left the theatre exhilarated, not only curiously moved by the high quality of the professionalism but also filled with unaccounted feelings of hope—about the future of the American musical, about the future of the American theatre, even a little bit about the future of America.

1997

The Descent of Man

(The Hairy Ape)

The plays of Eugene O'Neill have always presented problems, even for his admirers. His passion for large epic themes has rarely been accompanied by any great capacity to articulate them coherently, while his conceptual control, his effort to dramatize the ideas of thinkers like Marx and Freud, has always been shaky at best. As a result, intellectual critics, Lionel Trilling and Mary McCarthy among them, have usually been inclined to dismiss O'Neill as a pretentious windbag, and even the respectful Joseph Wood Krutch was forced to conclude that the dramatist had "genius without talent," by which he meant O'Neill lacked the verbal imagination to achieve his stated goals. Sadly enough, the playwright secretly agreed. If we are to believe his surrogate Edmund Tyrone, O'Neill always knew he was incapable of expressing his oceanic feelings in coherent speech: "I just stammered. That's the best I'll ever do," Edmund confesses to his father in *A Long Day's Journey into Night*, after trying to describe an epiphany at sea. "Well, it will be faithful realism, at least. Stammering is the native eloquence of us fog people."

That cruelly honest, deeply poignant passage is about the closest O'Neill ever comes to writing dramatic poetry. Most of the time all he is able to do is . . . well . . . stammer. In *The Hairy Ape* O'Neill tries to make a virtue of his speech defects, creating a character who can barely speak at all. Yank, the stoker, is one of America's earliest inarticulate heroes, a near relative of Stanley Kowalski in *Streetcar*. But whereas Stanley's crude proletarian idiom contains its own special spark and humor, Yank's mind is blunt and blank, his dialogue virtually impossible to read. "I start somep'n and de woild moves!" runs a typical passage. "It—dat's me—de new dat's moiderin' de old! I'm de ting in coal dat makes it boin; I'm steam and oil for de engines; I'm de ting in noise dat makes yuh hear it . . . ! I'm de muscles in steel, de punch behind it!"

This kind of exclamatory "toity poiple boids" language, in which Big Ideas are enunciated in a parody of Hobokenese, has kept plays like *The Hairy Ape* off the American stage for decades.

O'Neill's unprocessed expressionism hasn't helped much either—most of the characters in this play find their identity only as large abstractions.

A German production of *The Hairy Ape* some years ago by Peter Stein, however, proved such an enormous success against these odds that I imagined the only way to perform the play in this country was to translate it into a foreign language and then translate it back into speakable English. The current Wooster Group production offers another solution, which is to act the play so rapidly, through a razzle-dazzle of such technical wizardry, that you can barely make out the words. Oddly enough, the strategy works. O'Neill's underlying pulse and power, the dark side of his inarticulateness, have rarely been so potently revealed. Apparently the best way to receive this work is not to hear it.

The Hairy Ape was written in 1921, not long after O'Neill had completed his series of one-act sea plays. It is related to them in kind if not in length, taking place primarily in the fo'c'sle of a large ocean-going steamer. There the stokers, "hairy chested with long arms of tremendous power, and low receding brows," keep the ship's engines purring. Yank, the chief Neanderthal, is content with his place in the universe until a society lady named Mildred Douglas, paying a slumming visit to the engine room, is so appalled by his appearance and behavior that after calling him a "filthy beast" she faints dead away.

Yank's sense of belonging is severely shaken by this incident. Having "fallen in hate" with Mildred, he leaves the ship to confront the girl and discover his proper place in the chain of being. He visits Fifth Avenue, where he is first mocked, then thrown into prison. Later he tries to join the IWW (the Wobblies), who accuse him of being a government infiltrator (!). Yank ends up in a zoo where he is hugged to death by a gorilla, the only creature with whom he can feel any spiritual kinship. This ham-handed anecdote, an early study of alienation plunked inside a clumsy effort to dramatize Darwin's *Origin of Species*, might challenge and daunt even the most fearless performers.

Not the Wooster Group. Under the precisionist direction of Elizabeth LeCompte, this company has long enjoyed a well-earned reputation for doing deconstructed, unauthorized versions of anthology American plays. Among them have been Wilder's *Our Town* and

Miller's *The Crucible* (a production that so enraged the author he got an injunction to keep it off the stage). By comparison with these earlier efforts, LeCompte's production of *The Hairy Ape* seems relatively tame. The vanilla-ice-cream Americana of Wilder's play, for example, was interlaced with steamy pornographic movies and a blackface minstrel show.

Nevertheless the Wooster Group *Hairy Ape* is already mired in controversy. You enter the theatre past a group of picketers protesting that the presentation is busting various theatrical unions. The Wooster Group defends itself by claiming to be a "self-governing collective" that has never been a party to union agreements. This is unquestionably true. There is no doubt that the company's integrity, not to mention its longevity, has been inseparable from its commitment to common internal goals rather than to external controls and contracts. For years the Wooster Group has offered its work to a tiny audience in a small hard-to-find space in Greenwich Village. Critics have been admitted but not permitted to review the plays in progress. (I got lost once coming to see a Wooster Group show, arrived five minutes late, and found the door locked.)

Now the Wooster Group is performing a limited run of *The Hairy Ape* in one of those reconditioned 42nd Street theatres, with the backing of commercial producers. They hope to attract larger audiences with the lure of the movie star Willem Dafoe, a longtime company member, in the title role. What effect this move will have on the future of the group remains to be seen, but the present production is unsparing, uncompromising. The night I saw it there were so many outraged walkouts I thought I was back in Cambridge.

But a large number remained to cheer, and, indeed, there is much to cheer about. With the aid of dazzling klieg lighting by Jennifer Tipton, a thunderous sound score by James "J.J." Johnson and John Collins, and a metallic erector-set setting by Jim Clayburgh that rises and lowers like a steel trap, you look down on a claustrophobic space as dehumanized as its inhabitants. The event begins with looped videos of a prizefight that continue throughout the evening as a kind of leitmotif of combat and violence. Slowly the sooty-faced characters loom into view, rolling with the pitch and yaw of the ship, pressed into squatting positions by the metallic overhead cage. Dafoe's Yank is the sootiest of them all, his white eyes piercing through the grime like demented headlights, his white teeth bared in a monstrous grin.

The appearance of Mildred (Kate Valk) and her aunt (Peyton Smith) in the midst of this nautical *Walpurgisnacht*, mouthing O'Neill's tin-ear version of upper-class speech ("How naive age makes one!"), becomes a marvelous burlesque turn. Mildred strips to her negligee and starts prancing into the engine room wearing over-size ballet slippers that make her look like one of the ostrich chorus in *Fantasia*'s "Dance of the Hours." Her overstated expressions of disgust upon beholding Yank's repellent mug climax in an exaggerated balletic swoon that could have been choreographed by Balanchine.

In a yellow spotlight saturated with smoke, the stokers strip themselves naked to wash off the grime. And Yank, looking even more simian now that his features are visible, his reddish hair falling over his shoulders like a filthy towel, begins his long odyssey in search of the woman who insulted him. At times barking into a hand-held mike, at others glowering through a video screen, Dafoe's Yank perambulates the urban landscape like some exiled alien from a primitive planet. Confronting the Wobblies—a coterie of wise guys in green visors—he offers to blow up the Douglas Steel Works. The Wobblies respond by turning his video image negative. Dafoe's acting never deviates from a grotesque intensity. No wonder so many women walked out. They had come to see a matinee idol and found the monster from the black lagoon.

In the climax, against a video of a desolate moon, Kate Valk (or Mildred Douglas) puts on a fake gorilla head preparing to crush this hapless man to death. Yank has discovered his primal crime ("I was born"), and there's nothing left for him now but extinction. Still yammering about his failure to fit in ("I'm trou. Even him [the gorilla] didn't tink I belonged"), Yank experiences his *Liebestod* in the arms of an equally inarticulate primate as the rest of the apes celebrate his end in a crazy dance. Bells ring, the lights dim. *And perhaps* (O'Neill writes in a final stage direction), *the Hairy Ape at last belongs*.

In this production *The Hairy Ape* at last belongs to the rank of playable plays, having found its apotheosis in a dazzling experimental production that uncovers its secret heart. Many critics and most of the public see no value in directorial intrusions into the cloistered precincts of sacred masterpieces. But such gifted directors as Elizabeth LeCompte, and such creative companies as the Wooster Group, manage to show us how the spirit of a work can sometimes best be realized by ignoring the letter—in the case of *The Hairy Ape*, the unletter—of the text. Curiously O'Neill always considered this one of his most important if least appreciated creations, writing in a 1944 letter to Theresa Helburn: "It remains one of my favorites. I have an enduring affection for it—always will have—and an enduring respect for it as drama, the more so because so few people have ever seen what it is all about." Now that the Wooster Group has removed those obstructions that have blocked our appreciation, audiences are at last able to feel, if not to hear, what "it is all about." I suspect even O'Neill would have been pleased.

1997

Restoring a Ruined Colossus
(More Stately Mansions)

After various treks along 42nd Street's Theatre Row, vainly looking for something to review among those trivial pursuits that pass for serious drama these days, I chanced upon an unexpected treasure in the bowels of the East Village. For me it reaffirmed the power of theatre to make great art out of seemingly unreadable plays. I am referring to Eugene O'Neill's *More Stately Mansions*, in a production brilliantly staged at the New York Theatre Workshop by the Flemish director Ivo van Hove.

This extremely audacious offering, though honored abroad, was born for trouble in this country. Indeed, it ran into controversy before the very first preview. The nature of the flap is suggested in a program note by two of O'Neill's biographers, Arthur and Barbara Gelb—a spirited rejection of the whole enterprise written upon invitation by the theatre's artistic director, James C. Nicola. Inviting the Gelbs into the kitchen to criticize the cooking was a brave thing to do, though perhaps not as artless as it seems at first glance. Arthur Gelb wields a lot of power at the *Times*, having become chairman of the New York Times Company Foundation after holding other executive positions at the newspaper. Nicola may have been hoping to diffuse a potentially hostile reception by appeasing the cultural powers that be.

If this was his motive, it failed. The production was roundly assailed, regardless, by both of the *Times's* theatre reviewers, and for many of the reasons the Gelbs had cited. Their primary objection was that, being crude and unfinished, the play should never have seen the light, much less the stage, and that it was irresponsible of the Swedish adaptor, Karl Ragnar Gierow, to ignore O'Neill's instructions that his rough early draft for *More Stately Mansions* be consigned to the fire.

I'd read the adaptation two or three times since its publication by the Yale University Press in 1964—initially out of interest in O'Neill, later with the thought of production myself (Peter Sellars had expressed a desire to direct it at my theatre). Each time I found it of little other than archival value. As a piece of dramatic literature it's a very clumsy construct, written in that all-knuckles soliloquizing style that O'Neill employed in his early drafts—writings which, by the author's own admission, were "intolerably long and wordy" (a not inappropriate description, actually, for some of his finished plays as well). Without adding a word of his own, Gierow carved a three-and-a-half-hour work out of perhaps ten hours of material that was clearly not ready for prime time. And at first glance it's hard to dispute the Gelbs' contention that to rescue such an ill-formed child from oblivion was to contribute neither to the art of the theatre nor to the reputation of O'Neill.

But let's look at the situation from a more historical perspective. How many critic-biographers, for example, would have protested had someone found and reshaped an unpolished draft of a late lost play by Shakespeare? Or, if you find that analogy too remote, do we really think any less of Samuel Beckett because his early play *Eleutheria* was posthumously published against his express instructions and threats of legal action by his estate? How much in the long run is owed to an artist's dying wishes and how much to the world? Unlike Beckett's heirs, who tried to halt publication, O'Neill's widow and literary executor, Carlotta Monterey, actually gave the adaptor legal rights to proceed, having already ignored her husband's injunction that *A Long Day's Journey* remain in the drawer until twenty-five years after his death.

Publishing *More Stately Mansions* was arguably a disservice to O'Neill. But it was a singular service to O'Neill scholars, critics, and enthusiasts. And against all odds it has provided the occasion for a truly inspired evening of theatre. Van Hove's production demonstrates, as did the Wooster Group's stunning production last spring of O'Neill's generally incoherent *The Hairy Ape*, what a world of difference there is between the page and the stage. I am more and more convinced that the power of this playwright lies not in his words but in the tumultuous emotions that seethe beneath the surface of the words.

More Stately Mansions is the fourth work in a projected eleven-play historical cycle about America. As suggested by the awkward overall title, *A Tale of Possessors Self-dispossessed*, this epic was designed to dramatize the decline of early American idealism into the selfishness and greed of a mercantile culture. In form, *More Stately Mansions* is a family romance, retracing the incestuous graph of many other O'Neill plays, particularly *Mourning Becomes Electra*. But if *Electra* is essentially a quadrangle (husband and wife, son and daughter), *Mansions* is a triangle. The father of the house having died after the opening scene, two women—mother and wife—compete for ownership of the son/husband, thus revealing what O'Neill calls "the insatiable ambition of female possessiveness." Sara Melody, the Irish Catholic heroine of the previous play in the cycle, *A Touch of the Poet*, has married the sick man she was tending in that play, the sensitive Brahmin Simon Harwood. And now she and his mother, the regal and imperious dowager, Deborah Harwood, are contending for his soul (as well as for his estate).

At the beginning of the play, which takes place in the mid-nineteenth century during the presidency of Andrew Jackson, Simon is a naive dreamer, ambitious to write a Rousseauvian tract about the essential goodness of man. But having been persuaded to take over the family business, he soon turns into a ruthless capitalist, a pre-Nietszchean Superman beyond good and evil, who denounces the "stupid theory" that man is essentially virtuous.

This simplistic opposition—between the Poet and the Businessman, between American materialism and American idealism—was a well-worn theme of O'Neill's. It was his version of *Dr. Jekyll and Mr. Hyde*, and like R. L. Stevenson he sometimes used the same protagonist to dramatize the conflict, as he did, for example, in *The Great God Brown*. Deborah and Sara too, though separated by age, class, religion, and birth, also seem at times to be two sides of the same rusty coin. Simon clearly has a hard time distinguishing between them (he even suggests to each in turn that she murder the other). This crude reductionism makes the play seem raw and unformulated. What the production mines from this unfinished granite mass is a vein of raw strangulating power.

More Stately Mansions is on the surface a domestic drama. Van Hove transforms it into a Strindbergian dream play, partly through extremely stylized acting, partly through various abstract settings (pianos, machines, pipes) which form a background for the essentially bare forestage. By denaturing the visual environment and stripping the performances of their psychological dimension, the director manages to distract your attention from the bad writing and focus it on the boiling emotion. It is a process that permits the hidden lava of the work to flow more freely to the surface.

Each of the acts begins with the three central actors bowing to the audience, then to each other, like Sumo wrestlers. This is partly an effort to denaturalize the style, partly to prepare the audience for combat. For what transpires is an epic struggle in which each of the characters is stripped, both literally and figuratively, to the naked skin.

Joan Macintosh as Deborah, a character O'Neill describes as "deliberately deranged," is less a character than an icon, a woman blistered by hate. Her hair drawn tightly up from her face in a bun, her face and hands painted white, she looks like a ghost in a Noh play, a waxworks figure on two-inch-high white clogs. But then she moves, and the specter comes alive. She stalks the stage like a ravenous cheetah, rattling soliloquies, spewing acid, giving one of the most dangerous performances in my memory.

Two fine actors, Jenny Bacon as Sara and Tim Hopper as Simon, are almost as ferocious, and totally elemental in their relationship. At the end of the second act they create a remarkable moment together when he strips her naked, and—as she continuously tries to close her legs in order to preserve her modesty—he keeps opening them again, moving back to stare at her private parts. Aroused at last, she rips off his shirt, scattering buttons over the stage like hailstones, and yanks off his trousers. Both of them naked, they begin an abstract dance of extraordinary erotic grace, as, the lights slowly dimming, each takes a turn maneuvering the partner's nude body over the other's shoulders and around the other's waist. It is an event at the same time abandoned and controlled, fierce and tender, real and symbolic.

Deborah too has the opportunity to bare her body, exposing her breasts in a raw expression of incestuous longing for own son. Yet always permeating the erotic display is the implication that both love and lust are motivated by the will to power. At stake is the family business—a business that includes slave-dealing. Sara eventually gains possession of it in exchange for pretending to be her husband's whore. Even more at stake is the issue of which woman will gain possession of the husband-son. Each one, in turn, obtains hegemony over Simon, who becomes, in turn, the child of both his mother and his wife. (Van Hove illustrated this with two successive Pietas—at least one too many.) Simon pays a steep price for this accumulated maternal protectiveness, namely his growing infantilization. Van Hove staged this final moment in a manner that made my neck hairs crawl and tears spring to my eyes. (I think I'm describing what Aristotle called catharsis.) Sara moves to the side of the stage and beckons toward the dazed creature on the floor. He staggers toward her, hands in front of him, using the first unsteady and ungainly steps of a child.

Other moments stand out just as starkly in my memory: Sara humiliates an honest banker by demanding that he engage in the most squalid and degrading business practices. The man seems to dissolve into a liquefied mass before our eyes. In another typical van Hovian tableau, Simon and his brother Joel stand on either side of their mother, fighting like children over who gets the chance to touch her shoulder.

Joel (Robert Petkoff), by the way, is the comic butt of the play, "God's most successful effort in taxidermy," as he is described in an uncharacteristically humorous moment. "What an implacable bill collector you would make," sneers his mother Deborah. "How many times I wanted to pinch you to discover if you were stuffed." But these are among the few engaging and coherent moments in the play. The true eloquence of the evening is in the histrionic and visual arc of van Hove's production.

Yet the production would have been impossible without the text. And a true mystery is how, upon my returning later to this text, it began to assume a new dignity and magnitude that had escaped me before. O'Neill wrote *More Stately Mansions* at what would seem to have been a fearfully bitter period in his later life. He had been disappointed by his country, his family, and himself, and he was venting his disenchantment with all the inarticulate rage of a stillborn poet. As a result, *More Stately Mansions* is a colossus in ruins. Ivo van Hove's production reclaims the tragic masterpiece buried underneath the rubble.

1997

The Lionized Queen
(*The Lion King*)

Julie Taymor is the new lion queen of Broadway, universally acclaimed for having built a bridge between the avant-garde and the commercial theatre. Past experience reminds us that such a construction is less like a bridge than a conduit, since the traffic usually flows one way. (Typical is the fate of the experimental theatre director Tom O'Horgan, who never found his way back downtown after the Broadway success of *Hair*.) Still, there is no question that *The Lion King* is a brilliant amalgam of art and commerce. The Disney group has grasped something that still eludes most Broadway producers: It is the embrace of risk, not the repetition of tired formulas, that leads to a prestigious box-office success. *The Lion King*, being one long sustained *coup de théâtre*, is almost entirely a triumph of spectacle. In this it resembles most Broadway musicals. But for once the spectacle proceeds from fresh imagination rather than from cynical contrivance. A single Taymor puppet leaves an infinitely more indelible imprint on the imagination than the whole kaboodle of ascending saucers, descending helicopters, collapsing chandeliers, and similar such contraptions.

Perhaps Taymor's greatest achievement is to have proved that the Broadway audience is not a predictable population. *The Lion King* is a tourist attraction all right, but it is also a source of squealing wonder for thousands of kids who have hitherto sought their thrills in television cartoons, action figures, and computer games. Just to be present during the first stunning moments of the evening, when a silken sun rises and a whole menagerie of giraffes, cheetahs, gazelles, rhinos, and elephants begins to wend its way through the audience to the accompaniment of pulsing African music, is to watch the instant transformation of children from drugged spectators into wide-eyed participants in a compellingly live theatre event. One's attention is equally divided between observing the spectacle on stage and watching the kids jumping out of their seats.

I can't compare this piece of theatre to its source material, since I haven't seen the Disney cartoon. Some things are beyond a reviewer's bounden duty. (Perhaps perversely, I did see Disney's *Beauty and the Beast* and never saw the show.) Still, even in its theatrical, presumably more sophisticated incarnation, the plot of *The Lion King* is hardly a triumph of fairy-tale lore. Admittedly the book by Roger Allers and Irene Mecchi does try to capture some of the dreamlike psychology of a Grimm story. It is based on family conflicts, particularly the tensions between fathers and sons. Each time it threatens to plunge into any dark areas mediated by the unconscious, the plot jerks us back into conventional sentiment. Students of Bettelheim be warned: there is little here to excite psychoanalytical study.

Briefly, Mufasa, the king of the lions, warns his son Simba not to venture too far from the pride. The cub disobeys and, through the connivance of Scar, Mufasa's villainous brother, comes to believe that he is responsible for his father's death, when Mufasa, trying to rescue Simba from stampeding wildebeests, succumbs to their thundering hooves. Later Simba returns from a long exile, overcomes his guilt, kills the usurping Scar, and assumes the throne with his new bride Nala as the successor lion king.

Taymor uses this limp story as a clothesline on which to hang an array of spellbinding visuals. Her previous work displayed the fruits of her investigations into Indonesian and Balinese dance, Japanese Bunraku puppetry, and Javanese shadow play. In *The Lion King* she has also drawn on the energies of Zula warrior dances, choreographed by Garth Fagan, and the pulse of African music, some of it traditional, some invented by Lebo M. to enhance the original Elton John / Tim Rice score. For most of its length, *The Lion King* looks less like a Disney cartoon than a South African musical such as *Woja Afrika* or *Ipi Ntombi*. As if this were not enough of a stylistic mix, she throws in some amusing comic riffs derived from American vaudeville and movies. The result is an arresting multicultural unity—and if you think this is an oxymoron, go see the show.

Miraculously, Taymor's work shows little sign of Disney's patented anthropomorphic cuteness. Instead of investing animals with the character of humans, *The Lion King* shows us humans controlling the behavior of animals, thus managing to skirt all the cloying pitfalls of Disney conventions. This is accomplished, Asian style, by exposing the source of the puppetry, masks, and shadow play. The giraffes are actors on stilts using poles to maneuver their front legs. The faces of other actors appear through the jaws of grinning hyenas. The actor playing Zazu, the comic parrot who functions as the king's adviser, wears a clown costume (including a bowler hat) while carrying the bird in front of him like a breast plate. The actors playing the lions wear masks on top of their heads. The vaudeville team of the warthog and the meercat are visibly manipulated by their handlers. Wild birds fly through the air connected to poles held by puppeteers. Swaying grass fields in the veldt prove to be a chorus of African women. The stampeding wildebeests are represented by a series of painted drops which loom larger and larger as they thunder toward the forestage. Scar falls to his death, in slow motion, visibly suspended by wires. And so on: there are hundreds of such inventions during the course of the show.

The effect of this presentational technique is not to violate our suspension of belief but rather to reinforce it. What every theatrical tradition in the world has long understood—Western realism being the lone exception—is that the potency of the stage lies not in trying to hypnotize the audience into an illusion of reality but rather in continually reminding us we are sitting in a theatre. This understanding has been slow in coming to Method-dominated America, though it occurred to Yeats after discovering Arthur Waley's translation of Japanese Noh dramas, to O'Neill after experiencing Greek tragedy, to Pirandello after reading Bergson and absorbing *commedia dell'arte*, and to Brecht after studying Chinese and Elizabethan theatre. The single American form that has, almost unwittingly, continued to challenge representational realism has been the musical, with its direct address to the audience, its changing scenic metaphors, and its natural inclination to move abruptly from speech into song.

One of *The Lion King*'s many contributions to commercial theatre practice has been Taymor's capacity to forge a more obvious link between American musicals and nonillusionistic Asian conventions. Previously she had applied her voluminous theatre research to eighteenth-century Italian comedy (Carol Gozzi's *The King Stag* and *The Green Bird*), to Elizabethan drama (*The Tempest* and *Titus Andronicus*), and to South American fables (Horacio Quiroga's *Juan Darien*). Aside from a still embryonic musical called *Liberties Taken*, about the American Revolution, this is the first time she has applied her techniques to a native form.

Has she succeeded in creating a genuine work of art? Partially. There is no question about the brilliance of the first act, an absolutely ravishing series of scenic wonders. But in the second part, when the appealing ragamuffin who plays the young Simba (Scott Irby-Ranniar) transforms into a more conventionally acted adolescent (Jason Raize), the visuals are not quite sufficient to disguise the banality of the story. It is also in the second part that you begin to question a few of the stylistic choices. Max Casella and Tom Alan Robbins as Timon the meerkat and Pumbaa the warthog make such an amusing vaudeville duo that one is willing to forgive some of their more outrageous exchanges (Pumbaa to Simba: "Hey kid, what's eatin ya?"' Timon to Pumbaa: "Nothing, he's at the top of the food chain"). But there is an excess of low punning in the show, particularly among Scar's retinue of snarling hyenas, the most Disneyfied of Taymor's creations (Scar: "I am plagued by a profound emptiness" Hyena: "You're a regular Ennui the Eighth" Scar: "I need to be bucked up" Hyena: "You're already bucked up royally").

The villainous Scar, by the way, is played by the gifted John Vickery as a jaded and effeminate English aristocrat, in striking cultural contrast to his brother Mufasa (Samuel E. Wright), who is a noble warrior chieftain. This choice may have been influenced by the fact that Jeremy Irons provided the voice of Scar in the movie, but it makes a strongly anti-Western, if not vaguely homophobic, statement. Similarly Scar's trio of evil hyenas talks in the tone and idiom of ghetto street blacks while the members of the pride have a stately tribal bearing. So does Tsidii Le Loka as Rafiki, the female baboon / witch doctor, a character who frames the story with shamanistic dignity. Make of this what you will.

In short, no matter how manifold or perfectly realized the splendors of Taymor's *Lion King*, they cannot ultimately conquer the material. Listing the elements of drama in descending order of importance, Aristotle puts spectacle last, "of all the parts . . . the least artistic and connected least with the art of poetry." It is true that Julie Taymor, along with her splendid set designer (Richard Hudson) and lighting designer (Donald Holder), comes pretty close to making us revise Aristotle's estimate and move that element farther up the ladder. It is also true that spectacle is not her only contribution to *The Lion King*. She has also powerfully reinforced the characters and provided a splendid *mise-en-scène*. Still, let us her hope that her next project will display some of the Aristotelean virtues—strong action, powerful theme, compelling language, and dramatis personae—that evoke the deeper motions of the heart. That's the best way to prove that the traffic on the bridge between the avant-garde and the commercial theatre flows both ways.

1997

Musicals with a Message
(Ragtime; The Capeman; La Bohême Noir)

It's an old custom for churchgoers to listen to sermons on Sunday morning after visiting the whorehouse on Saturday night—a weekend ritual that may have inspired the Broadway tradition of mixing moral righteousness with musical entertainment. *Ragtime* and *The Capeman* are good examples of the way Broadway continues to merge the sacred and the profane. All of the considerable resources of the commercial theatre have gone into creating *Ragtime*. Based on E. L. Doctorow's powerful novel, it has been adapted for the stage by a very shrewd Broadway playwright, Terrence McNally. It has been driven by the epic imagination of a very gifted director, Frank Galati. It has been designed by some of the most brilliant visual artists in the business—Eugene Lee (sets), Santo Loquasto (costumes), Jules Fisher and Peggy Eisenhauer (lights), and Wendell K. Harrington (projections). And it is being sung and acted by an excellent cast, particularly Marin Mazzie as Mother, Peter Friedman as Tateh, and Brian Stokes Mitchell as Coalhouse Walker, Jr.

All of this promises us a musical of genuine distinction. What we often get instead is a self-congratulatory waxworks. Doctorow's kaleidoscopic novel roamed freely and broadly over the most colorful figures of the early years of the twentieth century: Emma Goldman, Harry Houdini, Evelyn Nesbitt and Harry Thaw and Stanford White, Henry Ford, Booker T. Washington, and Sigmund Freud (one of the few Doctorow celebrities missing from the musical). And while the novel took considerable liberties with historical fact, it compensated with an inventive writer's notions of how such figures might have behaved under imaginary circumstances. In the musical the historical characters exist only to flesh out an anorexic narrative line. In the novel they are people; in the musical only silhouettes. Little is left of Doctorow's broad panoramic view of America except his liberal pieties.

Like the novel, the musical splits up into three worlds: the world of Father, a rich Gentile explorer from New Rochelle; the world of Tateh, a Jewish socialist from Latvia; and the world of Coalhouse Walker, Jr., a black New York musician who impregnates one of Father's servants. Doctorow based Coalhouse Walker on Heinrich von Kleist's Michael Kolhaus, a German horse trader who became a symbol for unequal treatment by the law. After Coalhouse is accosted by some racist volunteer firemen, who vandalize his new car, and after Sarah, the mother of his child, dies in the act of trying to get him justice, Coalhouse turns terrorist and arsonist and occupies the Morgan Library. He is joined by a number of black followers in beige dusters and by Father's younger brother (an idealist ashamed of his race who "would shed this skin if I could stand with you and fight"). Eventually they agree to evacuate the library; Coalhouse is gunned down following his surrender.

In *Ragtime* Doctorow was trying to write the history of social diversification in America and predict its looming racial tensions. The musical tries to be faithful to this purpose, but as a form it is simply not equipped to provide depth and width at the same time. Stephen Flaherty's music and Lynn Ahrens's lyrics take their inspiration from the title. But aside from the opening number (called "Ragtime"), which is hammered rather insistently, the songs are not especially distinguished. McNally's book is faithful enough to the novel, but without Doctorow's rich abundance of detail, the plot seems overly schematic. And the ending—where Tateh marries Mother after Father dies, and they both adopt Sarah's black child—ends up looking like an artificial assimilation of its racial themes.

Frank Galati has already demonstrated his gift for creating Americana in his production of *The Grapes of Wrath*. In *Ragtime* he provides a number of deft nostalgic touches—particularly during the opening number when a child looking through a stereopticon conjures up the entire cast in sepia. But too much of the acting takes the form of that declaratory barking usually employed on Broadway to bridge musical numbers. Also, too much of the writing confirms the audience's previously held convictions. This musical version of *Ragtime* looks a lot like *Bloomer Girl* with a social conscience.

The Capeman looks like *Jack the Ripper* with a social conscience. The career of Salvador Agron, the Puerto Rican teenager who stabbed two innocent kids during a rumble and then bragged that his mother could watch him burn, would hardly seem to be inviting material for a Broadway musical. But Paul Simon apparently saw enough redemptive significance in Agron's life to turn him into a musical martyr.

To flesh out his concept, Simon enlisted the services of Derek Walcott to help write the book and lyrics, and Mark Morris (and later Jerry Zaks) to stage the production. None of these able people has been able to bring this dismal story to life. Neither Simon nor Walcott seems capable of creating a coherent narrative line or even a decent lyric ("Life is an ocean of endless tears" is fairly typical of the soggy sentiments expressed). The musical is bare of dance or even interesting movement, which is pretty surprising in view of the participation of Morris. And, with the exception of a couple of good salsa numbers ("I Was Born in Puerto Rico" is one), the score has a rhythmic monotony about it that will surprise Paul Simon fans (though all the songs sound better sung by the composer on the CD).

In conception *The Capeman* borrows heavily from *Evita* and *West Side Story*. From Andrew Lloyd Webber, Simon and Walcott take the device of a character on the sidelines—in this case the oldest of the three actors playing Agron (Reubén Blades, performing as if in a coma). Like Che, he offers sardonic commentary as the action proceeds. And from *West Side Story* the authors borrow the local barrio color, staged rumbles, and particularly the notion that juvenile delinquents are "depraved on account of we're deprived."

You probably recognize that phrase, written by Stephen Sondheim for "Officer Krupke" and intended to be ironic. In *The Capeman*, Simon and Walcott accept the notion with a perfectly straight face. The authors ask us to believe that Agron turned murderer not because of his nature but because of his nurture (or lack of it)—because his father deserted his mother, because his stepfather disapproved of him, because of a general prejudice against Latinos. Anyway, the killings were really a revolutionary act: "We share a history, the white man broke our nation. . . . The barrio is just another reservation. But the revolution is coming fast."

In short, Salvador Agron may have stabbed a couple of innocent kids, but he was basically a misunderstood sweetie—a Jesus Christ of the Barrio who took the rap for everybody else and bore their sins: "I am an innocent man," he cries, "and I paid you with my life." If Agron is innocent, then obviously white society is to blame: "Guilty by my dress," he sings, "guilty by the press / The world goes crazy for Latino blood when a white boy dies." After serving time in a number of prisons, he is finally released; returns home to his mother (whose hair has turned quite gold from grief); and finally, "a ghost wandering in the neighborhood," dies of a heart attack at the age of forty-three.

In his time Paul Simon has written some tender songs about romantic love, divorce, parenthood, and similar domestic issues. His muse is not up to wrestling with the concept of evil. *The Capeman* emerges as Radical Chic, vintage 1998. Apart from Bob Crowley's remarkable forced perspective settings, the show (which met a hostile press and quickly closed) is simply not *auténtico*. In fact, the only moments in the evening that seem convincing are the old newsreels in which the historical Agron, sneering self-consciously at the camera, tells an interviewer who asks him how he feels about the murders, "I feel like killing *you*." All right, what next? A musical extolling the tormented life of Jeffrey Dahmer?

On a recent trip to South Africa I found a wonderful antidote to the dyspepsia I get from American guilt musicals. It was an all-black version of *La Bohème*. Entitled *La Bohème Noir* and performed at the Nico Theatre Center in Capetown, this was a truly splendid rendering of Puccini's opera, subtly adapted to suit the circumstances of South African blacks under apartheid. The Nico Theatre Center was formerly a segregated cultural complex. Many whites boycotted it until Mandela became president and integrated everything. A lot of ANC cultural funds have been poured into the making of this opera. But although the conductor and the principals (wonderful singers all) were black, the audience was almost entirely white.

La Bohème Noir is set not in Paris but in Soweto, where the characters are suffering both from poverty and from oppression. Rudolfo has undergone a transformation from poet to playwright (he burns one of his plays to protect himself from the cold), and Mimi is now a domestic servant. Aside from a number of topical and geographical references, however, the libretto is essentially left intact. What has changed—and radically—are the social circumstances.

In the third act, for example, Mimi and other domestics are waiting for a bus in front of metal fences, shacks, and shabeens ("We have to go to work; we are the cleaners"). They are accosted by menacing Afrikaaner police who rudely examine people's faces and identity papers. The police pick out a suspect and haul him off for questioning, an action of a sort that raises the stakes of the opera considerably. In Puccini the bohemians have little to think about but love, jealousy, and their next meal. Here they are awaiting liberation, not just from starvation but from enslavement. "This is Republic Day in Soweto," goes one chorus, "where children's voices sing a new libretto." "What can we do for the struggle?" asks Rudolfo. Paint and write, comes the answer.

La Bohème Noir reminded me a little of those American musicals of the thirties and forties—period pieces like *The Hot Mikado* and *Carmen Jones*—where all-black casts performed in shows originally written for and by whites, without the slightest hint of self-consciousness or resentment. What was striking then, and now, was not just the robust talent but the exuberant good nature of the participants. They all contributed to a highly charged evening of opera, beautifully conducted and powerfully sung. Oddly enough, this version, though adapted so freely, managed to rescue the opera from divas, dress suits, and champagne suppers, and restore some of its original energies. Poverty for these characters is not simply a question of choice or lifestyle, as it is, say, in *Rent*. Nor are oppression and racism stimuli for cheap sentiment. No, they are grinding realities in a culture which, instead of wallowing in a guilty past, is seeking to improve the future.

1998

The Two O'Neills

(Ah, Wilderness!; The Emperor Jones)

Every serious modern playwright, no matter how sober his everyday work, likes to relax and take a vacation from time to time—Buechner with *Leonce and Lena*, Ibsen with *Peer Gynt*, Strindberg with *Lucky Peter*, Brecht with *The Caucasian Chalk Circle*. If humankind, as Eliot tells us, cannot bear very much reality, neither can the creative writers who remind us of this, which is why they need an occasional holiday away from their more remorseless themes.

O'Neill's season in the sun is called *Ah, Wilderness!*, and it is a holiday play in more ways than one. Celebrating the indomitable character of the American middle-class family, *Ah, Wilderness!* is set in Connecticut on Independence Day, 1906. Since O'Neill spent most of his career dramatizing the breakdown of the American middle-class family—a reflection of what he perceived to be the breakdown of our national values—this patriotic tribute to the American past is an interesting departure, to say the least. It is also significant that, despite the inordinate success of *Ah, Wilderness!* when first produced in 1933, O'Neill did not permit another work of his to reach the stage until *The Iceman Cometh* in 1946. Watching the play, moreover, makes us realize how, in *Ah, Wilderness!*, O'Neill's creative influence extended not just to somber writers like Arthur Miller and Tennessee Williams but to such cheerful spirits as Thornton Wilder (*Our Town*) and Neil Simon (*Brighton Beach Memoirs*). Here O'Neill reveals the flip side of his own imagination and of American drama as a whole.

In short, all the circumstances surrounding the play excite the mind and arouse the imagination. What provides little stimulus for either is the play itself. The current revival of *Ah, Wilderness!* in Lincoln Center does everything possible to spur this old warhorse into a canter. It has an attractive cast, led by Craig T. Nelson as Nat Miller (a role originally played by George M. Cohan), and featuring Debra Monk as Essie Miller and Leo Burmester as her alcoholic brother Sid. It also boasts, as their rebellious son Richard, an engaging actor named Sam Trammell, who may well become the next Matthew Broderick if his adolescent magnetism doesn't lure him into sitcoms. It has been affectionately directed by Daniel Sullivan, and beautifully designed with washes of tender nostalgia by Tom Lynch (a third-act love scene represented by a large moon, a distant star, and a derelict rowboat on a beach is especially evocative). And it contains some bittersweet speeches, particularly Nat's concluding "September Song" lines about the beauties of autumnal and wintry age as compared with the springy pleasures of youth.

But while the writing is controlled, it's just too comfortable. O'Neill defended the play, in a letter to his son, by saying it was a "new departure" which tried to capture "the spirit of a time that is dead now with all its ideals and manners and codes." And although O'Neill also claimed that the play contained very little of an autobiographical nature, one can't help noticing traces of the playwright's past life in some of the characters. In *A Long Day's Journey into Night*, a work set six years and written a decade later, the agreeable Miller family turns into the dysfunctional Tyrones. Dad has become a skinflint, Mom a drug addict, and young Richard, who spouts Swinburne, Wilde, and Omar Khayyam, has matured into a character with the same poetic tastes, the equally sensitive, if now sardonic and consumptive, Edmund Tyrone. Did that lost Eden of ideals and manners and codes ever really exist?

In a little-known essay on O'Neill, Lionel Trilling noted that he was "always looking beyond the social to the transcendental," and that his revolt was that "of the conscious middle class against its own sterile complacency." The opposite seems to be true in *Ah, Wilderness!* In that play O'Neill was writing about family values and community stability during a time when about the worst thing a child could do was drink too many sloe gin fizzes and visit a local whore, and when parents were there to provide a safety net for such mischievous behavior. These families still exist, of course, perhaps in larger numbers than we know, and their virtues deserve to be honored. But celebrating such homely values doesn't make for very penetrating drama, and, besides, such plays tend to invite middle-class audiences into the very "sterile complacency" that Trilling deplored.

Clocking in at about two hours and forty-five minutes, *Ah, Wilderness!* is a lot shorter than O'Neill's more epic creations. It just seems a lot longer. My wife compared it to a slow train ride that stops at every station. I think the reason for the sense of longueurs is that so little is at stake. Will Sid be forgiven his drunken lapses by Nat's sister Lily? Will Richard be rejected by his girlfriend Muriel because he kissed a prostitute? Who cares? The plot, the characters, and the theme of the play almost seem to call for reinforcement by song and dance, which is why the play's most appropriate incarnation was as a musical comedy called *Take Me Along*, starring Jackie Gleason as brother Sid. The Lincoln Center Theater has just announced a season of American musicals. Although it lacks a composer or a lyricist, *Ah, Wilderness!* may be the first event in that series.

The other O'Neill, the writer pursuing transcendence rather than domesticity, is also being represented on the New York stage these days, in a production of *The Emperor Jones* by the Wooster Group. This enterprising experimental troupe had already flexed its O'Neill muscles earlier this season with a powerful version of *The Hairy Ape*. *The Emperor Jones* is a reworking of a production it first presented in 1993.

This relatively early work, written in the same rush of inspiration that produced *The Hairy Ape* and *Anna Christie*, would seem to be virtually unplayable today because of its clumsy effort to render the black idiom. Look at this typical passage: "Think dese ign'rent bush niggers dat ain't even got brains enuff to know deir own names even can catch Brutus Jones? Huh, I s'pects not! Not on yo' life." Or even more problematical, "Feet do yo' duty!" when Jones is preparing to flee. Perhaps recognizing that O'Neill's tin ear made almost all his language sound stereotypical (Smitty's cockney dialect, even in the mouth of that superb actor, Willem Dafoe, is equally clumsy), the Wooster Group meets this problem head on. Brutus Jones, a role once played by the majestic Paul Robeson, is performed not by a black actor but by a white person in blackface, and a woman at that (Kate Valk). Rather than normalize Jones's speech, Valk chooses to exaggerate the already exaggerated dialect into minstrel show patter.

This is inviting trouble, but then so is the very act of producing the play. The only notes in the Wooster Group program are some generous comments from W. E. B. Du Bois, defending O'Neill against those "preordained and self-appointed" judges of how black people should be represented on stage, those who would "destroy art, religion and good common sense in an effort to make everything that is said or shown propaganda for their ideas." Du Bois believed that O'Neill in *The Emperor Jones* was trying to break through the defensive shells that prevent black people from being represented truthfully in the theatre. Today, when even such black artists as Kara Walker and Robert Colescott are being attacked for creating black stereotypes, O'Neill's early effort to open the doors of perception looks all the more brave and prescient.

As written, *The Emperor Jones* is a trip into the heart of darkness by an American black man who has persuaded himself that his Western reason and intelligence are protections against the voodoo spells of his native antagonists. He proves to be wrong. This former Pullman car porter and ex-convict is conquered less by external enemies than by his own "formless fears." Having set himself up as emperor of a West Indian island and looted all its treasure, Jones has invented the myth that he can only be killed by a silver bullet. He too eventually comes to believe the myth. Both Caesar the emperor and Brutus the assassin inhabit the same breast. In Trilling's words, Jones "goes backwards through social fears to very fear itself, the fear of the universe which lies in primitive religion." This is a great theme. O'Neill never lacked for great themes, only the art with which to express them.

Once again the Wooster Group, under its visionary director Elizabeth LeCompte, supplies that art by distracting attention from the play and the dialogue to the theatrical medium itself. The stage is bare except for a white linoleum floor, decorated with three television screens, and, for one blinding moment, three bright headlights. While the screens register ghost images, Valk and Dafoe engage each other, both displaying great vocal range and variety, sometimes as characters in O'Neill, sometimes as samurai warriors and dancers in a Kabuki drama. Two prop masters solemnly hand them their properties. Each actor carries a microphone, which also has a prop function (a walking stick for Jones, a bat for Smitty). Valk sits in a high chair on wheels, rolling her eyes and roaring her lines through a reddened mouth, a bit like Hamm in Beckett's *Endgame*. The mikes and the music (often raucous rock) are set at a high decibel level.

Those who emerge from the theatre without a headache can testify to a penetrating if painful encounter with the play. The Wooster Group's deconstructing of classic American drama can sometimes come perilously close to desecrating it. But when successful, such approaches also have the capacity to open up whole new avenues of understanding. "O'Neill's techniques," wrote Trilling, "like those of any sincere artist, are not fortuitous—they are the result of an attempt to say things which the accepted techniques cannot express." The same might be said for the Wooster Group.

1998

PART 3

PRODUCTIONS: FROM ABROAD

The Royal Shakespeare Company
(Hamlet; Artists and Admirers; Richard III)

The Barbican Theatre, where the Stratford-based Royal Shakespeare Company hangs out in winter, is a huge concrete complex largely subsidized by the Crown and wholly devoted to plays. No one really likes the building any more than its similarly endowed sister institution, the Royal National Theatre on the South Bank. But the RSC has the added problem of being located in a commercial part of the city underpopulated at night. It is unfortunate that neither of England's two major theatres are organically linked to neighborhoods. (The Royal Court and the Almeida, by contrast, are in the midst of street life, accessible to pedestrians, and surrounded by shops, bars, and restaurants.) Few people walk to these imperious complexes—you reach them by tube or by driving your car into large parking garages, like a shopping mall.

I confess my reserve over the architecture is partly inspired by envy over the resources—British theatre centers make visiting American professionals turn green. Even the Guthrie and the Vivian Beaumont pale in comparison. Bookshops, restaurants, child-care centers, cinema clubs, art galleries, handsome informative programs, a variety of stages, live music in production, and, above all, hordes of people intent on nothing but playgoing—these are perquisites that few American theatres can boast.

Nevertheless these portentous buildings do create something of a barrier to adventurous work, and the current Establishment theatre repertory, though often of high quality, lacks real excitement. Richard Eyre and Adrian Noble are each capable directors and administrators, but their theatres seem like institutional tourist meccas when compared with Laurence Olivier's National and the RSC under Peter Hall. At the Old Vic, Olivier and his literary manager, Kenneth Tynan, though hardly enthusiastic about cutting-edge experiment, were always alert to new voices in British theatre. At the Aldwych, Peter Hall and such associates as Peter Brook not only radically reinterpreted Shakespeare but created a home for Pinter, Arden, Weiss, Genet, and Bond. When you consider that arteriosclerosis set in at the National only after Hall, succeeding Olivier, moved to the massive bunker on the Thames, and at the RSC only after Trevor Nunn abandoned the Aldwych for the Barbican, it's tempting to conclude that the problem is at least partly architectural.

Unlike the National, the RSC still maintains a permanent ensemble of actors, and while the company still features new plays from time to time, it is essentially devoted to classics. I saw three of these RSC productions on my last visit to London: *Hamlet*, Alexander Ostrovsky's *Artists and Admirers*, and *Richard III* (which had moved from Stratford to the Donmar Warehouse).

Of these, Adrian Noble's Edwardian *Hamlet* was by far the most engrossing. An uncut four-hour-and-twenty-minute version, which allowed a five-minute break after the first two hours and a fifteen-minute interval after the first three, it proved to be not the endurance test one expected but rather a continuously fresh rethinking of the text. Like a number of contemporary British directors, Noble manages to make Shakespearean verse sound newly written. He's borrowed a few effects and ideas from his former associate Ron Daniels, whose similarly updated *Hamlet* with Mark Rylance was performed a few years ago at the RSC (and more recently at my own theatre). But otherwise Noble follows no established conventions or traditions, treating the play like an unsolicited script that just popped into the literary office. The result is a style of almost cinematic naturalism, embellished by radical interpretations of text, character, and relationships.

With a strong cast, designs of eloquent simplicity by the visionary Bob Crowley, sharp lighting by Alan Burrett, and ferocious music by

Guy Woolfenden, in fact, Noble had everything required for a memorable *Hamlet* except a memorable Hamlet. This is another of Kenneth Branagh's attempts to lay claim to Olivier's roles, the first being his stirring movie of *Henry V.* It is not an equal success. Branagh is essentially a rhetorical actor with a megaphonic voice which makes him seem marooned in Noble's naturalistic world. Excessively concerned with articulation, he appears embarrassed by the more emotional soliloquies, passages he invariably rushes. He whines through a self-pitying "To be or not to be," and his death scene is empty.

Only in the closet scene does Branagh display convincing feeling (disgust with his mother), though he rises well to the flourishes of "Oh what a rogue and peasant slave" and to the pyrotechnics of the Pyrrhus speech (this is the only Hamlet I've seen who performs more theatrically than the Player King). Branagh's Prince is not an appealing figure. Neither was Peter Stormare in Bergman's version of the play, but that was deliberate. Quite simply, Branagh lacks the requisite style and nobility. He has the artificial dignity of a Sotheby auctioneer and the potato features of a Yorkshire farmer. How does he illustrate "But break my heart, for I must hold my tongue"? He adjusts his waistcoat.

That this *Hamlet* nonetheless holds our attention is a tribute to Noble's meticulous direction and the confidence of the other performers. Clifford Rose's stumble-footed Ghost is a specter in white who thrusts his arm up through the ground (*Carrie*-style) in the swearing scene. Joanne Pearce's Ophelia, a playful young feminist, expresses both her high spirits and, later, her erotic dementia at the piano. Jane Lapotaire's Gertrude is a slightly dotty matron, though appealing enough to stimulate the lust of John Shrapnel's dapper and forceful Claudius. David Bradley's Polonius has the disapproving scowl of a Yankee banker, while Richard Bonneville's Laertes looks like a self-satisfied stockbroker. As for Richard Moore's First Gravedigger, he is appareled like a Victorian undertaker, and Guy Henry's Osric is a fop in spats. It is a tribute to this intelligent, well-fashioned production that it can be honestly described with a cliché: You think you're seeing the play for the very first time.

Which is more than I can say for the RSC version of *Richard III* at the Donmar Warehouse. The child of my companion, a stranger to Roman numerals, misread the title as *Richard One Hundred and*

Eleven, and that's how many times I felt I'd seen it after this laborious production (happily for my disposition toward the play, the 110th Richard was Ian McKellen's). At this performance, I should confess, the celebrated actor Simon Russell Beale, suffering from a slipped disk, had been replaced in the title role by a badly cast understudy, so it's unfair of me to review it. But the rest of the actors were sufficiently boring, and Sam Mendes's directorial concept enervating enough, to conclude that the replacement wasn't the major misfortune.

Paradoxically, the same naturalistic approach that distinguished the RSC *Hamlet* sabotaged its *Richard III*. In the extremely intimate space of the Donmar Warehouse, where the most significant object in Tim Hatley's bare design is a huge incandescent light bulb, the play is directed with the ostentatious simplicity of a movie documentary. The performers, costumed in Brechtian uniforms and jackboots, are devoted to "being" rather than acting, which is to say they suppress any high emotion or heroic behavior. For a play so dependent on lamentation, on "telltale women" raving and moaning, this is to rob it of its affective center. Gone too is any hint of regality—even Richard's crown is made of cardboard. The result is utter blandness, affected ordinariness, when the play is nothing without its powerful, riveting melodrama. Mendes scatters a few ideas through the evening. Each time someone is killed, for example, another character closes the dead man's eyes. But this is a "people's" version of *Richard III*, where all the characters are democratized and none of the actors is permitted to betray a hint of imagination or invention.

Artists and Admirers is a work that reads a lot better than it plays. English actors, who tend to colonialize foreign sounds into their own tongue, have even more difficulty with Slavic inflections than with French or German. It's disconcerting to hear talk of rubles by people more comfortable with pounds and pence, or to listen to Russian patronymics pronounced in cockney accents (a previous Russian work I saw in London was delivered in Scottish burrs). Ostrovsky's 1882 play is based on his long experience with the theatre. It is, in fact, partly a meditation on the censorship he experienced as a writer for the stage, though it is even more concerned with the hard financial lot of actresses.

Aleksandra Nikolaevna Negina, known as Sasha, is an actress with a provincial troupe, preparing for her benefit. Actors' salaries being extremely low, such supplements were required to rescue them from poverty. Although Sasha has a fiancé, a poor teacher, she is being wooed by two other men, a prince and a landowner, the second of whom offers to buy her benefit for five hundred rubles. By the end of the play she has abandoned them all, having determined that, though an actress exists not simply to create but also to be admired and loved, talent is preferable to wealth or happiness. She cannot live without the theatre.

There are rough sketches here for Nina in *The Seagull* and Lopahin in *The Cherry Orchard*, but the actress playing Sasha, with her poached-egg eyes and pinched demeanor, would have been better cast as Varya, or perhaps Sonya in *Uncle Vanya*. Ostrovsky understands the frustrations of trying to create theatre in the provinces—"Is art really understood here? Is art really needed here?" asks the troupe's despondent stage manager. But these questions seem out of place in an urban culture center like the Barbican, and this RSC production, under the direction of Phyllida Lloyd, contains no particular urgency. Not finding much appeal in the actors, I had trouble staying with the play. *Artists and Admirers* seems to have been chosen primarily to fill out the season schedule.

The poor acting quality of *Richard III* and *Artists and Admirers* is, I suspect, an aberration. The overall level of performance at the Royal Shakespeare Company is probably adequate enough. It's the level of inspiration that's low. Although most can hold a stage with confidence, there are few actors in these companies to match the legendary figures of the past. What is most conspicuously missing from the stages of the RSC and the National, however, is dramaturgical imagination. The new plays are unexciting, the modern revivals are insipid, and the classics are anthology favorites, recycled in new versions from season to season. It is true that such directors as Stephen Daldry, Declan Donnellan, Deborah Warner, and Richard Jones, working in tandem with inspired designers, have been opening up English audiences to European theatrical concepts, linking the nation's theatre, for the first time, to an artistic common market. But there's still something vacant in these Establishment buildings. I think what the English theatre most needs, to bust through the architectural barriers, is just one visionary playwright who could change the way people think about the stage.

1993

The Royal Court
(The Man of Mode; The Libertine; Blasted)

The Royal Court Theatre in Sloane Square is now entering its fifth decade as London's most friendly home for provocative new plays. Popularly known as the "Court" but actually named the English Stage Company, this theatre was founded by the legendary George Devine as a breeding grounds for Osborne, Wesker, Bond, Jellicoe, and other "angries" of the fifties and sixties. Forty years later it is still pulsing with impudent energy, still faithful to its mandate to flush out and facilitate young British talent. The Court continues to perform this function so well, in fact, that it is providing virtually the only things in London worth seeing at present.

The Court experienced a leadership change two years ago when Max Stafford-Clark ceded his position as artistic director to the thirty-four-year-old Stephen Daldry (Daldry's productions of *An Inspector Calls, Machinal,* and *The Kitchen* have now made him an international figure). At the same time Daldry was moving to stamp his imprint on the traditions of this historical playhouse, Stafford-Clark was forming a theatre of his own called Out of Joint. The two organizations have now joined forces to sponsor two plays in repertory at the Court, George Etherege's Restoration comedy *The Man of Mode* and Stephen Jeffreys's contemporary work *The Libertine.*

The plays are linked by more than the common stage they share. *The Libertine* is based on the later life of John Wilmot, Earl of Rochester, a notorious rake and pornographic poet, and the model for the character of Dorimant in *The Man of Mode.* The smell of the lamp hangs as heavy over this play as the stench of tobacco and the reek of alcohol. Indeed, *The Libertine* opens with Rochester, Etherege, and Charles Sackville drunkenly dishing their rival John Dryden's heroic verse. These literary resonances make the two plays virtually coextensive, and so does the fact that they share a common pool of actors. For the moment the Court is housing one of the few resident repertory companies still performing in England (like many theatres which use the word "company," the English Stage Company more commonly employs a pickup cast for each production). To watch these actors move so effortlessly from one role to another is again to be reminded of the almost forgotten pleasures of histrionic transformation.

Stafford-Clark told me he commissioned *The Libertine* from Jeffreys after waiting seven years for Heathcote Williams to write an appropriate script. He chose his successor dramatist wisely. Jeffreys's theatrical affinity with Rochester, coupled with a good historian's feel for Restoration manners and morals, has helped him fashion a more trenchant portrait of the period than did many of its playwrights, including Etherege.

The Libertine certainly features a more fully dimensioned portrait of a Restoration rake than one finds in the hollow cynicism of *The Man of Mode*. In the acerbic performance of David Westhead, Jeffreys's Rochester detests the world and no one in it more than himself. "You will not like me," he advises the audience, less as a warning than as a demand. This Rochester seeks not affection but attention ("I must not be ignored or you will find me as troublesome a package as ever pissed into the Thames"). The playwright invites us to regard Rochester's headlong descent into dissipation and debauchery not as a moral blank so much as the painful acting out of his own sense of absurdity. Trembling with despair, he betrays friends, wife, and sovereign, with the elegiac scorn of a self-hating sinner.

Rochester's cruel pranks get him banished from court at least twice (once for demolishing the king's cherished sundial), while his powerful literary gifts are consecrated to writing eulogies to whoring and drinking. When commanded by King Charles to compose a literary piece better suited to his talents, he contributes an obscene masque worthy of the Marquis de Sade called *Sodom*, "where the men deal only in buggery" and a chorus of women endowed with names like Fuckadilla and Clytoris perform a dance brandishing dildos ("A monument to your reign" he tells the unappreciative king). Like so many Restoration libertines drained by promiscuous lives, Rochester finally seeks solace in a romantic relationship—with the actress Mrs.

Elizabeth Barry, who later developed into one of the most truthful performers of her time, partly under Rochester's coaching. She nevertheless proved as stonyhearted toward him as she later did toward her even more besotted suitor Thomas Otway. Jeffreys perfectly captures, and absolves, the character of an ambitious creature for whom love is just a step on a career ladder that leads up from the pits of poverty and dependence.

In *The Libertine*, Rochester's anomie is partly attributed to his disenchantment with the leader on whom many hopes were riding, a sovereign who (in Rochester's famous characterization) "never said a foolish thing nor ever did a wise one." "We wanted a Sun King," he says, denouncing Charles for failing to become a god like Louis XIV. Whatever the reason, Rochester is drinking himself to death and when, in the final scene of the play, his wife grabs one of his wine bottles and empties it onto the floor, Rochester pours out the remaining bottle, sobbing and spewing out his guts as well. Before dying (at thirty-three), he embraces Christ, an act which only adds to his self-loathing. "Do you like me now?" he asks the audience in a fever of self-contempt. "Do you like me now?"

Westhead's dark, viscous voice, which seems to issue through Bose speakers, has the capacity to cut the air like a serrated knife. Combined with an edge of danger and reinforced by Stafford-Clark's authoritative direction, he turns the character into a pedigreed hound who bites himself when he is not biting others. Westhead is just one of the assets of a superb cast, two more exemplars being Katrina Levon as a passionate Mrs. Barry and Tim Potter as a playful if punitive King Charles. When these three actors switch to playing Dorimant, Mrs. Loveit, and Sir Fopling Flutter in *The Man of Mode*, they perform their parts, respectively, with elegant grace, jealous rage, and fatuous excess. But it is in the disintegrating mirror of *The Libertine* that the world of Etherege's comedy is best reflected. This was an age when idle courtiers had no greater purpose than to drink, shag, and display their wit, when sex was the expression not of love or pleasure but of power, when the lower classes were considered to have no other function than to service the appetites of a jaundiced aristocracy—an age, to borrow James Joyce's description of a previous era, of "exhausted whoredom groping for its god." That exhaustion is on display in *The Man of Mode*, on trial in *The Libertine*.

It is, however, in the smaller Theatre Upstairs, with a play called *Blasted* by a twenty-three-year-old writer named Sarah Kane, that the Royal Court is presently drawing the attention of London—almost all of it vituperative. Not since the 1965 premiere of Edward Bond's *Saved*, which also premiered at the Court before being closed by police, have the wattles of English critics shaken so angrily. Once again people are calling for the cancellation of grants and the heads of artistic directors. *Saved* culminated in the stoning of a baby. That action now seems pretty mild compared to what happens in *Blasted*, which culminates in the eating of a baby. If the capacity to give offense is your message of achievement, credit young Sarah Kane with provoking a level of outrage matched in our own country only by Robert Mapplethorpe and Andres Serrano.

Naturally all of London is flocking to see this new *succès de scandale*. Unfortunately, because of the extrinsic fuss, the intrinsic merits of *Blasted* will probably not be properly assessed for years. I found it at times crudely written, at times abruptly sensational, but also full of a strange integrity that had to be respected. This integrity was further reflected in the powerful commitment of the performances under the direction of James Macdonald. Actors won't normally do the sort of thing being asked of them in *Blasted* unless they truly believe in the script. Imagine the psychic wounds these three people have to lug home every night!

Blasted begins harmlessly enough with two people entering a motel room in Leeds: Ian, a macho Welshman with a shoulder holster, and Cate, a young thumb-sucking, stammering vegetarian with whom he once had a relationship. Ian is full of rage against what he calls "wogs," "paks," and "Lesbos," but most of all against his own life, which he is busy ending with the aid of gin and tobacco. Before he dies of emphysema, however, he would like to make love once more to the reluctant Cate, and when she refuses his demand for fellatio, he takes her brutally. In revenge, she rips up his leather coat and threatens to shoot him, an act he encourages ("Have a pop").

Ian may be a journalist for a scandal sheet. At one point he sends copy over the phone about a local serial killer. At other times he seems to be an underworld goon. Whatever the case, he is terrified of noises, of bugged phones, even of knocks at the door. While Cate is busy taking a bath, one of these knocks admits a soldier with an Uzi, and what was once a harmless motel room transforms into a bomb site with a huge hole in one of its walls. Without explanation we are somewhere else, possibly Bosnia. The soldier proceeds to terrorize Ian, first urinating on his bed, then assaulting his ears with accounts of shocking atrocities he committed against innocent civilians, including children. "This isn't a story anyone wants to hear," says Ian, "it has to be personal"—personal, that is, like the squalid material he shovels into the *Daily Mirror.*

The soldier retaliates for the rape and murder of his girlfriend by buggering Ian and then (are you ready for this?) eating his eyes. After a blackout we see Ian's face streaming blood and the terrorist dead on the floor. Cate returns carrying an infant that a woman gave her— "She's baby . . . innocent." When, soon after, the baby dies, she buries it under the floorboards of the motel room, then leaves to find a soldier who might exchange food for sex. In her absence the starving Ian digs up the baby and, retching, slakes his hunger. He then clambers into the baby's grave as rain falls from the ceiling on his exposed head. Cate returns, blood pouring down her legs, with a sausage which she proceeds to gobble washed down with Ian's booze.

Like Franz Xavier Kroetz's equally relentless *Request Concert,* almost all of this is mimed. What language there is consists of grunts and simple monosyllables, the syntax of the Second Coming. But underneath the repulsive stage action there is a stab at a theme—that a direct line exists between the carnal behavior of carnivorous males and the conduct of modern warfare. Many will reject this idea, and Sarah Kane does not make it transcendent enough to justify the incredible storm of horrors she rains upon the audience. But you don't have to agree with her theme to feel its power, or to recognize that the play is an honorable effort and not simply a dirty deed done publicly. Whatever the case, *Blasted* is beautifully acted by Kate Ashfield (Cate), Pip Donaghy (Ian), and Dermot Kerrigan (the Soldier). And whatever its limitations, *Blasted* is fulfilling the mission of this adventurous theatre to discover and encourage new young playwrights. The spirit of George Devine still haunts these halls.

1995

A Theatre Marking Time

(Medea; Tamburlaine the Great; The Tempest; King Lear)

At any given historical moment a nation's theatre is a dependable barometer of its cultural life. Whether that culture is moving forward or backward is related to whether the stage is dominated by playwrights or by directors and actors—which is to say, whether by new plays or by classics. To judge by my most recent visit to England, the British theatre now belongs more to its interpretive than to its creative artists. Lacking enough new works of any real quality, England is now primarily devoted to renewing its traditions through fresh looks at the great texts of the past.

This is an entirely honorable alternative to theatrical stasis, but it signifies a culture marking time. Harold Pinter and David Hare are still capable of giving the stage a jolt from time to time, and Caryl Churchill has just opened a (problematical) new work at the National. But the really big events this season are not new plays but rather classical masterpieces dominated by star performers and resourceful directors. The productions I saw were of varying quality, which sometimes made me nostalgic for remembered glories. Still, it was a joy to be again in theatres whose central objective was creating compelling works of art rather than delivering community services or promoting audience development.

The event that truly enthralled me on this visit was Diana Rigg's ferocious performance in Euripides' *Medea* at the Wyndham. This production, under the direction of Jonathan Kent, had originally opened at the Almeida Theatre in Islington where, in addition to new plays by Pinter and revivals by Rattigan, Kent and his partner Ian McDiarmid have been producing such arcane star-activated classics as Dryden's *All for Love* (also with Rigg), Racine's *Phèdre* (with Janet Suzman), and Ibsen's *When We Dead Awaken* (with Claire Bloom). For *Medea*, Kent chose a stark simple style of presentation, reducing the chorus of Corinthian women to three ladies in black, sitting on chairs and alternately chanting and singing. Together with the nurse, they reminded me of the keening Irish women who mourned the drowned Bartley in Synge's *Riders to the Sea*. And there was a lot to keen about here, given the shattering events of the play. Peter J. Davison's burnished-steel-panel setting reinforced the cruel sense of moral disintegration by literally bursting apart with a great racket at the bloody climax.

All the performances were strong, though Tim Woodward's ranting Jason failed to respond convincingly to the horrible death of his children, a scene as difficult to enact as Macduff's grief over losing "all my pretty chickens and their dam at one fell swoop." However, Diana Rigg more than compensated with a Medea that stands with the most riveting performances of our time.

I started applauding Miss Rigg's artistic progress in the early seventies when she first gave up the easy celebrity of *The Avengers* to explore the deeper demands of classical theatre. Her Medea confirms my conviction that an actor grows in proportion to the way she embraces the great repertory roles. To be sure, Rigg's feline grace had always seemed to me more appropriate for wit comedy than for classical tragedy. But although her Lady Macbeth with Anthony Hopkins and her Regan in Olivier's TV *Lear* had been admirable, I was not prepared for the scorching power of her Medea. The cat was transformed into a panther who roars and lacerates rather than purrs and scratches. Like few English actors of her generation, Diana Rigg now pulls her voice out of her internal organs, producing a sound of almost primitive savagery. The last Medea I saw was Judith Anderson in the 1946 Robinson Jeffers version (I believe John Gielgud was her Jason) where she skulked and scowled as if still playing Mrs. Danvers in *Rebecca*. Diana Rigg restores to the role its terrifying animal nature.

In a red dress, long ponytail, and bare feet, Rigg greets us with a piercing cry of pain. All her sacrifices for Jason have been rewarded with treachery, since he is preparing to contract a cynical match with Creon's daughter (the almost feminist theme of male advancement at the expense of women is heightened in Alistair Elliot's new translation). Describing her indignities and sense of abandonment, she coils like a snake, growls, hisses, and croaks like a fury, calling up images from jungle mythology. Perhaps inspired by how Olivier had trained his voice for *Othello*, Rigg has obviously worked hard to develop deeper vocal registers for this role. Yet her Medea remains consistently womanly, even when she materializes near the end drenched in the blood of her slaughtered children. (By comparison with the way

Medea repays her husband for sexual abuse, Lorena Bobbitt's revenge seems almost merciful.) At the conclusion Rigg disappears, not with the help of a *deus ex machina* but in a swirl of angry clouds, leaving us in the aftercalm of an emotional storm one rarely experiences on the stage these days.

Anthony Sher tries to kick up the same sort of dust in the Royal Shakespeare Company production of *Tamburlaine the Great.* And for five of the ten acts he manages quite effectively. Although Christopher Marlowe's marvelous two-part epic of imperial conquest is the first English play by a literary genius, it is very rarely produced, perhaps because the staging requires tactics and logistics cultivated less by theatre directors than by military strategists. In the first professional revival since the early seventeenth century, Brigadier General Tyrone Guthrie led his troops in a 1951 production starring Donald Wolfit and a huge supporting army (all I remember of that is a lot of swirling figures impaled by arrows). Terry Hands has now directed a big, boisterous, bludgeoning version of the show which allows Anthony Sher full scope to bellow and bluster.

Tamburlaine is Marlowe's first essay on the nature of aspiring minds. He is drawn to heroes who, in Berlioz's words, "make all barriers crack"—in *Tamburlaine* through world conquest, in *Doctor Faustus* through forbidden knowledge, in *The Jew of Malta* through absolute evil. The most modern of the Elizabethans, a government spy and uncloseted homosexual, Marlowe fathered a genealogical line of rebels leading to Sade, Artaud, Genet, and Orton (whom he resembles in the violent manner of his early death). A Theatre of Cruelty bloodbath, *Tamburlaine* is a play that exults in butchery and carnage. In his thirst for glory, the hero is loyal only to the captive Zenocrate. He scourges and pillages, batters and strangles, hangs up the slaughtered carcasses of virgins on a wall, even murders his own cowardly son. At the conclusion Tamburlaine is preparing to storm the heavens—"to set black streamers in the firmament to signify the slaughter of the gods." He is thwarted only by his own mortality. Through the character of Pistol, Shakespeare made fun of Tamburlaine's extravagance and hyperbole, but Marlowe, that "dead shepherd," is the one contemporary for whom he ever expressed any real admiration.

The most American-seeming of English actors (he is actually

South African), Anthony Sher makes Tamburlaine a crossbreeding of Al Pacino and Douglas Fairbanks. Sporting a Cherokee haircut, bare arms, and a huge black mustache, he gives an extremely calisthenic performance, complete with tumbles and handsprings, climbing a rope backward, shambling loosely around the stage like a boxer. Unlike some of his supporting cast, who often sound more like elocutionists than soldiers, Sher is capable of savoring Marlowe's swelling verse without sounding like a RADA graduate. And he has a really good time battling a variety of enemies, including four Turkish kings on mechanical stilts.

Ultimately, however, all the clanging music and bravura acting, not to mention a lot of heavy smoke, begin to wear you down a little. And after Sher's Tamburlaine turns fat and sluggish in the second part, his physical agility can no longer compensate for a certain lack of inner strength. Following the death of Zenocrate, having burned the Koran to signify his superiority to Muhammad ("on earth there's none but me"), Tamburlaine suddenly falls ill, and, in truth, it's time to die. We're left exhausted by the bombast, though grateful to have seen the play.

At Stratford I witnessed the final performances of two productions, the first being the new RSC *Tempest*, under the direction of Sam Mendes. It was the most disappointing experience of my visit. Alec McCowen, playing Prospero, still appeared to be reciting *The Gospel According to St. Mark* (his one-person show), contributing a sonorous milk-fed performance that not only put Miranda to sleep but also half the audience. If McCowen's milk was homogenized, that of Simon Russell Beale, playing Ariel, was curdled. Sour, sullen, and sulky as an ill-tempered Regent Street window dresser, Beale's Ariel was not only imprisoned against his will but beneath his class. Set free, he thanked Prospero by spitting in his face. Usually a capable actor, Beale in this role looked like the type that only does scornful parts.

There were two engaging performances in this deadly *Tempest*, those of David Bradley as Trinculo and Mark Lockyer as Stephano. Lockyer played the drunken butler with an Oxbridge accent (squeezed through a set of protruding false teeth) like a fantastical Bertie Wooster, and Bradley turned Trinculo into a red-wigged vaudevillian in a checkered suit and long shoes. Brandishing a ventriloquist's dummy dressed in the same clothes, with whom he shared Trinculo's lines, Bradley managed to contribute the few moments of real delight in an otherwise torpid production.

Finally there was Robert Stephens as King Lear, also at Stratford, in a heartbreaking performance, and I mean this in a number of ways. In his powerful debut in the Osborne-Creighton *Epitaph for George Dillon* in the late fifties, Stephens showed the sardonic power of a great English actor. But for years an alcohol problem severely limited his potential. Having freed himself of this affliction, he brings a ravaged persona to the most difficult role ever written, and the results are poignant and penetrating, though ultimately lacking in sufficient stamina to make the performance unforgettable.

In Stephens's hands, Lear's exhaustion is evident from his first appearance. Limping slightly, large-nosed, gaunt and hollow though endowed with an ample belly, the actor looks like a homeless wretch dressed up in a bright red coat. With his wispy beard and desperate eyes, he evokes the vague mental wanderings, the mad melancholy, of a derelict Don Quixote. His feelings for Cordelia do not constitute his most tender relationship, not surprisingly considering Abigail McKern's Yorkshire-pudding appearance in the part. She's too heavy to lug by himself (most Lears demand underweight Cordelias), so he allows some soldiers to carry her body instead. Enraged at her death, he kicks her over on her stomach.

Lear's warmest feelings are reserved for his Fool. And in Ian Hughes's beautifully modulated performance, these feelings are wholly reciprocated. I have not seen a more affectionate, touching engagement between these two characters since Louis Calhern and Norman Lloyd played the roles in John Houseman's Broadway production more than forty years ago. The seat of Lear's affliction, in Stephens's bittersweet rendering, is the heart. He suffers from angina pains and his "hysterico passio," or "climbing passion," looks very much like cardiac arrest. The Fool, leading Lear away, holds his master's breast as if to keep it from breaking. He hugs and fondles him, sharing moments of remorse and regret. For all his goading and nagging, Hughes's Fool expresses an almost physical love for Lear. He can't let him out of his sight, and when he disappears a crucial link is broken. I have never seen the relationship played so much like a marriage.

Adrian Noble directs this production with the same meticulous attention to detail and fresh approach to language that he showed in last year's *Hamlet*. Anthony Ward's design is dominated by a huge hanging sphere that opens, after the blinding of Gloucester, like a cracked moon to spill a mountain of sand on the stage. This literalized realization of Lear's desire to "Crack Nature's molds, all germains spill at once" has more impact than the hoarse thunderings of Stephens, who is both physically and emotionally dampened by the drenching rain. Stephens has beautifully rendered the ruefulness of the role but ultimately fails to convey its majesty and size.

A number of the supporting performances are disappointing, but David Bradley's tortured Gloucester (especially as seen in repertory with his jaunty Trinculo) identifies him as one of the strongest and most versatile members of this company. Bradley will undoubtedly be next in line to play the title part. It is actors like him, along with Stephens and Rigg, who make the English stage a blessing.

1994

England Reaches Out
(Mother Courage; Les Enfants du Paradis; Hysteria)

A recent journey to London provided me with some pleasures, a few pains, and one happy realization: England is reaching out. If, in the past, observers like myself could cavil about the insularity of the English stage, that term is no longer appropriate to what is happening in the subsidized theatres and on the West End. By contrast with a time when foreign plays were rarely seen, when foreign characters usually spoke with impeccable Oxbridge accents, and when about the only contact English audiences had with foreign companies was through the year-end World Theatre Festival sponsored by Peter Daubeny, the London theatre is now displaying a remarkable cosmopolitanism. Perhaps participation in the Common Market and construction of the "Chunnel" have extended the perspectives of this nation beyond the confines of its island parameters. Whatever the reason, of the five productions I saw on my visit, four were by non-English playwrights, and the fifth showed considerable Continental influences.

The best of the lot was the National Theatre's production of *Mother Courage*. Staging Brecht has always been a challenge for English directors. The last National Theatre production of this play took place in 1965, when the company was still in residence at the Old Vic. It proved a very limp evening, directed by William Gaskill with excessive devotion to Brecht's prompt books, and performed in an elegant manner by Madge Ryan, who tried to compensate for what she lacked in peasant grit by continually punching her fists into her hips and rearing back her shoulders.

The current Mother Courage is Dame Diana Rigg, a really classy actress of considerable artfulness and sophistication, but not exactly the type you would instinctively cast in the part of a salty peasant woman. Still, as she powerfully demonstrated playing Medea under the same director (Jonathan Kent), Dame Diana in middle age has managed to baffle all conventional expectations, developing new physical and vocal resources that have remarkably extended her range. Appareled in an ill-fitting greatcoat over a fading red dress, with a grimy turban wrapped around her head, her face smudged with dirt and her voice a cockney bark, she comes on stage straining away at her wooden wagon like an animated Breughel. Featured in the program, along with much commentary on the Thirty Years War, are sidebars describing the "entertaining" side of Brecht. This may be why Rigg plays her part so presentationally, throwing away rough asides to the audience, unearthing the mordant comedy of her hard-bitten dialogue, and delivering Jonathan Dove's bracing show tunes in a whiskey baritone worthy of Elaine Stritch.

The links between Epic Theatre and musical comedy are further illustrated by the other characters, particularly the cook, played with considerable brio by Geoffrey Hutchings. The prostitute Yvette remembers him as a man who (like the eponymous rascal of *Happy End*'s "Surabayo Johnny") always made love with his pipe in his mouth. Hutchings's cook not only mixes smoke with sex, but dialogue with dance. He is an engaging hoofer, belting out the Solomon Song to the accompaniment of music-hall patter, an athletic jig, even a smattering of cha-cha-cha.

By heightening the vaudeville values of the play, the production manages to underline the ironic disparity between the moral justification of religious warfare and its senseless carnage, its greed for land.

David Hare's English version is particularly effective with the scorching way Brecht uses hypocritical biblical imagery to expose human motives (indeed, Hare may be more successful adapting plays than writing them). Paul Bond's flexible and versatile setting is a bare stage with a turntable and upstage panel doors which are raised to reveal a variety of late medieval landscapes—many of them idealized. Only once does the production (and the design) betray the playwright—when the panel doors open on stacks of golden wheat being harvested by healthy peasant women singing a romantic Wagner-like air. Brecht would have plotzed.

But the show recovers in the great final scene when Rigg's Courage, having lost all her children to the war because of her irrepressible need to haggle, makes one last effort to pull her wagon off stage. Earlier, upon seeing the corpse of her son, Swiss Cheese, Rigg failed to do the famous "silent scream" patented by Helene Weigel (she chose instead to sit back limply in a chair). She was saving her big wallop for the end. Mourning Kattrin's death, Rigg's Courage appears to have lost all the flesh in her face. Gone a little daft, a staring death's head, she yanks at the battered wagon with all her feeble strength, and finally succeeds in budging it forward. Now a bruised and haunted skeleton, she has nonetheless managed to endure despite all the pressing arguments for her extinction. She leaves the stage to pick up the worthless remnants of her life as the final chorus ("Spring is here, the snows are melting") intones an ambiguous paean of hope.

The Royal Shakespeare Company at the Barbican is also making some effort to connect with the Continent through a feeble adaptation of the great Marcel Carné film *Les Enfants du Paradis*. The actor Simon Callow, who also directs, has elected to adapt Jacques Prévert's film script in what is clearly intended as an act of *hommage*. What he has produced instead is an act of *dommage*, an interminable ordeal during which you sit listening to subtitles for four hours, longing to see the original film.

In his recent biography of Orson Welles, Callow criticized the director for cutting, adapting, and reinterpreting classical works. Would that he had shown some directorial boldness himself. Imagine an untrained mime slavishly trying to imitate the fluid grace and aching passion of Jean-Louis Barrault's Baptiste. Imagine an unseasoned soubrette attempting to capture the sphinxlike mystery and enigmatic smile of Arletty's Garance. Imagine a hammy actor offering to duplicate the theatrical flair and swashbuckling charm of Pierre Brasseur's Frédérick Lemaitre. If the dialogue seems like a series of clumsy captions, the acting sounds as if it were dubbed. The enterprise succeeds only in inviting invidious comparisons.

Callow places his huge cast on a rotating wooden scaffold that is meant to convey—in the style of *Nicholas Nickleby*—the bustle and stir of an earlier period and place, in this instance the "Rue du Crime" in the time of Louis-Phillipe. But in place of bustle we get busyness, instead of stir, sterility. Callow is a competent actor and a scrupulous biographer. As a director-adaptor he needs to assert a stronger identity.

At the same time the National Theatre is commemorating a Bavarian and the Royal Shakespeare Company is sabotaging Parisians, the Royal Court is satirizing a Viennese and a Spaniard. Terry Johnson's 1993 play *Hysteria*, which the Court recently transferred to the Duke of York Theatre in the West End, is a work about Freud during the final night of his life in London, squeezing in an encounter he had weeks before with the surrealist painter Salvador Dali. Like a number of contemporary dramatists, Johnson has a fondness for writing about celebrities, often in unlikely pairings. His *Insignificance* featured Marilyn Monroe cavorting with Albert Einstein, and his latest play *Dead Funny* is about the late comedian Benny Hill.

Johnson is apparently trying to develop a method that encloses serious issues in farcical wrappings. This is a praiseworthy enough aim, but in *Hysteria* it accounts for some serious malfunctions. The dying Freud's efforts to put his life and thought in order are continually being interrupted not only by a woman visitor's effort to discredit his work on hysteria, but also by a distracting series of slammed doors, crowded closets, dropped trousers, mistaken identities, misassigned underwear, sudden disappearances via trapdoors, and other signs that the author is desperately trying to amuse. "A complete farce," says one of the characters, adding in a line you may have heard before: "If I saw it in the theatre, I wouldn't believe it."

The trouble is, you don't believe it. There must be some way to amalgamate English intellectual comedy with French farce—Shaw did from time to time. But here the real issues of the play are suspended for long periods while the author tries to entertain his audience. Similarly the presence of Dali seems to be superfluous until the final scene, a phantasmagorical conclusion modeled to a large extent on Joyce's Nighttown chapter in *Ulysses*. Mark Thompson's set collapses into a mélange of Dali paintings (including melting clocks, rubber doors, razor-slit eyeballs, and phones that transform into lobsters), during which Freud's four recently dead sisters and his long-dead Papa call his name.

The central question of the play, however (no doubt inspired by Jeffrey Masson's efforts to discredit Freud's thought), is whether or not Freud changed his views about the origins of female hysteria in order to protect his own father from charges of sexual abuse. He initially believed, and wrote in *Studies in Hysteria* (1895) and *The Aetiology of Hysteria* (1896), that hysteria was caused by infantile sexuality, thus giving credence to stories told by his Jewish woman patients about their sexually abusive fathers. He soon concluded, in *Sexuality in the Aetiology of Neurosis* (1898), that these recovered memories were too numerous to be credible and thus were probably examples of wish fulfillment on the part of sexually fantasizing children. As a result of this change of mind, and because of his controversial theory of "penis envy," Freud has been open to revisionist attacks on his integrity from a variety of quarters, attacks which *Hysteria* labors to confirm. The heroine, Jessica, turns out to be the daughter of one of Freud's hysterical patients ("Dora"?), who proves her mother's charge of having been seduced by her father when she confesses that the same man later abused her.

No matter what your opinion of "recovered memory" (mine is low), at least this is a solid dramatic event, which engages your brain so long as Johnson can desist from tickling your funny bone. And the play concludes powerfully when Freud's religiously observant doctor, Abraham Yahuda, gives him an overdose of morphine, and—as if the whole thing was Freud's dream at the moment of death—the action begins again with the entrance of Jessica.

Phyllida Lloyd's production is strongly performed: Henry Goodman as an anguished, pasty-faced Freud, Phoebe Nicholls as the hysterical Jessica, David de Keyser as Yahuda in a yarmulke, and especially Tim Potter as the wild egotist Salvador Dali, a part he plays like Franklin Pangborn hopped up on coke. His scrambled hair topping his wild eyes and waxed moustache, Potter expresses his passion for depilated armpits while confessing that he once called out a name ("My own") while making love. Now that's both funny and true.

1996

The Gaulois Duchess

(The Duchess of Malfi; Skylight)

John Webster's *The Duchess of Malfi* is full of danger and surprise, but it is a fearfully difficult play to produce. Lit by fitful lightning, this Jacobean tragedy proceeds, in contrast with the easy flow of Shakespearean blank verse, in jerks and spasms. It is a densely packed anthology of homilies, proverbialisms, epigrams, couplets, and Latinisms that could tongue-tie the most fluent of actors (one commentator called Webster "sublime by the aid of a commonplace book"). It also describes a world in which the boundaries between good and evil, innocence and guilt, have virtually disappeared, and about the only virtue left to admire is courage in the face of death. In fact, death and decay—what T. S. Eliot called "the skull beneath the skin"—constitute Webster's obsessive subjects. For that reason the fatality-averse Shaw dismissed him as a "Tussaud laureate." If so, the criminal waxworks Webster created still has the power to shock and terrify.

The title character of *The Duchess of Malfi* is almost unique in Webster for having more virtues than vices; yet her goodness is allowed to command the stage for only four acts before she is slaughtered by her vengeful brothers, with one whole act left to go. The heroine's untimely death helps to make *The Duchess of Malfi* a portrait of almost unrelieved evil blistered by the imagery of the charnelhouse. For this the recent plague in London was no doubt partially responsible. But the gloomy atmosphere also reflected the generalized Stuart pessimism shared by all of Webster's contemporaries (Shakespeare included) in contrast with the boundless Marlovian aspiration of Tudor England. Donne described this morbid period, in his first Anniversary poem, as a time of fragmentation, incoherence, and collapse ("If man were anything, he's nothing now").

The production Declan Donnellan brought to the Brooklyn Academy of Music with his Cheek by Jowl company embraced these challenges and added some new ones. Set in the twenties, during the period of Mussolini fascism, the play sat very comfortably amidst its modern trappings, as the characters drank cocktails, smoked cigarettes, and murdered each other in a variety of ingenious ways (once with a poisoned Bible, a wonderful symbol of the play's corrupt Catholicism). Contemporary moralists, Hamlet among them, thought a widow's desire to remarry was a sign of lasciviousness ("they are most luxurious who marry twice"). Webster's innovation was to treat this instinct as perfectly normal.

Donnellan's innovation, by contrast, is to regard the virtuous duchess, and her rather stiff consort Antonio, as something less than models of purity. Matthew Macfadyen's Antonio appears to be a rather cold and self-regarding narcissist. The duchess, as played by the strawberry blonde Anastasia Hille in the tarty "what a dump" tradition of Bette Davis and Faye Dunaway, is a willful, imperious, tempestuous, and deeply neurotic aristocrat—a provocative flapper in a variety of designer gowns who plays hard, drinks hard, screws hard, and smokes like a chimney. In fact (I thought), if the tool villain, Bosola, really wanted to drive this chain-smoker to despair, all he had to do was take away her Gaulois.

As for Bosola, played by George Anton with a harsh Scottish burr, he is a cold precisionist blackshirt, a voyeur of suffering who follows the duchess's fate with the fascination of a graduate student studying nihilism. When she lights one last cigarette before being strangled and says, "I am Duchess of Malfi still," Bosola is dazzled by her style. Her stoical contempt for death was never dreamt of in his philosophy. Paul Brennan's coldhearted, sexually depraved cardinal is the physical and moral double of Cardinal Pacelli, later Pope Pius XII. Scott Handy's Duke Ferdinand is a spoiled booby whom everybody smacks and ridicules, until he develops into a wolfish, incestuous madman, ravenous for his sister's blood.

Donnellan staged the play virtually on a bare stage, where the characters first appear as frozen chess pieces before assuming frigid life in this Gothic charade. The atmosphere is drenched in Catholic liturgy—even the madmen torturing the duchess sing a Gloria. Overlapping one scene with another, in cinematic fashion, the director has all his actors performing in a state of Dostoevskian brain fever. It is a fitting style for Webster's Cimmerian vision. Trying to comfort the duchess before he kills her, Bosola says, "Look ye, the stars shine still." But the heavens are muddy and the stars are dim. Bosola, like everybody else in this grim absorbing play, dies in a mist.

1996

David Hare's *Skylight* has the advantage of a really shattering performance by Michael Gambon, who at the present time may very well be the most powerful actor in the English-speaking world. You don't care a whit that this hulking figure is somewhat miscast as a natty capitalist, or that he's starring in a rather anemic play. The argument between Gambon's character, the middle-aged Tom Sergeant, and his considerably younger lover, Kyra Hollis (strongly performed by Lia Williams), echoes the debate Bernard Shaw concocted between the millionaire arms dealer Andrew Undershaft and his Salvation Army daughter, Major Barbara. Sergeant runs a group of hotels and restaurants, and passionately defends his accumulation of wealth, while the even more passionate Kyra defends her commitment to improving the minds of poorly educated kids.

Informing this conflict is the continuing tension between Thatcher's Tory England and that of the Lib-Lab opposition. And it must be admitted that the playwright, despite his own liberal sympathies, doesn't try to load the deck. "I'm disqualified from having any feelings," Sergeant moans, "because I made some money." Kyra, he notes, is always drawn to the injustice of the world: "The question is, why you went out to look for it."

Kyra replies that she hates those "right-wing fuckers" who sneer at social workers. Who else would perform the tasks they're willing to do? "What makes sense," she later says to Tom's rebellious son, "is finding one really good pupil . . . one private target and that's enough."

Still, the intellectual argument of *Skylight* is weak and perfunctory. Hare seems considerably more interested in the emotions of the personal relationship. Sergeant has returned to see Kyra following his wife's death, partly to ask forgiveness, partly to reignite their love affair. And although they spend one last night together, Kyra sends him into the cold morning air alone. The reason? He told his wife, before her death, about their affair.

But forget about the play. The evening is worth the price of admission just to watch Gambon crumple into fragments, disintegrate before your eyes the moment he realizes his love is futile. With his potato face and sleepy features, his Asiatic eyes hooded like a hawk's, Gambon looks more like an Irish coachman than an English plutocrat. And he wears his expensive overcoat as if he had just found it in a yard sale. Yet there is something immensely attractive and commanding in the way he inhabits this role. Dancing and feinting in a manner that belies his considerable bulk, he leaves us in no doubt that this character once took up ballet. His resonant voice barking and nattering through a remarkable range of human music, somewhere between an English horn and a Bach trumpet, Gambon can make the most declarative lines ring with irony and power. In perfect harmony with Lia Williams's vigorous Kyra, and under Richard Eyre's effortless direction, he manages to give a tragic Lear-like weight to an essentially weightless character. Acting of this magnitude makes the stage a place of rare beauty and rude strength.

1997

Death March
(The Mountain Giants)

At New York's Istituto Italiano, while introducing Giorgio Strehler, renowned leader of the Piccolo Teatro Milano, I expressed the not very original opinion that, in the first half of this century, theatre was dominated by playwrights (Pirandello, Brecht, O'Neill, and Beckett) and in the second half by directors (Peter Brook, Ingmar Bergman, Robert Wilson, and Giorgio Strehler). In his speech, Strehler modestly disclaimed any central role for himself or his colleagues, insisting that throughout his career his major theatrical purpose had merely been to realize the intentions of the playwright.

This of course is the declared purpose of every interpretive artist, but in the act of "realizing" a playwright's intentions, the director is often found reinventing them. Strehler's version of *The Mountain Giants*, which enjoyed a brief run recently at the Brooklyn Academy of Music, not only reinvented Luigi Pirandello's last work. The production literally reconstructed it. The play was unfinished at the playwright's death, the first three acts being unrevised and the fourth act unwritten. Using notes provided by Pirandello's son, Stefano, Strehler undertook to imagine how Pirandello would have brought it to completion.

In theory this was a noble enterprise. *The Mountain Giants* was clearly intended as Pirandello's last will and testament. It sums up, in monumental fashion, his oft-expressed views concerning the antinomies between life and art. Unfortunately, ideas that were sharp and penetrating in such plays as *Six Characters in Search of an Author* are saturated with self-pity in his later, more subjective work. In his final years Pirandello seemed to believe that he was insufficiently appreciated and often misunderstood, despite his Nobel Prize and his election to the Italian Academy. As these attitudes suggest, he was suffering from a highly bloated ego—inflated even further by the idolatry of his companion, the actress Marta Abba. Perhaps in gratitude for a series of meaty roles, she made him the object of almost religious veneration (Abba probably called him "Maestro" even in bed). Their letters are a record of mutual adoration and shared vanity. "The only thing I have been able to do," he wrote to her in 1929, "is to think beautiful and lofty things."

The Mountain Giants is full of such beautiful and lofty things, which is why it sometimes seems even more bloated than Pirandello's ego. While his earlier plays examined universal themes of reality and illusion, this one is essentially a lament about the coarse unfeeling environment in which the artist is forced to create and to which he is obliged to submit. A touring company of actors, led by the count and his wife, the actress Ilse, show up at a strange villa in the Italian countryside owned by the "magician" Cotrone. On his suggestion they perform a play before the "giants" who inhabit a nearby mountain. These spectators behave in a brutal, insensate manner, and when Ilse rebukes them, they riot and kill her. As the actors carry out Ilse's lifeless body, Cotrone cries that mankind has destroyed poetry in the world. But according to the way Stefano Pirandello interpreted his father's intentions, "it was not poetry that was refused, it was just that the poor, fanatical slaves of life, who today have no taste for spiritual things but who someday might very well have, had innocently killed the fanatical slaves of art the way they would break rebellious puppets."

At a time when art is facing its own mountain giants in this country, few can dispute the poignance of this message. Yet there is something unsatisfying in the way Pirandello delivers it. Marginalized though they often are, and though it is true they can sometimes cause riots, modern artists are rarely murdered, except in totalitarian countries. And rather than being hothouse plants withering in a hostile atmosphere, they are capable of showing considerable resistance to tyranny and philistinism. In *The Mountain Giants* Pirandello encourages artists to join the crowd of victims and martyrs flocking to the whining wall. He might have done better to invest his characters (and, through them, us) with a little more spine.

Strehler's effort to complete the play (mostly in pantomime) provides some compelling theatrical images. If those images also seem a trifle familiar, that may be because this is his third production of *The Mountain Giants* (the first going back to 1947, the second to 1966), and he hasn't always managed to edit out dated ideas. His use of large puppets as the mountain giants never develops beyond Bread and Puppet conventions, his acting company has the outsize behavior associated with large histrionic temperaments, and his final image— when the actors carry the body of Ilse through the audience, their faces contorted with sorrow—evokes memories of the Living Theatre. The two previous productions Strehler brought to these shores—*The Servant of Two Masters* in 1949 and *The Tempest* in 1984—were afloat with grace and originality. *The Mountain Giants* leaves us marooned in the attitudes and gestures of the sixties.

1995

The Rebirth of Irish Drama

(The Steward of Christendom; The Beauty Queen of Leenane; The Cripple of Inishmaan)

No theory has yet been able to account for the way the arts seem to flower for a period in one country and then, like Canada geese or rambling roses, migrate to other climes. Was it democracy at home and foreign conquest that stimulated the tremendous outpouring of plays, poems, sculpture, and architecture in Periclean Athens? Was it homage to an idealized Virgin Queen and the spirit of exploration that animated the verse drama of Shakespeare and his numerous playwriting contemporaries? Was it the looming Russian Revolution that ignited the creative spark of Chekhov and Gorky? Did the disillusionment of the Weimar Republic galvanize the febrile German neoromantic art of Wedekind, Brecht, Grosz, and Pabst? Possibly a national destiny is linked to a burgeoning culture, but if so, how do we account for the sudden efflorescence of Ibsen and Strindberg in sleepy Scandanavia, and how do we explain the fact that Switzerland, a land noted primarily for Alpine resorts, milk chocolate, and cuckoo clocks, suddenly engendered, almost simultaneously, the plays of Friedrich Dürrenmatt and Max Frisch?

Irish drama is another of those national anomalies. After a renaissance led by Yeats, Synge, and O'Casey among others, and commonly linked to the struggle for independence, Irish drama lay dead or dormant for forty years. Now at the end of our century Ireland again promises to be the spawning ground for some of the strongest dramatic writing in the world. Two playwrights (others would include Brian Friel and make it three) have recently emerged to justify this statement: Sebastian Cabot and Martin McDonagh.

Of these, only Cabot has made it to these shores as yet, and only with his fifth play, *The Steward of Christendom*, which received glowing reviews when it opened at BAM's Majestic Theatre. As for McDonagh, he has had two of his plays performed in London this year, each winning major prizes and public acclaim, though both were written when the playwright was still a mere stripling in his early twenties. His very first work, *The Beauty Queen of Leenane*, produced at the Royal Court in association with the Druid Theatre, has dramaturgical weaknesses, but it is clearly the product of a major writer. Indeed, on the basis of this play alone I would have been willing to make the rash claim that McDonagh was destined to be one of the theatrical luminaries of the twenty-first century.

The play concerns a forty-year-old spinster named Maureen, caring for her infirm mother Meg (a ghastly old crone) in a small town in Connemara. Maureen embodies the despair of the unmarried Irish woman. A victim of her age and domestic circumstances, ensnared in a loveless environment like a marmoset with one foot in a trap, she snarls at her mother and her fate with the eloquence of a foul-mouthed Medea. After a neighbor, Pato, invites her to a family outing, she brings him to her home and tries to make love to him, indifferent to her mother's self-righteous and selfish disapproval.

Having left for London to work as a bricklayer, Pato sends Maureen a letter asking her to accompany him to America as his wife. Meg reads the letter before Maureen comes home, and burns it. When Maureen discovers this betrayal—too late to preserve the relationship—she scalds the old woman with hot water and kills her. Previously Maureen had been institutionalized with a mental disorder. Now delusional, half mad, and turning into the very image of her mother at the end, she locks herself in the house and consigns herself to eternal loneliness.

The plot of the play (like that of Ibsen's *Doll's House*) depends too much on an undelivered letter. Nevertheless it has the remorseless, inexorable drive associated with the greatest tragedy. As in *Othello*, we know what's going to happen, yet we pray that it won't. McDonagh's uncanny insight into the dynamics of a sour symbiotic mother-daughter relationship is exceeded only by his understanding of the mean-spiritedness and small-mindedness of Irish provincial life. *The Beauty Queen of Leenane* would be an extraordinary achievement for a mature playwright. It was a dazzling debut for a writer of twenty-three.

His next play, *The Cripple of Inishmaan*, is an even finer work. Currently playing at the Royal National Theatre's Cottelsloe with a wonderful cast under the scorching direction of Nicholas Hytner, it concerns the stir aroused on a small Aran Island when the inhabitants learn that the great documentary filmmaker Robert Flaherty is coming to a neighboring island to film his movie, *Man of Aran*. John Millington Synge had already discovered the verbal splendors to be found among these islanders, language that converted this would-be bohemian expatriate, then living in Paris and trying to imitate French symbolist poetry, into the national playwright of Ireland. "In countries," wrote Synge, "where the imagination of the people, and the language they use, is rich and living, it is possible for a writer to be rich and copious in his words. . . ." *The Cripple of Inishmaan* fulfills Synge's command that dramatic speech be "as fully flavored as a nut or an apple."

Like Synge, McDonagh has no illusions about the heroic nature of his countrymen, whatever the musical quality of their language. Most of the inhabitants of Inishmaan seem like Irish versions of the Jukes and the Kalikaks—crude, vindictive creatures just a cut above the bestial. There is Jimmypateenmike, the professional rumormonger, who would sell his mother for a bit of gossip, and no wonder—in this deadly wasteland, the discovery of "a sheep in Kerry with no ears at all" is big news. There is his ninety-six-year-old mother, Mammy O'Dougal, who has kept herself alive by pouring gallons of whiskey down her throat. There is Helen, a wild fulminating wench who delights in breaking eggs over people's heads. Pretty enough to have her ass groped by priests who like to show her their cocks ("I don't know why"), she scorns all mankind as "boring feckers." There is the boatman Babbybobby who, though endowed with a little more human feeling than the others, also displays a violent temper when he feels he has been crossed.

And there is Billy, the cripple of Inishmaan, a kind of sacred fool on the order of Prince Mishkin, a sweet-natured man with a hundred troubles, including bad arms and bad legs, who spends most of his time looking at cows. Desperately in love with Helen, and even more desperate to get off the island, he cons Babbybobby into taking him across the seas to audition for the role of the cripple in Flaherty's movie, and actually wins a Hollywood screen test.

But Billy doesn't get the part, and when he returns to Inishmaan he is riddled with consumption and disillusionment. He has seen America—a fantasy land for the population of Inishmaan, but for Billy no better than Ireland, "full of fat women with beards." Badly beaten by Babbybobby for having deceived him, and spurned in his love for Helen, he seems just as trapped as Maureen in *The Beauty Queen of Leenane*. He loads a bag with cans of peas for the purpose of drowning himself. But, at the last minute, Helen accepts his invitation to take a walk ("no kissing or groping, cos I don't want you ruining me feckin' reputation"). Despite this caution, she nevertheless deigns to give Billy a kiss, though not before poking him hard in his bandaged face. Elated after she leaves, Billy is soon wheezing and coughing blood, doomed to die at the very moment when life at last seems worthwhile.

McDonagh is a natural storyteller who well knows how to tell a tale through action, and he knows how to create a gallery of fascinating rogues. The energy of his plays is prodigious. And while most of the younger British dramatists (like Mark Ravenhill, whose *Shopping and Fucking* is currently shocking London) are drawing characters sunk in anomie and despair, McDonagh has managed to celebrate what remains enduring and alive in human nature even in the most appalling circumstances.

Sebastian Cabot is another extraordinary Irish writer, though probably more of a poet than a playwright. *The Steward of Christendom*, like his other plays, is pulsing with vibrant language, often in the form of monologues spoken by the central character, Thomas Dunne. A former constable in the Dublin National Police, now in his mid-seventies, Dunne is being confined in a mental institution (to judge by Cabot and McDonagh, half the Irish population lives in madhouses). Dunne has been characterized by *Newsweek*'s Jack Kroll as "Lear in longjohns," which seems an apt way to describe him. He has three daughters, he's mad as a hatter, and he spends most of the play lolling about in dirty long underwear.

But like Lear's madness, Thomas's dementia is informed by deeper insights into the human condition than that of the sane. His "sleepy sleepy" ramblings have some of the visionary power of the sleeper in Joyce's *Finnegans Wake*. And while being beaten by his keeper for failing to use his bedpan ("a deserted house needs no gutter"), he has recurrent memories that evoke his entire past.

As a loyal servant of the Crown ("a steward of Christendom") at a time when Michael Collins was storming Dublin Castle, Dunne shares the guilt of many Irish royalists who resisted the unification of Ireland, mixed with pride in his uniform over having performed his job well. Reliving the moment when Collins was killed in Cork, he sobs uncontrollably over a time when Ireland was once loyal, unified, and true.

His relations with his daughters are equally ambiguous. One of his girls has escaped to America, another is married with children, but the third, a woman with a deformed back as a result of polio, is like Cordelia still around to tend to her father in his distress. Dunne's greatest despair, however, is over his dead son Willie, a victim of the First World War, who reappears in his delusions as a mute child consoling his father, much like Leopold Bloom's dead son Rudy in Joyce's *Ulysses*. In the exquisite closing moments, Dunne tells a moving story of how his own dad (showing "the mercy of fathers, when the child sees at last that he is loved") forgave him for disobeying his wishes: Dunne had spared a dog who killed a sheep. After hugging him, Willy lays his head on his father's chest, as Dunne goes off into the silent consolation of sleep (or death).

Apart from this moment and a few others, not much of *The Steward of Christendom* is dramatized. Often you feel as if you're absorbing monologues rather than watching enacted scenes, and the continuity of Dunne's story is fuzzy. But the language is so rich, and the acting (under Max Stafford Clark's direction) so powerful that the structural lapses of the play can be forgiven. Donal McCann, in particular, his head shaved to emphasize his jug ears, is giving the performance of an already celebrated career. Like the character he is playing, he has eyes that look inward rather than out, into a moment in Irish history when things could have been different. Sebastian Cabot's work, and that of Martin McDonagh, transform that history. Their plays are enduring testimonies to how the power of art can redeem the past.

1997

The Comédie Française

Frederick Wiseman—and let me confess at once he is a friend of mine—has been making documentaries about institutions for over thirty years. Most of these were developed from an adversary position. Wiseman's very first film, the grainy, black-and-white, long-suppressed *Titicut Follies*, ran into legal trouble over its depiction of horrific conditions at Bridgewater State mental hospital. And *Welfare*, perhaps his finest sustained work—a wry, relentless record of the humiliations experienced by both workers and recipients in the bureaucratic New York system—made a strong if implicit case for welfare reform two decades before the current debate. With his latest documentary, *La Comédie Française Ou L'Amour Joué*, Wiseman has at last made a totally positive case for a human institution. The result is a glowing cinematic tribute to the achievements of this long-lived repertory company and to the talents of its bighearted actors.

Clocked at three hours and forty minutes, *La Comédie Française* sometimes seems as long and leisurely as the company's 316-year history. It is certainly a lengthy sit for anyone but those enchanted with the process of making theatre. It is also possible that not everyone will come away as fascinated as the filmmaker with the rather unadventurous productions of this venerable institution. Still, for all its longueurs and repetitions—and *répétition*, we should remember, is the French word for rehearsals, of which we see many—the cumulative effect of the documentary is curiously moving, sweet and endearing. Wiseman spent eleven weeks at the Comédie, shooting 126 hours of film. He steeps us in the day-to-day process of the company—play selection, casting, set and costume construction, administrative meetings, union negotiations, ticket purchases—continually cutting back to exterior shots of its handsome five-story theatre building and stage house, along with cinematic snapshots of the city in which it is located, a city he obviously adores.

Unlike most theatres in our own country, the resident company, the building, and the city are inseparable: the Comédie Française is among the best-loved cultural institutions in Paris. As a filmmaker who must scrounge continually among recalcitrant funding agencies in order to ply his trade, Wiseman is obviously struck by the theatre's entrenched place in the hearts of its countrymen. "What particularly impressed me about the French," he writes in a press release, "is the large amount of money the state invests in cultural activities—one-percent of the national budget. The Comédie Française has existed for more than three centuries because the government recognizes the importance and value of the theatre and other arts to the proper functioning of a civil society." His film, therefore, while celebrating

French culture, also functions as a kind of implicit rebuke to our own miserly, culture-adverse, uncivil society—a dramatic demonstration, by indirection, of the impact of a nation's arts investment, or lack of it, on the confidence of its artists and the spiritual constitution of its people.

The Comédie is alternately known as the House of Molière, the great comic playwright who originated this theatre in the late seventeenth century. The film begins and ends with actors celebrating the founder's birthday in front of his bust with responsive readings of lines from his plays. One of these plays—*Dom Juan*—is in rehearsal, along with Racine's *La Thébaide*, Marivaux's *La Double Inconstance*, and Feydeau's *Occupe-toi d'Amélie*. All are French classics (two of them, the Molière and the Marivaux, recently toured to the Brooklyn Academy of Music). Conspicuously missing from the schedule are any works from abroad or even from the contemporary French repertoire, nor can it be said that the classical productions, however vigorously performed, appear particularly fresh in their approach.

At a meeting of the company, some actors compare the current administration of Jean-Pierre Miquel (directing the Marivaux) with that of past artistic directors such as Jacques Lasalle (directing the Molière). One actor observes that, although the company has an obligation to innovate, there had been public indignation in the past over such radical production ideas as having Caligula make his entrance on a moped. Perhaps as a result of the uproar ("How can the Comédie-Française produce such nonsense?"), the current administration has become considerably more cautious and conservative.

Watching Miquel rehearse *La Double Inconstance*, we see the best of that conservatism in action. Miquel is a strikingly handsome, suave, and cosmopolitan individual with a deep sonorous voice. He is obviously immensely intelligent and deeply read, and he conducts the rehearsal like a scholar in a classroom, always responsive to the opinions of his students, yet gently prodding them toward the proper approach to the text. Clearly tradition weighs heavily on his mind—some very great actors have played these roles in the past. Still, we are again and again reminded of how actor-director discussions (a process known as table talk) can manage to evoke subtle new meanings. Miquel's exchanges with the actors range from readings of lines and interpretations of character to reflections on the ambiguities of great playwrights to comments on the nature of politics, which he compares to Marivaux's game of love, a hypocritical defense against boredom.

Clearly Miquel is no stranger to politics, being the prime mediator between the permanent acting company and competing pressure groups—the cultural ministry on the one hand, the unions on the other. He regrets the recent cuts in subsidies which have forced the company to dig into munificent reserves and reduce the number of new productions by one ("We can't appear to be rich"). He presides over the admission of new *societaires*—four contract actors voted in by the company. He averts a threatened electricians' strike by granting them a small "rotation bonus," already provided the stagehands, while giving a "technical bonus" to the flyhands. At a long table decorated with Vichy water, he informs the company of the 3.2 percent ceiling allocated for raises, and describes the way civil servants depend on tax-free bonuses. Witnessing these discussions and negotiations is equivalent to watching paint dry, but it is precisely the kind of tedious business that makes possible the exciting life of the stage. It is heartening to see how Miquel maintains his good nature without ever relinquishing his sense of command.

By contrast, the other directors seem either too dictatorial or too laid back. The celebrated Roger Planchon, rehearsing the Feydeau farce, is a precisionist, marking every move and every intonation, while Jacques Lasalle, rehearsing *Dom Juan*, is not entirely in control of his process. He watches, with transparent fatigue, as Roland Bertin, the actor playing Sganarelle, dominates the rehearsal with a long and tedious debate about the original meaning of Molière's phrase "Tout la même" (Andrezej Seweryn, the mesmerizing Polish actor cast as Dom Juan, maintains a bleak but eloquent silence during the whole harangue). Bertin is what we in the theatre call a "high-maintenance actor." He takes up a lot of air, but the patience of the others in the room is a tribute to their preternatural tolerance. American actors would more likely tell him to shut up and sit down.

In contrast to American Method actors, often embarrassed by good articulation, the French actors glory in language. They are taught to "take delight in every verb." Even in the dressing room applying their makeup, they are rehearsing their lines. This plangent declamation, the sound of actors reading verse, however, is continuously undercut by silences, as Wiseman focuses the camera on seamstresses sewing pleats on costumes, technicians building and mounting sets, workers eating in the cafeteria, audiences lining up for tickets. For all the interesting detail of performance (Seweryn's Dom Juan seducing a peasant girl by slowly lifting her sleeve and kissing her arm), it is almost an anticlimax when the actors finally take their places on the stage and the curtain rises to reveal the rather tame results of all this careful preparation.

Perhaps the most interesting thing about Wiseman's film is the way it documents the family life of the Comédie Française. It is a family that looks after its own. Three scenes in the film reveal concerns about the well-being of elderly members. One shows a retiring actor being celebrated for his thirty years in the theatre, presented with a gold watch so he can keep time in his new life. The actor breaks down expressing *beaucoup de chagrin* (a heavy heart): "All that's left of my acting days is stage fright." In another episode the *doyen* of the company, Catherine Samis (who plays Jocaste in *La Thébaide*) makes an impassioned plea to the ministry for home care for aging actors who deserve to have eyeglasses and false teeth and, above all, a telephone to keep touch with the outside world: "We communicate, and we've never been so alone." And in one of the last scenes of the film, also its most moving, Samis visits a former Comédie actress, Suzette Nivette-Paillard, who is celebrating her hundredth birthday in a retirement home for artists. (A wall photo of her as a young woman suggests she was once a dead ringer for Danielle Darrieux.) After the mayor of Versailles presents the new centenarian with a silver medal, Samis, who has inherited many of her roles, speaks of Nivette-Paillard's seventeen years with the Comédie, remembering her stage fright, her smile, her kindness to young actors like herself. She concludes the ceremony by giving this toothless, wizened, but wonderfully alert and obviously delighted old woman a kiss from the entire company. Together they testify to the almost religious nature of their profession ("They call me Sister Catherine") and how deeply it has ennobled their lives.

At a time when people in our own country tend to distrust institutions, Wiseman has managed to dramatize how a generous artistic organization, endowed with an honored tradition and generous government support, can be a source of extraordinary nourishment, both for its members and its audiences. The Comédie Française may not be at the height of its artistic glory now. It features no actors of the magnitude of Louis Jouvet, no productions of the brilliance of his *L'École des Femmes*. But as a compassionate institution, sensitive to the needs of all its constituencies, it has few peers.

Lacking established roots or firm traditions, the American theatre has no choice but to innovate. Yet we pay a price in rivalry and careerism. The faces of the Comédie actors in rehearsal and performance display no strain or neurosis; their behavior toward one another is that of support, not competition. Wiseman's film is a testament to the positive influence of a benign environment on the character of a people. It reinspirits the effort to establish a humane theatre culture in our own benighted nation.

1996

The Moscow Art Theatre

In June 1997 the Moscow Art Theatre organized an international conference to celebrate its approaching Jubilee. MXAT (pronounced Mahat), as the Moscow Art Theatre is locally called, actually opened its doors officially in October 1898. But it was a year earlier, on June 22, 1897, that the founding directors, Konstantin Stanislavsky and Vladimir Nemirovich-Danchenko, first sat down at a table in a Moscow restaurant called Slavyansky Bazaar to plan a new theatrical institution for Russia. It was to be an art theatre with a program that would do away with the reigning artificiality, conventionality, and contrivance; revolutionize scene design; and bring a new standard of naturalistic acting to the world stage.

The three-day affair celebrating this historic meeting included banquets, student presentations, informal gatherings, satirical cabarets, visits to the graves of the founders, and a tour of Stanislavsky's rather seedy Lyubimovka estate (the inspiration for Chekhov's *Cherry Orchard*) in a nearby suburb. But the pivotal event was the Slavyansky Bazaar conference on Sunday, preceded by a performance of Chekhov's *Three Sisters* on Saturday night. Both occasions took place on the vast reaches of the Moscow Art Theatre stage.

For the conference this steeply raked stage was simply furnished with two chairs and a table, simulating the restaurant site where the two men had held their first meeting. Huge photographs of the founders stared down at the participants, who included over eight hundred directors and actors from all over Russia and the former Soviet states. Some of the more well-known invitees from abroad—among them Peter Brook, Ingmar Bergman, Robert Wilson, and Meryl Streep—had failed to show. But there were still a significant number of foreign guests in attendance, including Declan Donnellan of Great Britain, Franco Quadri of Italy, François Rochaix of Switzerland, and Tadashi Suzuki of Japan.

I was invited as a U.S. representative. It was my first visit to Russia, and I was filled with wonder and regret. What particularly piqued my envy was the healthiness of Russian theatre by comparison with the underfunded theatres of my own country. Although institutions like MXAT still receive large government subsidies, Russian theatre is in the process of being partially privatized. And it remains to be seen how well theatre will continue to flourish in this brutally capitalist society, where the garish features of McDonald's restaurants now share the landscape with the "onions" of Byzantine churches, and the Russian Mafia takes a substantial cut, on pain of death, from the profits of every budding businessman.

Nevertheless the theatre still commands large, enthusiastic audiences from a population that considers both the solitary arts—literature and poetry—and the performing arts—theatre, dance, and music—to be indispensable features of public life. This passion for culture is further reflected in the way Moscow avenues and squares, especially since *perestroika*, are increasingly being renamed after Russian artists. Pushkin, Gorky, Chekhov, Tolstoy, Mayakovsky, and other literati appear as often on street signs as politicians, generals, and martyrs, and many of their Moscow apartments have been turned into shrines.

I'm not exactly sure what the conference accomplished except to canonize the founders of MXAT. The whole complicated affair had been carefully engineered by the theatre's brilliant and personable literary director, Anatoly Smeliansky—an expert, ironically enough, on Mikhail Bulgakov, one of Stanislavsky's most unforgiving critics. Bulgakov, in his novel *Black Snow*, had satirized Stanislavsky as an egotistical ogre who tyrannized young dramatists, especially if they had the temerity to include gunshot sounds in their plays (the aging director preferred his stage deaths to come by sword or bow and arrow).

Still, in Smeliansky's capable hands, the conference generally avoided any direct criticism of the author of *My Life in Art*. Indeed, both founders were blessed with a telegraphed endorsement from Boris Yeltsin and the significant presence of the cultural minister with his two vice-ministers. They also enjoyed considerable reverence from a majority of the conferees, even though the two founding directors had ended up as bitter enemies who refused to talk to each other for sixteen years. (This division recently found a modern parallel when the MXAT split into two separate institutions—one the Chekhov Theatre, the other the Gorky Theatre, popularly known as "his" and "hers.")

The chorus of praise for Stanislavsky and the ecumenical atmosphere of the conference were somewhat surprising considering how many present had broken off into radically different theatrical directions. Yet occasionally the conference managed to arouse some of the old rivalries. At the very beginning, in fact, Yuri Lyubimov, former director of the Taganka Theatre, rudely interrupted Yefremov, the current artistic director of MXAT, in mid-sentence, before he had had a chance to complete his introductory remarks. Lyubimov, a great bear of a man with a shock of white hair, lumbered threateningly to his feet, behaving as dictatorially as the apparatchiks who had made him flee Russia, to demand a moment of silence from the conference "in the name of the fallen."

Lyubimov is a former political dissident who followed the techniques of another defector from Stanislavsky, the futurist and surrealist director, V. E. Meyerhold. Here he was asking recognition of the fact that on this very date the Nazis had begun their war with the Soviet Union. Deftly sidestepping another potential conflict, Yefremov graciously yielded to Lyubimov's request, though the silent moment had already been scheduled for later in the day, closer to the exact hour of the outbreak of hostilities.

Following this interruption, the five-and-a-half-hour conference proceeded more routinely with a number of speeches, which Lyubimov, holding a bottle in his hands and glowering at the stage, sometimes greeted with audible rumbles of disagreement. (His own speech included the curious complaint that he had to go abroad to hear Dostoevsky's name mentioned with respect.) The procedure involved about ten minutes of commentary from each participant, after which he or she was asked to turn to the empty chairs and pose a question to the two absent founders. My own query, after I had made some remarks about how the American version of the Stanislavsky system (the "Method") created many more movie stars than theatre artists, was directed to the ghost of Stanislavsky. I asked him how much responsibility he was willing to take for Lee Strasberg.

The question would have been rhetorical even had Stanislavsky been alive to answer it. After visiting Stanislavsky in Paris in the thirties, Stella Adler had already reported on the Master's disapproval of Strasberg's use of "private moments" and "emotional memories" as unwarranted intrusions into the actor's psyche. But more significant than Strasberg's technical deviations from the Stanislavsky system was his indifference to Stanislavsky's ethical purpose. Stanislavsky had famously demanded of his company that they love the art in themselves rather than themselves in art, which was his way of urging them to be dedicated actors instead of egocentric careerists. By contrast, one of Lee Strasberg's leading examples of a great American actress was Marilyn Monroe.

The best witnesses at the conference to the preservation of the Stanislavsky ethic in Russian theatre were the actresses. One of them, the ninety-one-year-old Angelina Stepanova, testified to her love of theatre and her anguish at having grown too old to project over the footlights. Suggesting that some theatrical fashions are universal, she also lamented the current Russian tendency to celebrate ethnic differences rather than to use the theatre as a locus of mutual understanding. Alla Demidova of the Taganka, a veteran of thirty years' devotion to the stage, spoke of the "beauty of still force" and the need to renew and restore the old masterpieces, since tradition is the enemy of the new.

One of the most eloquent of the speakers was the Irish director Declan Donnellan. He scorned the stereotype of actors as people who like to show off, who compulsively seek attention, preferring to call them "sophisticated lawgivers." Donnellan, who is highly selective about the countries where he directs, said he had come to hate the "banal" cleverness of directors, including himself, longing instead for those moments when actors bring life to the stage, when you "collapse at a sense of the truth." "To preserve the freedom of the actor," he concluded, "we sometimes have to impose laws—and then admit they are failures, because all laws are the symptom of the breakdown of love."

For all this spirited discussion of actors and directors, it was disconcerting how little talk there was of playwrights, and how few had been invited to the conference. This was particularly odd, considering that it is the image of a seagull—symbolizing Stanislavsky's stunning reincarnation of Chekhov's play, a failure when it was earlier produced—that still adorns the curtain and the façade of MXAT. Chekhov's quarrels with Stanislavsky over the misinterpretation of his work ("he turns my characters into crybabies") are legendary. So I thought I was in something of a time warp when Oleg Yefremov told me, during one of the banquets we attended, that Chekhov really didn't understand his own plays, because when he tried to direct a scene himself he failed miserably. Obviously the old tensions between the "author of the play" and the "author of the production" still prevail, as they did in the early days of MXAT. Stanislavsky and Chekhov are buried in the same Moscow graveyard (called "The Cherry Orchard" after Chekhov's last play). But the director's grandiose stone monument virtually dwarfs the playwright's tiny marker.

Still, I had the sense that the spirit of Chekhov was hovering, yet unsatisfied, over the heads of the conferees. Appropriately it was Chekhov's *Three Sisters* that was the artistic centerpiece of the weekend. Despite his unhappiness with Stanislavsky, I think the playwright would have been well satisfied with Yefremov's current version, which is new to the repertory. It is a production that takes some liberties with the play yet leaves it thoroughly refreshed. Because Yefremov suffers from a debilitating form of emphysema (like many Russians, he is a very heavy smoker), the director was ill during some of the rehearsals, so some of the production seemed unfinished. But I came away from this *Three Sisters* with a renewed appreciation of Chekhov's singular *fin-de-siècle* vision.

Although only Act Four is actually an exterior setting, Yefremov began each of the other acts in front of the Prozorov family home. In Act One, for example, the sisters are returning home from a visit to their father's grave. This provincial homestead is a haunting piece of architecture that sits on stage like an island surrounded by three huge, gorgeously lighted drops of birch trees before a revolve brings us inside for the beginning of each action. All of the acting is extremely detailed, and every character has been newly interpreted. Natasha, for example, usually played as an insensitive parvenu, is here a good-natured, highly sexed, blowsy blonde (Natalya Yegorova) whose adulterous relationship with Protopopov is partly caused by the indifference of her husband. At the beginning of the second act, she mounts Andrei as he is working in the drawing room. He sits passive as a stone with his back to the audience, while she, chattering away, achieves sexual satisfaction without any participation whatever from her partner.

The actresses playing the sisters (Olga Barnet as Olga, Yelena Mayorova as Masha,* Polina Medvedeva as Irina) are also fully dimensioned. Their shared sense of having been passed over by life is influenced both by external circumstances and their own lack of nerve. Indeed, there is deeply textured playing by the entire cast. As a result, I've never seen the fourth act of deaths and farewells more wrenchingly performed. Tusenbach, preparing for his duel with Solyony, bids a merry goodbye to Irina, walks to the back of the deep MXAT stage, then turns and shouts her name in a manner that resounds like the gunshot that is soon to take his life. Masha, saying farewell to her departing lover, Vershinin, gives him a brave, perfunctory pat on the arm, brushes past him, then falls grief-stricken to the floor. Hearing the play performed in its native language made me aware for the first time how often the word *nichevo* (Russian both for "nothing" and "there, there") reverberates through the dialogue, how often Chekhovian comfort alternates with Chekhovian despair.

The first time I saw MXAT do *Three Sisters* was in 1965 during its last visit to New York. Then, the company seemed a little dusty, a little haloed by the past. For what might have been ideological reasons—the need to leave a positive message—Tchebutykin's despairing response ("It doesn't matter") to the awful events of the last act had been excised, though Chekhov intended it as a nihilistic counterpoint to the sisters' final paean of hope. Yefremov cut it too, not to placate a political regime but in order to achieve a stunning

*Mayorova committed suicide a few months after this review appeared.

theatrical effect. The entire Prozorov house moves to the backstage wall. The birch trees descend to form a looming enclosure. And the sisters wander in aimless circles before coming together in a final embrace within the vast expanse of nature.

MXAT is experimental without being avant-garde, daring without being cutting edge. Under Yefremov's direction for the past twenty-seven years it has managed to bridge radical changes in political and theatrical fashions. It is hardly the most adventurous theatre in Russia. That distinction surely belongs to the Maly Theatre of St. Petersburg. But at present it is preserving the rich heritage of the theatre not just through ceremonial tributes to its founders but also through powerful and penetrating works of art.

1997

PART 4

PEOPLE OF THE THEATRE

Stella for Star

A splendid woman of the theatre, Stella Adler, died in the final days of 1992. The *Times* obituary put her age at ninety-one. She was probably somewhat older—at the least her life spanned most of the century. Stella's mother, Sara, also died at a very advanced age, after a distinguished career in the Yiddish theatre at the side of her father, the famous Yiddish tragedian Jacob Adler. Stella once revealed to me how she knew her mother was approaching death. The woman was accustomed to holding a teacup with her pinkie cocked, and one day—the day she died—Stella noticed her little finger droop. What small sign—what slight interruption of her customary seductiveness and grace—signaled the death of Stella Adler?

In her last three decades Stella was known primarily as an inspiring acting teacher running studios in New York and Los Angeles, but she was, like all her clan, essentially an actor. Beginning her career as a four-year-old on the Yiddish stage, she abandoned the theatre permanently in 1961 after being critically pummeled in a London Production of Arthur Kopit's *Oh Dad, Poor Dad.* But her every act, her every gesture, her every class, was a performance. Stella's low commanding voice, which could also tinkle with coquetry, was an instrument ideally equipped to make ideas and emotions theatrical. I don't mean that Stella was "actressy." Naturally endowed with regal dignity, she hated fakery in life as well as on the stage. But if she was larger than life, that was because she knew that life was larger than life. Though she occasionally held her gowns together with safety pins and was known to paste on an eyelash backward, she dressed like an elegant courtesan and also lived like one. Her roomy Fifth Avenue apartment, where she entertained so many notables, was furnished like a Venetian bordello with low-hanging chandeliers, burnished mirrors, and overstuffed furniture. And she was always happiest holding court with artists and intellectuals over a table groaning with food.

She equated style with size, which may be why she so despised the kind of "truth" and "reality" associated with the Method. Her quarrel with Lee Strasberg, centering on his obsession with "affective memory" exercises, was really over the way Method actors reduced everything to the level of their own meager lives. How could anyone hope to find the raging majesty of Lear in the limited experience of working-class stiffs or middle-class householders?

Stella admired plays with big ambitions because she loved a large imagination as much as she loved large floppy hats. Though her formal schooling was thin, she was an omnivorous reader. Her celebrated script analysis course displayed a familiarity with dramatic literature well beyond the domestic play syllabus of most scene-study classes; her understanding of text often exceeded that of most scholars. She was famously tough on female students, some of whom she bullied and cowed into near paralysis. (By contrast she bewitched the men in her class, among them her most celebrated products, Robert De Niro, Warren Beatty, and Marlon Brando.) This is not to say that women didn't adore her, but they usually felt intimidated by her powerful theatricalism. The fact that Stella had forsaken the stage as a result of wounds she never revealed—and the way she spoke about the cruelty of critics, the insensitivity of directors, and the difficulty of acting—made some of them conclude that the profession was not worth the hardship.

But if Stella believed that acting was arduous, she also believed it to be profoundly honorable and worthy of respect. She allowed no gum chewing, smoking, slouching, or lateness in class. She was appalled by the sloppy dress and rude manners of her Yale students in the sixties. For her the actor was a figure of the highest dignity, and anyone who didn't understand this had no place in the profession.

After a performance of *Troilus and Cressida* at my theatre, Stella wrote praising the performers for "giving us all they had—all their richness and spirit. And by the time they lined up to bow, I understood that there is no more noble man in the world than the actor."

Stella's rhetoric was often Shakespearean, but what a contrast with the usual view of actors as either unemployed wastrels or meat-market celebrities. She had grown up in a rich Yiddish acting tradition where, when the noted tragedian Boris Thomashefsky died, people lined up on Second Avenue from Fourteenth Street down to Houston Street to view the corpse on stage. She was familiar too with the Russian theatre where actors shared state honors with statesmen and scientists. And as one of the founding members of the Group Theatre, she absorbed its passionate idealism, though not without a characteristic dose of skepticism. Like most Group Theatre actors, Stella spent time in Hollywood, playing the "other woman" in a few inferior films. She temporarily changed her name and permanently bobbed her nose, and perhaps she might have stayed there if her career had prospered. But I doubt it. Her first allegiance was to the theatre. It was in the theatre that she formed her strongest relationships, particularly with her second husband, Harold Clurman, the Group's most visionary figure. By his own account (in *The Fervent Years*), Clurman "rushed" this "spiritually vibrant" woman into marriage, and their tumultuous union had the internal strains of any relationship that mixes love with work. One famous point of conflict came when Clurman forced Stella, then in her thirties, to play Bessie Berger (the mother in Odets's *Awake and Sing!*) instead of Bessie's daughter, Hennie. She was a triumph, but after Clurman cast her in yet another older role, there were more flare-ups.

Stella's reluctance to play a series of character parts was not just a matter of vanity. She truly believed that actresses were spiritually affected by their roles and that Clurman was aging her prematurely. For the same reason, years later, she rebuked me for casting my late wife in the wordless part of the Mummy in Strindberg's *Ghost Sonata*. Norma was required to wear pasty old-age makeup and a costume that appeared to be disintegrating on her body, besides being instructed to play the role as if she were looking into her grave. Didn't I know, Stella asked, how this could affect the psychic poise of a sensitive woman?

Stella's contributions to the Group Theatre were crucial not only as an actress but as a director and an educator. It was she who, after journeying to Paris to inform Stanislavsky that his theories were ruining her love of acting, discovered that Strasberg had all the while been misinterpreting the Stanislavsky system (her belief is confirmed in Richard Hornby's recent book, *The End of Acting*). Stella's schism with Strasberg, always a little personal, grew wider. She quarreled with other Group members, including her brother Luther, their arguments sometimes spilling into curtain calls. And she did not endear herself to her more indigent colleagues by flaunting what Clurman called a "taste for the first-class," including European travels and her apartment on Fifth Avenue (one story, perhaps apocryphal, has it that she joined a protest march wearing a mink coat and carrying a poodle). Ultimately her temperamental clashes with Clurman dissolved the marriage, despite their artistic affinities, just as internal quarrels and an indifferent culture dissolved the Group, for all its radical idealism.

It was then that Stella first found professional satisfaction in teaching (she found romantic fulfillment in marriage with the novelist Mitchell Wilson). Later, in 1966, she accepted my invitation to head the acting department at Yale, where she captivated President Kingman Brewster (upon being introduced, she asked him in her most imperiously charming manner, "And what does a Yale president do?"). I saw this appointment as an opportunity to bring her back to the stage. Her friend and colleague Bobby Lewis had proposed a production of *The Seagull* with Stella in the role she was born to play, the grand actress Arkadina. Swearing me to secrecy because she didn't want to hurt Bobby's feelings, Stella told me she would accept the part, but only if the Russian George Tovstonogov agreed to direct her. Tovstonogov had been doing experimental productions of Chekhov at the Gorky Theatre in Leningrad, and Stella, criticized by some Yale students for being "old-fashioned," wanted her comeback to be audacious. Unfortunately at that time American-Soviet relations had deteriorated to a low point. Also, the mails were very slow (I sent Tovstonogov a letter in early October; he replied in late December). When the Soviet authorities refused to let him out of the country, we dispatched a messenger to Canada, where the cultural minister, Madame Furtseva, was visiting Expo '67, to beg her permission for an exit visa. She brushed past our emissary brusquely. We collected supportive letters from Sol Hurok, Bobby Kennedy, and Lillian Hellman, and sent them to the Soviet Union. No response. Finally, and with great regret, we were forced to cancel the production.

Stella showed no great disappointment, and I have often wondered whether she knew in advance she had created impossible conditions. Whatever the case, she continued to limit her performances to the classroom and the living room. These were wonderful, but Stella was not happy in the revolutionary Yale atmosphere of the sixties, especially when the "pishers," as she called the young student directors, claimed to know more about acting than she did. "It's the blind leading the blind," she said scornfully, and went back to New York in her big floppy hat, lugging her carpet bag.

After that, Stella connected her studio to the NYU acting program but spent more and more time in Los Angeles. She returned to Yale from time to time for productions, dinner parties, and, finally, to see Norma play Arkadina in *The Seagull*. Norma, who had been her student and assistant before we met, was terrified at playing Stella's role, but her teacher's response was warm and generous. At the end, when Dr. Dorn enters to tell Trigorin that Treplev has shot himself, Stella put her hand to her mouth and shouted, "Oh my God!" as if she had never seen or read a word of her favorite play.

Stella Adler lived long enough to see all but Bobby Lewis, Phoebe Brand, and Elia Kazan, among the leading members of the Group Theatre, predecease her: Clurman, Strasberg, Morris Carnovsky, Frances Farmer, John Garfield, Franchot Tone, her brother Luther— a funeral cortege of great American talent. She was a witness to how ideals could tarnish and hope grow dim in the struggle to survive in the American theatre, but she never lost her own commitment. She was of a generation that produced many grand ladies of the stage, including Helen Hayes, Katharine Cornell, Eva Le Gallienne, Judith Anderson, Katharine Hepburn, and others. It is now a lost tradition, and Stella didn't belong to it long, if indeed she ever did. But she maintained an indelible place in the pantheon of Olympian theatre people through the strength of her convictions, the integrity of her character, the brilliance of her mind. She and I approached the theatre from somewhat different directions, but I always held her in the highest esteem. I also adored her, and not just as another of her smitten cavaliers. In her deepest being, Stella embodied the art of our profession, and what it could become. Her loss impoverishes us in more ways than I want to think about.

1993

Joe Papp's America

Helen Epstein's compendious new biography *Joe Papp* is subtitled *An American Life*. This is as good a way as any to characterize the arc of this theatre impresario's development, even though Papp's America was invariably seen through New York spectacles. Joe Papp was a quintessential municipal figure with a quintessentially metropolitan vision. Whatever his other triumphs, his most heroic achievement, indeed his unwavering goal, was to bring free Shakespeare to a diversified New York audience. Still, it is not amiss to use the word "American" in regard to this Brooklyn-born child of immigrant Jewish parents. Papp's Americanness helps us understand what was so impressive about his career—and may explain, if not entirely eradicate, the blemishes on his life.

During the seventy years of this life, Papp participated in many of the characteristic events of the American century, from naval service in World War II to a twenty-year membership in the Communist party to appearing before the House Un-American Activities Committee where he took the Fifth Amendment (costing him his job as stage manager at CBS) to demonstrating for peace in Vietnam (and getting arrested in Washington) to challenging the NEA over creative freedom (making him reject a sizable federal grant rather than endorse the obscenity clause). Papp was nothing if not a public figure, and the positions he took on the various fractious issues of our time were always brave, and often, if not always, correct.

But more notable than his political postures were his cultural contributions: he built a major producing organization from scratch and made his name synonymous with postwar American theatre. After three and a half years with the left-wing Actors Lab in California, where he developed his notion of "art for the people" as opposed to "art for art's sake," Papp returned to New York in 1951 to lay the foundations for two major popular institutions, the New York Shakespeare Festival and the New York Public Theater. Perhaps the most compelling sections in this rigorously researched book are Epstein's retelling of Papp's journeys from a little church on the lower East Side to an East River amphitheater to winter quarters at the Heckscher on Fifth Avenue, and—after emerging victorious from an epic struggle with the imperious Parks Commissioner Robert Moses—into permanent quarters at the Delacorte near the Belvedere Tower in Central Park. Papp's combative nature was always fired up by controversy, and he had the good fortune to pursue a profession that is always embattled. The same obstinacy and persistence that forced CBS to reinstate him in the job he lost through HUAC compelled Papp to resist strong pressures (from Moses and Walter Kerr, among others) to charge admission to Shakespeare in the Park.

Like Ibsen's Solness, Papp was driven to attempt the impossible. And, impossibly, he persuaded the City of New York to purchase the Astor Library as the home of the New York Public Theater. It was there on Lafayette Street that Papp was to nourish a host of brilliant playwrights, directors, actors, and designers, all of them collaborating in hundreds of adventurous productions (*A Chorus Line* being only the most lucrative). Papp even devoted three years to supervising the Vivian Beaumont Theatre at Lincoln Center until deciding that running a cultural center was not only violating his populist aesthetic but depleting his capital.

The story of Papp's professional donnybrooks is familiar enough from media accounts and from Stuart Little's 1974 biography *Enter Joe Papp*. What Epstein adds, after a process of arduous investigation and countless interviews, is a wealth of new detail about Papp's early struggles and later achievements, and, more disturbingly, about his personal relationships. For behind the famous public figure lay the shadow of a considerably more hidden private man, whose story, as Epstein tells it with utter frankness but obvious discomfort (she is a family friend), is not always pretty. Yeats believed that the human intellect must choose perfection of the life or of the work. Papp made his choice early, and the result was a distinguished career and a less than distinguished personal life. Born Yussel Papirofsky, he concealed his Jewishness until 1962, even from close Jewish friends and one of his wives, claiming a Polish Christian father and a British mother who served tea every afternoon. Lacking a college education, he pretended for a time to be a graduate of Columbia (later he would scorn all university-trained intellectuals). Until his exemplary marriage to Gail Merrifield (his fourth wife), he was a philandering husband who underwent therapy to curb his womanizing. He was always an indifferent father. Of his five children (one of whom he did not meet until she was thirty-five), he saw only his son Tony on a regular basis and then only when he was twenty-nine and dying of AIDS. And his relations with colleagues at the theatre revealed a pattern not only of generosity and reinforcement but of imperiousness, dogmatism, and territoriality.

As the years passed, Papp's rule over the Festival grew increasingly despotic and self-important, and his growing refusal to brook dissent made him eventually part company with virtually all his trusted advisers. He fired his associate producer Bernard Gersten, a close friend since the Actors Lab days, because Gersten wanted to produce on Broadway a Michael Bennett musical that Papp had rejected for the Festival (Papp refused to reconcile with Gersten until he was near death). He sacked Merle Dubuskey, his press agent for thirty years, in an economy measure designed to save an $18,000 fee. To fill Gersten's job, he passed over Robert Kamlot, his longtime general manager, in favor of the brash, unlikable Jason Steven Cohen (Kamlot thereupon resigned). A long parade of directors—Stuart Vaughan, Gerald Freedman, Ted Cornell, Jeff Bleckner, and others—also failed the Papp Test, sometimes abruptly removed from productions, sometimes banished from the Festival for reasons they couldn't comprehend. Papp valued loyalty above all other human qualities, but his own commitment to friends and associates was often based on what Dubuskey bitterly called "an unqualified adoration of the producer."

As a result, the admiring memorials and flattering obituaries following his death were mixed with asides of an entirely different nature. The playwright David Rabe, with whom Papp had had a complicated filial relationship, spoke of his "powerful artistic, human side" mixed with "a tremendous ambition and desire for power and control." Stuart Vaughan, his first artistic director, dismissed Papp as "just one more fast-talking con man who latched onto the nonprofit structure" ("Arrogant and anti-intellectual autodidact," Vaughan erupted in an interview after his death, "have done with you"). Gersten, diagnosing Papp as suffering from "anhedonia," an inability to enjoy pleasure, spoke of his "inflated ego, encouraged by sycophants."

Anyone so combative and powerful is bound to attract resentment from those he has offended or ignored, and anyone so populist in his taste is bound to be trashed by the likes of John Simon. (Deriding Papp's "vulgar, nouveau riche" sensibility, Simon sniffed, "Joe came out of the gutter and had a gutter mentality.") One is tempted to dismiss remarks like these as the screeches of sweating eunuchs staring on Don Juan's sinewy thigh. Still, Epstein has documented a number of instances where Papp could properly be spanked for behaving like a gutter rat. It is one thing to dispute a critic's dismissive treatment of a play (I can hardly fault Papp for this myself). It's quite another to shout at Clive Barnes over the telephone (after the critic brass-knuckled Rabe's *Boom Boom Boom* as "chic filth"): "Listen, Clive, you're trying to fuck me up the ass and I'm going to fuck you up the ass. You're trying to kill me and I'm going to kill you. You son of a bitch. You cunt. I'm gonna get you fired." Papp's relationship with the media exposed him at his most brazen and his most craven. He claimed to be struggling "with the monopoly that is the *New York Times*" and once banned Walter Kerr from his theatre. But he also cozied up to *Times* editors and reviewers (including his enemies, Barnes and Kerr) and, through his close relationship with Arthur Gelb, always maintained access to the *Times*'s cultural pages, which often printed his story ideas as well as his replies to negative reviews.

Epstein mentions an old article of mine about Papp in which I wrote "whom the media would destroy they first make famous." Although Papp scorned my fears that his high visibility was dangerous for his health, there is little doubt that his later years were plagued by media backlash. *New York* magazine observed that it had become "very hip to knock Papp." When he created the Shakespeare Marathon, he became prey to every young gunslinger in the West. Chief among these was Frank Rich, who regarded Papp (along with everyone else over thirty-five) as "out of another era." In a Sunday column in 1989, Rich, who had been repeatedly panning Papp's Shakespeare productions, attacked the whole idea of the Marathon, calling it the work of "a shrewd impressario" engaged in "promotional expediency." This "snide" article, according to Epstein, angered Papp "more than any single piece of writing had for years." It made him sit down and write a point-by-point rebuttal, chiding Rich for ignorance about the creative process. Touchingly, Papp later called Rich to commiserate about the death of Rich's mother. Papp was dying himself, and the two men had a highly emotional conversation.

It was, in fact, when he was facing death that Joe Papp seemed at his most appealing and most poignant. His bond with Gail—always deeply dependent—grew stronger than ever, and his devotion to his son Tony partially redeemed his past parental indifference. Papp, whose compassion for minorities didn't always extend to gays, at first denied Tony's homosexuality, then blamed himself for it. Exhausted as he was from battling advanced prostate cancer, he nursed Tony in his house after his son had grown blind. Tony later died in a hospital after Papp, unable even to care for himself any longer, had moved to Gersten's Manhattan house. "Oh my son," he cried, having suffered the ultimate tragedy of a parent, outliving your own child. Five months later he too was dying. He had finally met a challenge he couldn't conquer ("I don't know how to do this. I don't know how to die"). An hour before his death, his mind was still "teeming with ideas."

"What is consistent in my work," Papp once told an interviewer, "is that I have always wanted to provide access to the best human endeavor to the greatest number of people." Papp's emphasis on "the best human endeavor" distinguishes him from today's diversity ideologues and their indifference to quality, at the same time that his concern for "the greatest number" revealed his warm democratic ideals. He compared his idea of theatre to the concept of the New York Public library in that it was free and open to people of all races and classes. It was a comparable social idealism that first attracted him to the Communist party—though like a number of like-minded egalitarians, he had trouble extending a love of the masses into a feeling for individuals.

Still, Papp's politics were best realized through culture, where he was among the first to demand that the actors on the stage have the same kind of faces as those in the audience (what today is called "nontraditional casting"). From the evidence of Epstein's book, Papp was often a cold and unapproachable man, with more offenses at his beck than time to act them in. But he was brimming with civic virtues, and an unflagging belief in the responsibility of municipal, state, and federal agencies to support the arts. Ultimately, and ironically, his major funding source turned out to be a capitalist investment, namely *A Chorus Line*, which brought $40 million to the Festival by charging top dollar in a Broadway theatre—playing not to multicultural urban audiences but to expense-account executives from out of town. Yet he never lost his faith in an affordable theatre for the masses. His success in building that theatre, against impossible odds, remains his greatest legacy. That achievement will continue to be celebrated long after the stains on his character have faded from memory.

1994

Orson Welles:
The Poor Caretaker

The chronicle of wasted American talent is a long and melancholy one, but few careers have ever seemed so profligate as that of Orson Welles. In the first volume of his new two-part biography, *Orson Welles: The Road to Xanadu*, Simon Callow consigns that woeful condition to a conflict in Welles between the artist and the careerist, which is to say between the self-expressive and self-publicizing elements of his character. Callow has unusual credentials for a biographer. He is an English actor and director of considerable wit and grace (you may remember him as the laconic aging gay in kilts who gets buried instead of married in *Four Weddings and a Funeral*). And so he writes about this conflict from inside the whale.

He is also an accomplished theatre writer who has published books both on his own acting experience (*Being an Actor*) and on the life and career of that outsize histrio, Charles Laughton. Corpulent theatre artists would appear to have a special attraction for Callow, as if waist and waste were both homonymous and synonymous (I wouldn't be surprised if his next subject were Marlon Brando). "The main questions asked of [Welles] when he died," he writes, "were: what went wrong after *Citizen Kane*?; and why did he get so fat?" Adding to an expanding body of works about the expanding body of Welles, this new biography suggests that things went wrong well before *Citizen Kane*, and that Welles's precocity and obesity were the results of the same unappeasable appetite.

The Road to Xanadu takes us from the period preceding Welles's birth in 1915 to the year (1941) immediately following the release of his first film when he was barely twenty-six. The book finds its dramatic climax in the well-told tale, now amplified with copious research yielding many fresh details, of the making of *Citizen Kane* and the resistance that celluloid provocation encountered from Hearst, studio moguls, and, surprisingly, its earliest critics and spectators. Since most of Welles's work prior to his Hollywood days was in theatre or radio, Callow is primarily preoccupied in his first volume not with the failed promise and aborted projects of his movie career but rather with his remarkable work in theatre and broadcasting when this "boy wonder" was amazing the world with his youthful inventiveness.

After recounting Welles's meteoric career at the Todd School and telling the incredible story of the way he managed, at age sixteen, to land a leading part at the Dublin's Gate Theatre (in *Jew Süss*), Callow goes on to describe how he parlayed this opportunity into significant roles opposite Katharine Cornell without even taking an audition. Through a combination of seductiveness, exaggeration, manipulation, and outright lies, and with the aid of an infatuated and gullible press corps (the one holdout being Mary McCarthy who continually panned his acting and directing), Welles set about constructing his own legend as not just a star but a major constellation.

Despite the author's effort to maintain a balanced view, his book is not very fair to its subject. Callow finds Welles to be less a pure artist brought down by a corrupt system—the official view Welles virtually dictated to admirers like Barbara Leaming and Peter Bogdanovich—than a basically flawed being whose faults were apparent almost from birth. *The Road to Xanadu* is a somewhat obsessive account of how, time after time, Welles betrayed his closest relationships, both personal and professional, in the ruthless pursuit of his own ambitions.

Callow's indictment is well documented but seems at times a bit too relentless. He often appears to be taking posthumous revenge on behalf of his profession for the many indignities Welles visited on actors in the same boat as Simon Callow. Those of us who regarded the legendary Mercury Theatre—created by Welles and his partner John Houseman following an earlier collaboration on the Federal Theatre Project—as the classical counterpart of the idealistic Group Theatre are bound to come away disenchanted. Rather than a cohesive ensemble of committed artists subordinating their own interests to a greater artistic goal, the Mercury was, in Callow's view, a vehicle organized exclusively for the celebrity of its leaders. Houseman himself, the elder of these two "opportunists and buccaneers," admits as much in his memoir *Runthrough*. Describing the death of their theatre after barely two seasons, he writes: "The Mercury had fulfilled its purpose. It had brought us success and fame; it had put Welles on the cover of *Time*." Callow bitterly adds: "The only real casualties were a few actors who had for a moment thought that they were engaged in the remaking of the American theatre."

Although contemporary critics found Welles to be the "wonder boy of acting," if not the greatest actor in the world, Callow considers him an essentially external performer who demanded praise without working for it. He never bothered to prepare his roles, indeed barely bothered to learn his lines, being too busy gobbling triple steak sandwiches washed down with one or two bottles of brandy when he wasn't on the town betraying his newly married wife with ballerinas. Callow even dismisses Welles's most celebrated performance—that of Charles Foster Kane—as too icy and reserved to reach the depths of the character, calling it the "most linear performance in the history of film."

I disagree with him about Welles's performance in *Kane*. It represents for me one of the very few times his irrepressible personality managed to truly inhabit another character. But there is no question that Welles was always a little too outsize, clumsy, and self-conscious to be a convincing actor. Acting for Welles was usually something of a stunt, like playing the ancient Captain Shotover, swaddled in tons of makeup, when he was only twenty-two—though even under his makeup, as Lehman Engel remarked, he seemed like a Peter Pan too heavy to fly. And his great booming voice, issuing from that pudgy baby face like "trombones doubled by cellos" (Callow's phrase), was an instrument more appropriate for radio than for stage or film. It is for that reason, perhaps, that his most effective performance in movies (if we discount his self-portrait in *The Third Man*) was as the narrative voice-over in *The Magnificent Ambersons*, taking a bow at the end, with his signature "your obedient servant Orson Welles," personified by a microphone. Indeed, his physical absence from that film may explain why it still remains his most concentrated cinematic achievement, regardless of the studio-imposed ending.

Despite the rhetorical and sentimental nature of his acting, however, he was one of the greatest directors in the history of theatre or film, with a splendid design sense that made his productions pulse with metaphorical power. Callow tends to discount his staging achievements as well, ofen sounding like a Mercury actor griping about directorial intrusions and conditions at the theatre. For Callow, it would seem, Welles's successes were due primarily to luck, nerve, and salesmanship, his greatest gifts being as a fabulist and publicist.

But this does not explain away the unbroken string of artistic achievements Welles produced for the Negro Theatre Unit (*Macbeth*) and for Unit 891 of Hallie Flanagan's Federal Theatre Project (*Horse Eats Hat, Doctor Faustus, The Cradle Will Rock*) until that federal agency was killed by Congress for exactly the same specious reasons leveled against the National Endowment for the Arts. Nor does it account for Welles's brilliant unbroken record with the Mercury Theatre (*Julius Caesar, The Shoemaker's Holiday, Heartbreak House, Too Much Johnson*), until his one flop, *Danton's Death*, closed it down forever ("Welles's flops are louder than other men's," remarked Houseman ruefully). As for Welles's radio shows, Callow finds these not so much examples of Welles's brilliance as illustrations of his personal vanity.

Admittedly that vanity was prodigious. His name was mentioned nine times in three minutes on the first "Mercury Theatre of the Air," without identifying any other actors, authors, or technicians, while the "Campbell Playhouse" spent a third of the first broadcast introducing him as "the white hope of the American stage" ("he writes his own radio scripts and directs them, and makes them live and breathe with the warmth of his genius"). Still, in spite of all the hype, many of those broadcasts were rich theatricalizations of classic novels (the panic-inducing "War of the Worlds" being only the most notorious). Compared with today's feeble and infrequent offerings on NPR, they seem like a golden age of American radio drama.

While acknowledging Welles's showmanship in creating these theatre and broadcast triumphs, Callow is particularly severe about a directorial method that not only failed to credit other actors but reduced them to mere puppets in an egotistical marionette show. It is true that Welles never directed a play "straight." As an early "concept" director in the tradition of Vakhtangov, he always imposed his own ideas on the classics, ruthlessly cutting down the texts, transposing speeches, rearranging scenes, and otherwise playing havoc with the authors' intentions. He was among the first to modernize a classic play by updating the text and changing its geography, setting his voodoo *Macbeth* in Haiti and his antifascist *Julius Caesar* in Mussolini's Italy, always for the sake of "recapturing their original energies."

This was also the declared purpose of the conceptual directors who followed him (Andrei Serban, Peter Sellars, Jonathan Miller, Robert Wilson). And like them, Welles was often charged with being a militaristic choreographer, better at giving actors marching orders than helping them find their own steps. Unable to submerge his personality inside his roles, he didn't know how to help his cast transform either. And although the Mercury Theatre company included some excellent people (Joseph Cotten, Hiram Sherman, Norman Lloyd, Agnes Moorehead, Vincent Price), there was always a lot of green-room grumbling about Welles's insatiable lust for headlines. An artistic leader who dominates the reviews and announces to the press, "I am the Mercury Theatre," is not likely to hold a company long.

The charge of Welles's credit-stealing has been raised before, notably by Pauline Kael in her introduction to the *Citizen Kane Book*. It is the one area where Welles's vanity found no creative compensation. Determined to be regarded as the sole auteur of each of his works, Welles was not reluctant to claim authorship of others' writing as well, even when his contribution was minimal or nonexistent. He couldn't very well deny appropriate credit to Shakespeare, Marlowe, and Dekker, though he cut his productions of *Doctor Faustus* and *Shoemaker's Holiday* down to little over an hour each. But he forced Howard Koch to sign away his role in the writing of the "War of the Worlds" adaptation, and refused even to allow the ambiguous credit "written by Howard Koch under the direction of Mr. Welles," when the account of the broadcast was being compiled. To the author of that account, Hadley Cantril, he wrote magisterially, "I should most certainly think that the word of the producer-director-star and star of the broadcast which is the subject of the book would hold more weight with you than the word of one of the authors employed by him at the time." He added unconvincingly, ". . . My interest in this matter is not to receive credit. My only interest, like yours, is accuracy" (in the interest of which Cantril nevertheless listed Koch as the author of the script when the book was published).

His conduct regarding the authorship of *Citizen Kane* was even more shocking. There is much evidence that the movie script was the sole work of Herman J. ("Mank") Mankiewicz with some editorial help from John Houseman, but Welles's lawyer insisted on inserting a clause in the contract saying that all of Mankiewicz's work was the property of Mercury Productions Inc. (i.e., Orson Welles) which was henceforth to be deemed "the author and creator thereof." Accustomed to the ways of Hollywood, where the screenwriter is considered only slightly more important than the best boy, Mank was more philosophical than Koch about the theft of his work, though he threatened exposure after Welles told Louella Parsons he had "written" *Citizen Kane.* No action was taken, but the witty Mank fantasized giving an Academy Award acceptance speech in which he said, "I am happy to accept this award in mr welles absence because the script was written in mr welles absence."

Callow speculates on the profound insecurities, dating from childhood, that inspired Welles's compulsion to consider himself the "onlie begetter" of a creative collaboration, the sole star of his own self-created drama, a Renaissance man in an age of narrow specialists. Callow's psychologizing is perhaps the weakest and most facile aspect of his book (he does too much "father figure" analysis as well as implying that Welles was bisexual, on no more evidence than some ambiguous remarks). But there is no question that Welles had become as bloated with egotism as with meat and drink. On the other hand, he possessed more writing skill than Callow allows. Aside from three unproduced plays, a book on directing, and a best-selling series on *Everybody's Shakespeare,* written when he was a mere stripling in collaboration with his mentor from the Todd School, Roger Hill, Welles was a brilliant improvisational wit (he once characterized Basil Rathbone as "two profiles in search of a face"). He also had considerable insight into his own vanity, his craving for flattery, and his rage for stardom.

Callow's most telling point is that although Welles hated Broadway and everything it stood for, he often behaved like a Broadway press agent. Perhaps he recognized that, the business of America being salesmanship, survival in the theatre was essentially a question of learning how to control your own image. "If we could sell the end of the world," he remarked after being invited to run the "Campbell

Playhouse," "we could sell tomato soup too." But he not only sold soup, he sold himself, lavishing as much care on publicizing his theatre productions as on creating them. Callow has the good sense to note how one's relationship with the press, "like any dependent relationship," is fraught with danger. And when the critics turned on Welles after *Danton's Death*, they had once again demonstrated that the only story that sells more newspapers than success is failure.

Welles defended himself by saying he had been denied the right to fail. "The Mercury has many faults, including its inability to produce an unbroken succession of smash hits, which is exactly and with absolutely no exaggeration essential to the maintenance of the permanent repertory company devoted to elaborate experimental productions under present Broadway circumstances." Although the critics' ignorance of process was the same problem that brought down the Group, Callow is skeptical about Welles's defense, emphasizing that the press had been remarkably indulgent toward the Mercury, and that Welles's complaints were essentially self-serving. Whatever the case, it is clear that publicity for Welles was like supper for the dead Polonius—not where he eats but where he is eaten.

The only time I saw Welles on stage was fifty years ago in *Around the World in Eighty Days*, acting, directing, and performing his magic acts (I can't remember if he claimed to be the adaptor). He took his bow carrying a kitchen sink, as if to say, I defy anyone who complains that this show has everything in it but. . . . He hadn't yet reached his full corpulence, but he was still pretty enormous, as if he had feasted too much on his own publicity and salesmanship. Some years later, and fatter still, he would be peddling Paul Masson wine on television (around the same time that his former partner Houseman was shilling for Smith Barney). Whether Welles deserved to become such a disappointing failure, a case Callow will no doubt try to prove in his second volume, it doesn't make the loss of his great theatrical promise any the less disheartening. What we come away with from *The Road to Xanadu* is a sense of sadness not so much over how Welles failed his genius and consumed his substance as how, Saturn-like, the vast American celebrity machine eats up its most gifted children and spits them out as showmen.

1995

Brecht and His Women

John Fuegi's *Brecht and Company* is a work of massive scholarship and deep rage. It is a rigorously researched, densely written, and generally complete account of the life of one of the great masters of the modern stage. It is also a frantic and furious effort to deny Brecht the authorship of most of his works. I think that Fuegi has plotted at least three different books here—a detailed biography of a hugely influential poet and playwright, a compelling history of the ghastly times in which he lived, and a revenge play featuring all the women whose love he betrayed and whose talents he exploited. Only two of these books are objectively documented. The third has an agenda which is convincing in part but finally too sweeping and speculative. For all its compendiousness, *Brecht and Company* tells us less about Bertolt Brecht and his ideological times than about John Fuegi and *his* ideological times.

Fuegi, who founded the International Brecht Society and edited fourteen volumes of its proceedings, clearly detests the man he has committed his life to. He reminds us a little of Chekhov's Vanya who, after years of slavish devotion, finally perceives that his idol, Professor Serebryakov, is a charlatan. There is hardly a page of this biography that does not deliver some fundamental judgment on the fraudulence and loathsomeness of Brecht's character. And while any number of witnesses have testified that Brecht was a horrid human being, I am not certain that the moral nature of a creative artist is all that central to an evaluation of his work. Eric Bentley's comparison of Brecht with Shaw's Dubedat in *The Doctor's Dilemma* ("a scoundrel but an artist") seems to me a more illuminating way to understand this playwright than Fuegi's constant harumphing about his immoral conduct. And as a matter of curious fact, the author does not seem very interested in the artistic side of Brecht. Full of detail about his life (and thefts), the book is thin and sketchy regarding his plays.

Fuegi's exploration of Brecht's creative work is limited to its sexual themes, and then only as a means of determining how much he stole from women collaborators. It is as if the present-day journalistic fashion of ruining public figures by exposing their erotic adventures had now entered the realm of literary scholarship.

The diary of this scoundrel nevertheless makes for compelling reading, especially since he performed on an historical stage where the most horrible events of the twentieth century were also played: World War I, the collapse of the Weimar Republic, the rise of Nazism, the Reichstag fire, the Spanish Civil War, Stalinist labor camps, the Moscow trials, the Holocaust, World War II, and later the considerably less harrowing but still oppressive pall of McCarthyism and the HUAC inquisitions. (All of these events are described by Fuegi in scrupulous detail.) Born into a middle-class Augsburg family in 1898, Brecht was conducting five simultaneous love affairs by the age of eighteen, and never thereafter was he involved with less than three women at a time. Like his character Mackie Messer, he was capable of simultaneous marriage proposals and multiple impregnations while continuing to declare undying love for all. Fuegi fully documents the "omnivorous sexuality" of this Bavarian Don Juan and his lifelong dependence on (and contempt for) women lovers. Although Brecht's most intense early affairs were with men (as reflected in his youthful poems and plays), he was not averse to attacking homosexuals when it suited his purposes. He called the poet Rilke's way of dealing with God "wholly faggot" (the German insult word Brecht used was *scwhul*), and, in order to undermine the reputation of Thomas Mann, he circulated his own homosexual sonnets under Mann's name.

Politically Brecht was also inconsistent. In his youth he behaved with cool indifference toward the revolutionary movements of the day, contemptuous of bolshevism and apathetic toward the Spartacist revolution that formed the background for *Drums in the Night*. Fuegi hints that Brecht, who occasionally expressed anti-Semitic sentiments, had a more natural affinity with the Nazis than with the Soviets. More than one witness has compared his screaming and raving to Hitler's.

Nevertheless it was to communism that Brecht finally committed himself, and whatever his private reservations about the development of Stalinist totalitarianism, and despite the fact that one of his ex-mistresses (Carola Neher) was exterminated in a Soviet camp, this allegiance was total, at least in public. Fleeing from the Nazis with his second wife, Helene Weigel, their two children, and his current mistress, he went first to Denmark, then to Finland, and finally to the United States where he worked on movie scripts and an ill-fated production of *Galileo* until in 1947 he ran afoul of the House Un-American Activities Committee. After giving specious testimony that won the congratulations of the committee at the same time less wily witnesses were naming names or taking the Fifth or going to prison for contempt, Brecht escaped to East Germany and founded the Berliner Ensemble. There he became rich and famous by remaining reticent and cautious, a theatrical radical who never stuck out his political neck, even during the East Berlin uprising. In a concluding passage Fuegi lists Brecht's unattractive contradictions: "master and child; a wealthy man who compulsively represents himself as poor; a Communist who mercilessly exploits those around him; a man who denigrates women and then proudly presents their work under his own name."

It is this last charge on which Fuegi's book will eventually stand or fall, for it is the leitmotif that plays through its seven hundred pages. In fact, one of the reasons for the book's inordinate length is that, along with his life of Brecht, Fuegi has submitted biographies of the three women he claims had written Brecht's plays: Elizabeth Hauptmann, Margarete Steffin, and Ruth Berlau. These three hapless mistresses, along with other women who play a less important contributory role, represent the "company" of the title. And if we are to believe John Fuegi, they are responsible for the major share of all of Brecht's published writings—without credit, without royalties, without gratitude, without a place in history.

Where Fuegi's conspiracy theory fails to convince is in explaining why these women chose to remain silent for so many years, and, more important, how so many different hands could have created such a unique and individual style. To answer the first question Fuegi cites contemporary victimology. The women were all too mesmerized by Brecht's charismatic appeal, or too sunk in traditional roles, to claim their proper due. Fuegi believes that, as a dramatist, Brecht, along with Molière and Chekhov, comes first after Shakespeare, but he nevertheless insists that, aside from a few poems and perhaps the early plays, his brilliant body of work was written by a woman's conglomerate with Brecht marketing and publicizing their unacknowledged labors under his own name. Seeking analogies, the author cites Virginia Woolf's famous essay "A Room of One's Own," in which she imagines an equally gifted sister of Shakespeare prevented by the mores of her time from realizing her gifts. "If 'Shakespeare's sisters,' to use Virginia Woolf's formulation, wrote much of the works," Fuegi concludes, "why should not women everywhere be able to draw strength from the free and open acknowledgment of that fact?" The sentiment is warm but the analogy is weak. It suggests the kind of leaps in logic the author makes throughout the book. Woolf never said that Shakespeare's fictive sister wrote *Macbeth* and *King Lear*. A more accurate comparison would have been with Colette who allowed her husband, Monsieur Willy, to take the credit for much of her work.

Fuegi's evidence is partially external—interviews with people in the Brecht circle and latter-day testimony by some of the ghostwriting women. Hauptmann, for example, dropping her "usual classical . . . understatement," is quoted as saying: "Up until thirty-three I either wrote or wrote down most of the poems," while claiming in a 1970 interview, that "her contribution to the *Lehrstucke* was as high as 80 percent." While one has less difficulty conceding her contributions to such frozen and flavorless ideological pieces as *Der Jasager* (*The Yeasayer*) and *Die Massnahme* (*The Measures Taken*), there is a big difference between the creative act of writing and the stenographic act of writing down. Fuegi nevertheless insists that instead of inflating her role "she radically understated the source and magnitude of her contributions."

The reason for Fuegi's confidence seems to be largely internal, based on Elizabeth Hauptmann's knowledge of languages Brecht couldn't read. His claim, for example, that Hauptmann wrote "*at least* 80%" of *The Threepenny Opera* is mostly derived from the fact that she knew enough English to translate into German John Gay's *Beggar's Opera* (its eighteenth-century source) along with the Kipling ballad that informs the "Cannon Song." What Fuegi fails to understand is that Brecht, like any artist, might have exploited Hauptmann's translations for his own purposes, adapting them to his own distinctive idiom. *The Threepenny Opera* is not simply a translation of *The Beggar's Opera*. Stylistically it is a whole new work.

But Fuegi is less interested in examining style than in reading sexual politics into the plays. Assigning almost everything else in *The Threepenny Opera* to Hauptmann, Fuegi allows Brecht, discounting a few "nips and tucks," only a single lyric, "Mack the Knife," because of its "strictly male orientation." But the most telling evidence for Brecht's authorship of *The Threepenny Opera* is something Fuegi cites as proof of Hauptmann's authorship, namely her contribution to *Happy End*. Originally attributed to a magazine story by a fictitious American named "Dorothy Lane" with lyrics and music credited to Brecht and Weill, the book of *Happy End* was clearly written by Hauptmann and just as clearly represents the work of an inferior dramatist. Although Fuegi calls it "a superb creation," which would have been "a great success, a kind of second *Threepenny Opera*," had it not been "sabotaged" by Brecht and by Helene Weigel's inflammatory curtain speech, *Happy End* is generally considered a very poor piece of writing. Lotte Lenya found it too mediocre to be performed in America, though it contained some of her husband Kurt Weill's finest songs. Only when Michael Feingold submitted a radical reworking of the clumsy text did Lenya allow the Yale company I directed at the time to do the premiere, and still the book could not match the power of the lyrics.

Even these lyrics Fuegi denies to Brecht. "Weill and Brecht were credited with the songs," he writes, "though several of them bear the usual traces of being more Hauptmann than Brecht texts"—namely English words and kind feelings toward women. Weill, on the other hand, is allowed to have composed his own songs because he is "consistently considerate of the difficult role of women in male-dominated societies." This bizarre criterion is used throughout as the yardstick Fuegi brandishes to determine authorship. *Saint Joan of the Stockyards*, for example, belongs to Hauptmann because a "typical central character in Hauptmann's work cares about other people, puts her own life on the line, and works to change the world for the better." His other reason is that the play is set in Chicago, like Hauptmann's *Happy End*, as if Brecht didn't first use the Chicago setting in *In the Jungle of Cities*. A more persuasive argument for Hauptmann's authorship of *Saint Joan* (though Fuegi fails to mention it) is that, as in *Happy End*, the play's Salvation Army heroine is appropriated from *Major Barbara*. If Brecht and Company includes Elizabeth Hauptmann, Hauptmann and Company would have to include George Bernard Shaw.

Not only are we to believe that Hauptmann wrote all of Brecht's Berlin plays (and many of his poems), but, in Fuegi's view, Steffin and Berlau wrote most of the plays in exile. Yet the sections Fuegi quotes from Steffin's rather gushing diary make no mention of her literary contributions, aside from serving as Brecht's stenographer and typist, while the plays she composed under her own name are far from distinguished. Once again Fuegi's reason for assigning work to female pens is that some scenes treat women kindly or some characters display tender feelings—notably the mute Kattrin in *Mother Courage*, whose personal heroism "reflects the values of Steffin and Berlau."

As for *Simone Machard*, "the young woman's straightforward and successful heroism is highly unusual in the Brecht canon," so it must have been written by Ruth Berlau. And as for *The Good Woman of Setzuan* and *The Caucasian Chalk Circle*, these texts have to be Steffin's since they feature "a strong woman seeking to do good in a world that demands evil" (only the Groucho Marx–like comic Azdak is attributed to Brecht and only because, in Fuegi's view, he is guilty of "sexual harassment"). Fuegi finds Brecht's plays "filled with males beyond the law, men who deny their feelings and preach a philosophy of hierarchy, control, and dominance. . . . Nowhere is there a strong, caring, and committed adult male in an enduring relationship with either a female or a child."

Although he uses this women's studies language throughout, it is only at the end of the book that Fuegi declares his underlying feminist theme: "Should people in future years still be asking the question, Where were the woman dramatists of world rank in the first half of the twentieth century, point them under the mask of the brutal male 'lover' Shui Ta, at the hidden face of the woman who loves him despite his brutality, Shen Te in *The Good Woman of Setzuan*. Or, having heard the boasting of murderer, rapist, racist Mack the Knife, we can urge people to listen to words sung 'in a different voice,' the voices of Hauptmann's Polly and Jenny as they dream of a tomorrow when women are recognized in their own right, no longer brutalized and silenced by Mackie and his kind."

If what you seek in literature is confirmation of Carol Gilligan's *In a Different Voice*, then it goes without saying that Brecht will never satisfy you—nor for that matter will many major writers. But the notion that the "brutal" "masculine" Brecht of *Baal* and *In The Jungle of Cities* was incapable of writing tender female characters is tantamount to charging that the misogynistic, domineering Strindberg of *The Father* and *Miss Julie* could not have composed *A Dream Play* or *The Ghost Sonata* because they feature compassionate heroines. Great artists rarely conform to our efforts to classify them; they are always in development. Brecht's mind was dialectical, and the violent surface of his plays was usually tempered by inner controls—early on by rational constraints and later by a Confucian calm (something Steffin found "enormously reactionary" because of Confucius's indifference to women's rights).

I have no doubt that Brecht stole ideas, themes, characters, and even plots from all his collaborators, including other playwrights, lovers, wives, patrons, actors, designers, composers, stenographers and typists. "In literature as in life," he once wrote, "I do not recognize the concept of private property." I believe that Fuegi is correct in saying he should have shared his own private property with all those who helped him. But the distribution of royalties is hardly the same as the disintegration of authorship. Works of art are not completed by committees, and however much Hauptmann, Steffin, or Berlau may have suffered from Brecht's voracious plundering, I remain unconvinced they could all have mastered the singular style of his greatest work.

Brecht's gifts were, I believe, as much directorial as authorial, and like most *auteurs*, he was accustomed to cannibalizing other's talents to suit his own stage purposes. Not just *The Threepenny Opera* but virtually all of Brecht's plays are adaptations from other literatures, and adaptations are always a form of theft. On the other hand, no matter how it developed and changed throughout the years, the bulk of his writing (the *Lehrstücke* and a few minor pieces excepted) bears the stylistic imprint of a unique and idiosyncratic artist.

And no matter how detestably he behaved toward the people who loved him, he remains a pivotal figure in modern drama. Certainly Brecht is not a man you would have chosen to share a meal or a weekend in the country with. He was selfish, vain, promiscuous, and unscrupulous, his politics were hateful, and he smelled bad. He threw in his lot with the totalitarians and sometimes used his poetry to validate oppression. But since he was also supremely gifted, to drop Brecht down an Orwellian memory hole because of sexist behavior, as Fuegi does, is to be complicit in the charge the biographer accurately makes against his subject, that simplistic politics sometimes drives his work. Obviously twentieth-century ideologies come in many shapes and flavors. Subtitled *Sex, Politics, and the Making of Modern Drama*, Fuegi's study would be better described under the subtitle *Sexual Politics and the Remaking of Modern Drama*. For all its scholarly paraphernalia, this revisionist biography, which could have been definitive, will probably find its place less on the shelves of theatre scholars than on the reading lists of courses in gender theory.

1994

Shakespeare and
Harold Bloom

Some time ago the celebrated scholar-critic Harold Bloom gave two Tanner lectures under the auspices of the Center for Human Values at Princeton, with the titles "Shakespeare and the Value of Personality" and "Shakespeare and the Value of Love." Along with three other scholars (Stephen Greenblatt, Stanley Cavell, and Lisa Jardine), I was invited to participate as a discussant. The lectures were pretexts for Bloom to ruminate on his favorite Shakespeare characters, notably Falstaff, Hamlet, and Lear, and to pigstick his favorite *bête noire*, namely ideological criticism. Like all of his brilliantly conceived and gracefully composed literary reflections, the talks were constructions of such original insight, studded with so many provocative barbs, that they were bound to raise hackles among the other respondents. As for me, I was uncertain whether to devote my allotted fifteen minutes to praising Caesar or trying to bury him.

As suggested in his book *The Western Canon*, Bloom rightly holds Shakespeare to be the canonical center not just of Western literature but of world culture. And one must respect him for continuing to defend the centrality and integrity of Shakespeare against the radical feminists, cross-dressers, historicists, multiculturalists, and all the earnest myrmidons of political correctness whom he memorably calls "The School of Resentment." In "Shakespeare and the Value of Personality," the paper on which I was asked to comment, this self-proclaimed "Bloomian Brontosaurus" holds the old-fashioned position that Shakespeare valued personality above any other element in his drama. "Personality and eros," he says, "were for the poet-playwright Shakespeare primarily aesthetic values." With this bold statement Bloom joins the rearguard ranks of such eighteenth- and nineteenth-century critics as Maurice Morgann (*The Fortunes of Fal-*

staff) and A. C. Bradley (*Shakespearean Tragedy*) who held that character was the supreme dramatic element in Shakespearean drama.

I see two paradoxes here. Although Bloom is properly critical of Plato for dismissing Homer (along with all other Greek poets) from his ideal Republic, it was nevertheless Plato who believed that *ethos* or character (in its morally elevated sense) was the only proper concern of art. And although Bloom is clearly an Aristotelean in his essentially aesthetic approach to literature, his preference for what he calls "personality" challenges those early twentieth-century revisionist critics who believed with Aristotle that the soul of tragedy was not *ethos* but rather *mythos* (variously translated as action, plot, or simply myth).

It also strikes me as paradoxical that almost in the same breath that Bloom is celebrating the value of personality he is expressing the age-old academic's conviction that Shakespeare should be read aloud rather than performed. "I am so weary of badly directed Shakespeare," he moans in typical Bloomsian despair, "that I would prefer to attend public readings rather than performances of the plays, if only such readings were available." I find this paradoxical because who more than actors share Harold Bloom's passionate belief in personality as the crucial element of drama? Who more than actors share his interest in analyzing, probing, interpreting, and dissecting Shakespeare's characters, though admittedly for the anti-Bloomsian purpose of impersonating them on stage?

I suspect that Bloom's fatigue with bad Shakespearean production is motivated not just by his quarrel with modern conceptual directors but by a secret conviction that he could perform the plays better himself—and he may be right. Harold Bloom is not only our leading academic critic: he also may be one of the great American actors *manqué*. I can never watch him at a lectern for more than three minutes without imagining him on stage. His melancholy air, his mournful, heavy-lidded eyes, his exquisite gloom, coupled with a certain rabbinical paternalism, make him ideal casting for all those parts that Charles Laughton and Zero Mostel are no longer around to play: Falstaff, Henry VIII, Simon Eyre in *The Shoemaker's Holiday*, Leopold Bloom in *Ulysses in Nighttown*, Max Bialystock in Mel Brooks's *The Producers*. Though possessed of a less than magniloquent voice, he has the colorful temperament we associate with actors of size and appetite.

It is therefore altogether fitting that the histrionic personality named Harold Bloom should be preoccupied with the histrionic personalities of William Shakespeare. And his lectures are notable for defending their variety and depth. Bloom, for example, believes that William Empson is "morally reductive" in assigning a "villainous" side to Falstaff, and he is right. But it was E. M. W. Tillyard, if I remember correctly, who first conjectured that Shakespeare originally conceived Falstaff as a villain—a vice figure in a medieval morality play about the moral education of a True Prince. In this design, Hal, like Everyman, torn between the sinful permissiveness of Falstaff and the tough love of virtuous father figures like the Lord Chief Justice, would eventually reach a stage of moral awareness that would make him reject his evil companions and choose the path of "virtue"— though it is difficult to understand a "virtue" defined by such things as repudiating his best friend Falstaff, hanging Bardolph, killing helpless prisoners, and slaughtering so many French on the fields of Agincourt.

But since Shakespeare was a poet before he was a Tudor apologist or English nationalist, the play got away from him and the character of Falstaff escaped—much the same way that Mother Courage, that "hyena of the battlefield," escaped the poet-ideologist Brecht and took on a vital life of her own. Put another way, Shakespeare began the play as a Platonist, preoccupied with moral aspects of character (*ethos*), then developed, against his will, into an Aristotelean, allowing Falstaff's character—a character revealed through action (*mythos*)—to exceed its restricting moral outline. This has always struck me as the truest reading of *The Henriad* and the most convincing explanation of Falstaff's complicated nature.

Falstaff, Hamlet, and Lear form a pantheon of Bloom's favorite personalities, perhaps because they represent the triple poles of his own personality. But in treating Hamlet as a personality, he seems to ignore the fact that the play *Hamlet* also embodies a conflict between *ethos* and *mythos*. Hamlet is not only a courtier, soldier, and scholar but also an amateur playwright who turns *The Murder of Gonzago* into *The Mousetrap* with the addition of some dozen or sixteen lines. I disagree with Bloom about what those lines are. Bloom votes for the Player King's speech beginning "Purpose is but the slave to memory." I think it more likely that Hamlet composed the Player Queen's protestations about second marriages ("A second time I kill my husband dead / When second husband kisses me in bed"), especially since Hamlet says pretty much the same thing to his mother in the closet scene, albeit in much better verse (Shakespeare's, not his own).

Bloom recognizes that Hamlet is self-consciously theatrical—in short, another actor—and, of course, he speaks some of Shakespeare's finest poetry. But as Hamlet himself recognizes ("I am ill at these numbers"), he is an inferior poet and a worse playwright—and not just because of his weakness for doggerel. His artistic horizons are limited. Nietzsche called Euripides the poet of aesthetic Socratism. He might have leveled the same charge against Hamlet. If Hamlet's *Poetics* are encapsulated in his phrase "the play's the thing wherein I'll catch the conscience of the king," then he obviously shares with Euripides, Socrates, and Plato the belief that the main purpose of art is to expose the guilty, chasten character, and improve the state.

But whatever Hamlet believes, the playwright who conceived him was an artist who knew, if only subliminally, that poetry had functions considerably more important than rewarding virtue and punishing vice, more important than arousing the remorse of "guilty creatures sitting at a play," even more important than trying to solve the inequities of society. Today, when our intellectual wells are being fluoridated by well-meaning Platonists who measure the value of art by its political, social, and moral utility, Shakespeare stands as one of our last defenses against such mindless utilitarianism. And so does Harold Bloom, who skewers those reductive thinkers and "scholarly detractors who love Sir John rather less than they love moral virtue and its alliance with the nation-state."

Something puzzles me though, and that is why Bloom talks about the value of *personality* in Shakespeare rather than the value of *character.* My objection may sound pedantic. After all, the dictionary defines "personality" as "the state or quality of being a person," which suggests the word may be interchangeable, if not synonomous, with character. However, the word "personality" has now come to carry an additional layer of meaning, namely "a person of prominence or notoreity"—i.e., a talk-show celebrity of the kind featured in gossip magazines. Personality is a quality measured by external attributes—its etymological roots are found in the Latin *persona* or mask—while character suggests a certain quiet internal integrity. Or to revive

David Riesman's well-worn terms, personalities are other-directed while characters are inner-directed.

The distinction between character and personality, in fact, is a major theme of modern drama. It obsessed the playwright Luigi Pirandello, who wrote innumerable plays about the tension between what you are and what society expects you to be (or thinks you are). For Pirandello, personality was the rigid mask we place over our features in order to placate the busybody's hunger to define and classify, while character for him was the suffering face, spontaneous, evanescent, unknowable. And that is why actors are often our most celebrated personalities. Being role players, constantly shifting skins, playing a multitude of characters, they represent the masks used in drama (or *dramatis personae*). In Pirandello's *Trovarsi*, an actress sitting before her dressing-room mirror learns that she has no self or character, only a compound of her past roles, while the suffering hero of *Enrico Quattro* can preserve his character only by assuming the personality (i.e., playing the part) of a medieval king. Likewise Ibsen's fantasist Peer Gynt is loaded with personality, but his Gyntian self is like an onion, layered with the masks of all the characters he has previously played (storyteller, lover, merchant, emperor, etc.). A superficial personality like Peer is best described with a phrase I once heard used about another shallow individual, "What a character that guy needs." All this is my long-winded way of saying that the qualities Bloom admires in Hamlet, Falstaff, and Lear are more accurately described as qualities of character.

And Shakespeare himself was very conscious of this distinction. When Hamlet says, "I know not seems," he is disdaining a role-playing personality and claiming to have a sincere character, just as when Iago says, "I am not what I am," he is celebrating his capacity for role-playing. Iago is an actor who plays at *seeming*, at dissembling, at dissimulation, at being other than what he is, which explains his obsession with reputation (so similar to the actor's preoccupation with his reviews or the politician's with his image). We believe him when he tells Othello, "Good name in man and woman, dear my Lord, is the immediate jewel of their souls," and we don't believe him when to Cassio he says the very opposite, that "Reputation is an idle and most false imposition." In common with his fellow Machiavels in Shakespeare, notably Edmund in *Lear*, Iago builds a semblance of reputation, outward show, good name—the constructs of personality—in order to compensate for, and disguise, his lack of character. Stage manager and director of Othello's tragedy, he is also the main supporting actor, hiding his evil face beneath an invented mask of directness and affability.

Though equally concerned about his "wounded name," and also endowed with an actor's self-consciousness, Hamlet nevertheless strikes us as more a character than a personality. Like Iago and Edmund, he dissimulates, assuming the mask of an antic disposition, but by compulsion, not by choice. (He also becomes a mass murderer by compulsion—a bloodbath Stephen Dedalus characterizes in *Ulysses* as, "Nine lives are taken off for his father's one.") But to *seem* is as foreign to Hamlet's character as it is native to Iago's personality. Seeming is the way of villains, flatterers, and actors. Hamlet's true nature is more like that of all those blunt, plainspoken soldiers—Kent in *Lear,* Enobarbus in *Antony and Cleopatra,* Benedick in *Much Ado About Nothing*—who speak their minds regardless of the consequences.

It is worth remarking that such soldiers were the icons of the age, men who purged their blood in battle rather than, like idle courtiers, through sexual activity (according to contemporary humours theory, sperm was thought to be dried blood). Indeed, these gruff soldiers had evolved into such conventional figures of virtue, in the satires and plays of spitting critics like Jonson, Marston, Nashe, *et al.,* that when Iago chooses a disguise for himself, he enacts the role of the military plain dealer. But Hamlet is a natural plain dealer. His directness is not a performance, not an act, not a pretense in a borrowed costume. Hamlet has "that within which passeth show, these but the trappings and the suits of woe."

Trappings and suits are crucial garments in *King Lear* as well, and for much the same reasons. "Thou ow'st the worm no silk, the beast no hide, the sheep no wool, the cat no perfume," the battered old king says to Edgar on the heath. Furs, woolens, perfumes, and face paints are the costumes and makeup of courtly histrionic personalities. But it is total nakedness, and nakedness alone, that best displays the reality of character. The way Shakespeare plays on the word "accommodations" in *Lear* underlines his belief that only unaccommodated man, that poor bare forked animal, is capable of virtue. The word *accommodated,* as Justice Shallow pedantically reminds us in

Henry IV, part ii, stems from the Latin *accommodo,* which means to borrow or to lend. And Lear must divest himself of all the lendings of royal personality—his troupe of retainers, his kingship, his clothes, his illusions of power, even his five wits—before he can truly gain his own character. In that great speech "Come, let's away to prison," Lear has discovered that one finds true happiness only by shunning the great stage of fools—the stage of actors performing their futile roles. He has learned to disdain the vanity of courtly celebrity, "who loses and who wins, who's in, who's out," the red-hot center of histrionic personalities and *Entertainment Weekly* fame. When forced, if only for a moment, to divest himself of his last lending, the illusion of salvation through Cordelia, and look into the naked abyss of life without hope, it kills him.

In conclusion, I would like to beg Harold Bloom not to take Lear's way and shun the stage, however foolish it may seem. For all the growing theaterophobia that he and other academics are now displaying, the best place to observe the distinction between character and personality is not in the study but in the theatre itself. All of us have suffered through bad productions of Shakespeare—I perhaps more than most—and the theatre continues to be the most provisional of the arts. Nevertheless it is only through the assumed *personalities* of actors—through their fleshly embodying of great roles—that the major *characters* of Shakespeare, the doubleness, complexity, and variety Bloom correctly finds in Falstaff, Hamlet, and Lear, can be fully manifested.

1995

Shepard's Choice

Challenging the camera over a period of thirty years, Sam Shepard's face appears in sepia and black-and-white on the jackets of three newly issued books. The chiseled bones, the two deep furrows in his forehead, the uncombed mane and dimpled chin are physical constants. What the camera also reveals is how the acid of time and circumstance have etched radical mutations in Shepard's appearance. Something is responsible for his transformation from the youthful hipster depicted in Bruce Weber's unposed photo for *The Unseen Hand (and Other Plays)*, to the engaging, rather shy young man of Weber's cover shot for *Simpatico*, to the unshaven, haggard, vaguely anguished figure in Brigitte Lacombe's portrait for *Cruising Paradise*, to the harrowing, glowering desperado in Richard Avedon's recent celebrity mug shot for the *New Yorker*. Avedon's black-bordered photograph shows the face and neck of its now middle-aged subject creased by a life in the weather and the barroom, his brow threatening, his mouth drooping at the edges with surly contempt. You can almost sense him tapping his foot, an unwilling subject, impatient to return to his horses in the open air, who doesn't know what in hell he's doing in a New York photographic studio.

Why, he might be asking, is someone who prided himself on being a private, even reclusive writer now willing to cooperate with this cosmopolitan world of hype and fashion? Once a mysterious taciturn presence behind a wealth of cryptic plays, today he finds himself a highly publicized celebrity, not through his theatre work, which never managed to draw a mainstream public, but largely as a result of screen appearances, particularly in *The Right Stuff* which brought him momentary fame as the new Gary Cooper. It is true that Shepard's movie roles have been occasional, even desultory lately, and that the once prolific dramatist has produced only three plays in more than a decade. Yet, we are told, this will be Shepard's jubilee year. He has just enjoyed his first Broadway premiere—a revised version of the 1979 Pulitzer Prize–winning play *Buried Child* in a splendid production directed by Gary Sinese. The Signature Theatre will stage a series of Shepard works next year, some old, some revised, some newly written. And Knopf and Vintage are issuing a series of Shepard volumes, the latest among them his collection of tales called *Cruising Paradise.*

Reading *Cruising Paradise* after seeing *Buried Child* reinforces the impression that Shepard's writing is becoming increasingly autobiographical, if not self-absorbed. *Buried Child* was the beginning of a relatively new phase in Shepard's work. Not long before he was discovered by Hollywood, he turned away from the rock-and-rolling hallucinogenics of *Tooth of Crime* and *The Unseen Hand* ("impulsive chronicles," as he now calls them, "representing a chaotic, subjective world") to compose domestic plays in a relatively realistic style. It was around the same time that this itinerant road warrior settled into domesticity with Jessica Lange and permitted the studios to replace his broken front tooth. What was jagged and chaotic and parentless in the Shepard persona was now turning familiar and familial.

Indeed, *Cruising Paradise* suggests that the characters depicted in *Buried Child* (and other plays of the period: *Curse of the Starving Class, A Lie of the Mind, Simpatico*) bear a family resemblance to Shepard's own ancestors. Even a few *Buried Child* character names—Dodge, Vinnie, Ansel—are invoked in these brief terse tales (though in different guises) along with some of Shepard's favorite weird Western locales (Azusa, Cucamonga).

Dodge, a cantankerous drunkard in *Buried Child*, reappears in the stories as the name of his great-great-great-grandfather, Lemuel Dodge, who lost an ear fighting for the North and an arm fighting for the South (these amputated parts may have inspired Bradley's prosthetic leg in *Buried Child*). But Dodge, the dramatic character, is probably much closer to Shepard's own father, whose bourbon-soaked presence dominates the first half of *Cruising Paradise*. In "The Self-Made Man" Shepard remembers his father as a World War II fighter pilot in a silk scarf, who mournfully concluded that "aloneness was a fact of nature." In "The Real Gabby Hayes" he recalls him as man who loved the open desert and loaded guns, two passions inherited by his son. In "A Small Circle of Friends" he describes the way his father gradually became estranged from all his close companions as a result of his drinking bouts and temper tantrums. At one point he attacks a man he suspects is having an affair with his wife, smashing his face on his raised knee and splitting his nose. And in "See You in My Dreams" he recounts (in an episode recapitulated in *A Lie of the Mind*) how his father was run over by a car in Bernalillo after a three-day binge of fighting, fishing, and drinking with a Mexican woman. His son buries his ashes in a plain pine box in Santa Fe's National Cemetery, feeling "a terrible knotted grief that couldn't find expression."

Most of these tales, like many of his plays, take place in motor courts—Shepard may be the most relentless chronicler of motel culture since Nabokov wrote *Lolita* (both writers recognize that nothing better suggests the bleak rootlessness of American life than a rented room). In one of the stories—"Hail from Nowhere"—a man (the author?) is looking for his wife in another motel and discovers that she has abandoned him. He can't remember what they fought about, but in a companion piece, "Just Space," the woman describes him to her mother as someone "who carries guns" and tried to shoot her. I was reminded of a time when Shepard, having driven to Boston with a brace of shotguns in his car trunk, threatened to use them on a *Herald* photographer who was stalking him and Jessica Lange through the streets of Beacon Hill. Rage, alcohol, and a profound respect and awe for trackless nature—these constitute the basic Shepard inheritances.

They also constitute the essence of *Buried Child*. Set in Central Illinois in 1978, the play is about an alcoholic couch potato (Dodge), his hectoring unfaithful wife (Halie), two dysfunctional sons (the half-wit Tilden and the sadistic amputee Bradley), and a grandson (Vince) and his girlfriend (Shelley). Some past nastiness is afflicting this family—Halie has borne a child out of wedlock by her own son, Tilden—a secret that is gradually exhumed (along with the child) in Ibsenite fashion.

Shepard monitors this story through strong and violent metaphors. At the end of the first act, Bradley cuts his father's hair until his scalp bleeds, and, at the close of the second, thrusts his fingers into Shelley's mouth, in a gesture equivalent to rape. When Vince returns to the family, no one recognizes him. He responds by drinking himself into a stupor with his grandfather's whiskey. By the end of the play Dodge has quietly expired, Vince has inherited his house, and Tilden—who earlier carried corn and carrots to dump them into Dodge's lap in some vague vegetative rite—enters with the decaying remains of the child that was buried in the garden. It is a remarkable moment, contrasting fertility and drought, invoking the lost innocence and failed expectations not just of a family but of an entire nation. *Buried Child* reverberates with echoes of *The Waste Land, Tobacco Road, Of Mice and Men*, even *Long Day's Journey into Night*, but it is at the same time an entirely original Shepard concoction.

And the production Gary Sinese has fashioned with the Steppenwolf company is a corker—easily the finest staging of a Shepard work I have ever seen. Robert Brill's vast set is composed of an endless staircase ascending to nowhere and wooden slatted walls decorated with the head of a lopsided moose that seems to be as drunk as the owner. The accomplished cast fills this space entirely, investing the dark gothic colors of the play with considerable comic luminosity. James Gammon, a quintessential Shepard actor, is especially powerful as Dodge, rasping his part as if he were swallowing razor blades. Leo Burmester as Bradley drags his leg along the floor like Walter Slezak stalking John Garfield in *The Fallen Sparrow*. Terry Kinney plays the lobotomized Tilden in filthy boots and trousers, as if he had just been plucked out of the earth himself. And Lois Smith is an eerie, frenzied, nattering Halie.

While *Buried Child* uses the family as a commentary on an entire nation, *Cruising Paradise* is oddly insulated from anything but Shepard memories. In most of these stories this is not a pressing problem. Whether told in first or third person, they are drenched in a powerful nostalgia. "I found myself lost in the past more often than not," Shepard writes in "The Devouring Lion," which may explain why he has chosen the reflectiveness of narrative rather than the immediacy of drama for evoking his family history. But if the short tale is the perfect medium for reminiscing about yourself and your ancestors, it is not an ideal medium for talking about your experiences as a movie star. What weakens and finally enfeebles *Cruising Paradise* is the self-regarding, oddly conflicted nature of the final stories.

Here, in a series of twelve impressionistic vignettes, mostly written on location in 1990 for a film he was shooting at the time (Volker Schløndorff's *Voyager*), Shepard goes by train to California for an initial meeting with a German director, then by car to Mexico for the filming. "I'm an actor now," he writes. "I confess, I don't fly. I've been having some trouble landing jobs lately because of this not wanting to fly; plus, I refuse to live in L.A." He also doesn't own a fax machine or a word processor, and he won't do "press junkets."

During appointments with costume and makeup, he realizes that he is going to be thrown together with perfect strangers on a long shoot. This makes him want to "either run or puke." He gets in a hassle with an assistant to the director who, because of Shepard's fear of flying, is making arrangements for a limo, which are complicated by Mexican border regulations. "I don't want a limo. Just get me a Chevy." The L.A. weather reminds him of murder, "the perfect weather to kill someone in." Passing some "very chic people" in the hotel, "sinking into paisley, overstuffed sofas, reaching for silver trays full of cashews and almonds," he thinks of murder again. He remembers what Céline said in his very last interview: "I just want to be left alone."

Because he won't fly, or use technology, or engage himself socially, he manages to create more trouble for the studio than the most demanding star. He harasses an Austrian driver who insists on wearing a tux while driving through the desert. He feels alienated from the director when, sick with *"la turista,"* the fellow cries over a lost love ("I barely know the man"). In short, he behaves, uncharacteristically, like a real pain in the ass.

He arrives in Mexico finally after a series of harrowing adventures. The limo is stopped and stripped by some narcs, looking for drugs. Shepard can only get a work permit by lying to a female bureaucrat, telling her he's Spencer Tracy. "I'm not an actor. I'm a criminal," he muses. "Maybe there is some inherent crime attached to pretending." These last stories contain some finely observed paragraphs about the Mexican landscape, the local villages, the Indian extras. But the very act of writing them while making a movie he despises reflects a determined effort to maintain his self-respect.

Shepard knows there is something inherently grotesque in the prospect of someone with his talent and sensibility functioning as a Hollywood actor. It is bizarre to find a man noted for his reserve talking about "this scene I'm playing now," about having "no idea whatsoever how to play this character." He is trying to enjoy the perquisites of a public personality without sacrificing his privacy as an artist. This is not an easy choice. The face in the Avedon portrait suggests it's a choice that is tearing him apart.

1996

Christopher Durang's
Poison Pen

I have been reading and watching Christopher Durang's plays for over twenty-five years now, ever since he entered the playwriting program of the Yale School of Drama in the early seventies when I was the dean. I write this less in the role of critic than of proud parent.

Durang was a member of a now-legendary class, many of whose members not only performed, directed, and designed his work at the school and the Yale Rep but were to be his regular collaborators for many years to come. He is a famously loyal friend, but also someone who is stimulated by talents compatible with his own.

In a sense, Durang set the tone for this witty and brilliant, sometimes acerbic, sometimes disaffected generation. I once described him as an angelic altar boy with poison leeching through his writing fingers, which was my clumsy way of saying that behind his shy and courteous demeanor lurked a literary Jack the Ripper. After rereading the seven full-length works in the new volume of his *Collected Plays*, I realize that this characterization is only marginally true. There is a great deal of anger in his work, all right, often proceeding from genuine pain and wounded innocence. But except on rare occasions—when a demon leaps out of his skin and starts pitchforking some fatuous damned soul—Chris is much too kindhearted to go for the jugular.

It's probably more accurate to describe him as a Catholic lapsarian, troubled over the meaninglessness of life and heartsick over the absence of God—when he is not being dumbstruck by His malevolence and delinquency. Durang's surrogate Matt says it best in *The Marriage of Bette and Boo:* "I don't think God punishes people for specific things. . . . I think He punishes people in general, for no reason." This has a Dostoevskian ring, doesn't it? I've always suspected Durang of being the reincarnation of Ivan Karamozov, assuming that Dostoevsky's heterodox character had been reborn in New Jersey, educated at Harvard, and forced to achieve his liberal arts baccalaureate by wading knee-deep through the swamps of American pop culture.

Does that sound too sober? I think so too. It certainly does little justice to Durang's anarchic sense of humor. So let me wash my brains, as Chris might say, and start again.

Christopher Durang's unwashed brain is an uneasy compound of Hollywood movies and sitcoms, Eugene Ionesco plays, and Monty Python skits. Like Ionesco, Durang certainly knows how many crimes are committed in the name of language. (I adore the female analyst in *Beyond Therapy* who for the life of her can't remember the word for "Porpoise. Pompous. Pom Pom. Paparazzi. Polyester. Pollywog. Olley olley oxen free. Patient. I'm sorry, I mean patient.") It was Ionesco who told us that philology always leads to calamity. For Durang, calamity is more often the result of stupidity. Don't his people sometimes remind you of John Cleese selling a half-hour of "abuse" to Michael Palin? Sudden explosions of fury, followed by an overwhelming sense of relief, this seems to be the trademark behavior not only of the playwright's characters but of us who watch them. Perhaps of everybody.

Durang began his writing life as a parodist. In *The Idiots Karamazov* (co-authored with his classmate, Albert Inaurato), he turned his mocking eyes on the whole corpus of Russian and American literature, fashioning the revenge of an innocent undergraduate who, having had Dostoevsky, Chekhov, Dickens, Anaïs Nin, Djuna Barnes, James Joyce, and Eugene O'Neill forced down his throat for four years, regurgitated them in the form of demented Cliff's Notes. The four Karamazov Brothers transform into the Three Sisters (with a touch of the four Marx Brothers), Aloysha turns into Pip, Constance Garnett into Miss Havisham, and Mrs. Karamazov becomes Mary Tyrone. It was the first full-length Durang I ever read, and it still makes me laugh out loud. Chris is kind enough to mention in the preface to his collected plays that I have always been a supporter of his work. Well, it is true I recognized that each of his plays had special genius, if not necessarily equal value. And thank God I did! Otherwise I might have found myself in them. There is nothing that so damns a producer (or a critic) to the lowest circle of a satirist's hell than failing to recognize a genuine talent.

Pardon the note of nostalgia—reading this volume has been a trip into the past for me—but I shall never forget the two Yale productions of *The Idiots Karamazov*. Both featured the divine Meryl Streep, a wart on her nose, her eyes oozing gum, playing the "ancient translatrix" Constance Garnett, bane of all lovers of Russian literature. Brandishing her cane and fixing us all with a baleful scowl, she concluded the action by circling the stage in her wheelchair, screaming at the audience "Go home! GO HOME!" Lying in ruins on stage was the detritus of Western literature, having been jammed into some crazy blender which spewed it out as pulp and seeds.

It was assumed at this time that Durang's great talent was for satiric cabarets. And, indeed, in his next play, *The Vietnamization of New Jersey*, he ridiculed the antiwar plays of the age, particularly *Sticks and Bones* by the hugely gifted but (at the time) overly conscience-stricken David Rabe. The poster we made for the Yale production was a sardonic variant on the famous Norman Rockwell Thanksgiving dinner painting, this time featuring a family you wouldn't dream of taking home with you, much less sharing a drumstick with. Skewering right-wing warmongers and left-wing guilt-mongers alike, like Lenny Bruce before him, Durang managed to make comedy out of the unthinkable and the unspeakable. The play showed a brave, outspoken generation beginning to find its voice—before political correctness gave it laryngitis by shoving a great big bone down its throat.

The History of American Film was Durang's last dramatic parody. After this he was to explore the more difficult terrain of his own life and his own family, without ever abandoning his almost Swiftian indignation. (His parody was now reserved for short plays and nightclub cabarets, many featuring his Yale contemporary Sigourney Weaver.) *American Film*, however, was the ultimate cabaret parody—a whirlwind tour through four decades of Hollywood shlock, featuring most of the movie characters who still haunt our dreams: Jimmy and Loretta, Hank and Bette, etc. These and other celluloid archetypes are encountered so frequently in so many guises—most hilariously as the (" 'cause we're the People") Joad family in *The Grapes of Wrath*—that we come to realize they are always playing the same parts. Someone once advanced the theory that the mark of a really fine mind was the capacity to find not differences but rather similarities among several species or things. *The History of American Film*, like *The Idiots Karamazov*, proves the theorem.

When I first read *Beyond Therapy*, Durang's most mainstream comedy, it disappointed me. I thought it no more than a cute meet. I missed the Durangian outrage. Either the play has changed since, or I have. Indisputably Durang's wittiest and most lighthearted work, it also contains a hidden lode of fury and resentment. It's like a dose of laughing gas that doesn't quite manage to subdue the toothache. Psychoanalysis in particular gets the full impact of the dentist's drill, as the therapists prove to be more aggressive, and often more looney, than their patients. And this is Durang's first play, to my knowledge, to examine his complicated feelings toward bisexuality, a theme to which he returns in *Laughing Wild*.

Durang's preoccupation with dead babies (they first appear in *American Film*) becomes an obsession in what is clearly his finest play to date, the thinly disguised autobiographical drama *The Marriage of Bette and Boo*. In this play Durang reveals himself as another child of O'Neill, entering the action as a character (he also entered the production as an actor) in much the same way O'Neill did in *A Long Day's Journey* and for much the same reasons. "Unless you go through all the genuine anger you feel, both justified and unjustified," Durang writes in his poignant introduction to the play, "the feelings of love that you do have will not have any legitimate base. . . . Plus, eventually you will go crazy." *The Marriage of Bette and Boo* is an extremely touching tribute to a recently dead mother, to an alcoholic father, and to a son who has finally learned to forgive his family and himself.

Baby with the Bathwater, which also deals with dead or abused children, is another comedy about a dysfunctional family, an emphasis which led one of Durang's critics (Benedict Nightingale) to accuse him and other American dramatists of writing "diaper plays." (An even more overworked and wrongheaded epithet for Durang is "sophomoric.") But if Durang writes diaper plays, so did O'Neill, Odets, Miller, Albee, and Williams. Indeed, the quintessential American drama is and always has been a family drama—a work in which the writer lays his ghosts to rest at last, making peace with his past by exorcising the dead.

Laughing Wild is the last play in the volume and one of the strangest: two stream-of-consciousness monologues and a very bizarre dialogue in which the pair of speakers share each other's dreams. It features some of Durang's most experimental writing and free-floating connections (consider the character who sees father in a baked potato, smears him with butter, and eats him!). And it contains an extremely eloquent diatribe against the paleocons who regard AIDS as a punishment for sexual deviation. Worth quoting from this play is one of Durang's most telling witticisms, characteristic in the way the playwright combines metaphysics with show business. Recoiling from an egotistical actor who blesses his Creator for an award as featured performer, the male speaker says: "God is silent on the Holocaust, but he involves himself in the Tony Awards? I don't think so."

Christopher Durang doesn't think so either, and this conflict between conventional wisdom and perceived reality continues to be a prime trigger of his anger. Another is the arrogance and muddleheadedness of us theatre critics, particularly Frank Rich, who had the distinction of panning many of the plays in this volume. Appended to *Laughing Wild* is Durang's wrenching description of how Rich, during his tenure as *New York Times* drama critic, was controlling the stage and disheartening playwrights. But of course there is much more to be found here than a display of wounded feelings—namely, seven extremely fine plays, complete with eloquent introductions, that now have a permanent life in published form, impervious to critical abuse. They represent a brilliant and daring dramatic mind at work. And they make me very very proud.

1997

Ionesco's Memories

Eugene Ionesco's *Past Present / Present Past* is a personal memoir that was first published in France in 1968. It represents a melancholy excursion by this Rumanian-born dramatist into the precincts of his past life. The book is a record of profound alienation. Not altogether certain whether he has lived this life or dreamed it, whether he is sleeping or remembering, Ionesco sits at his desk, piecing together autobiographical fragments to shore against his ruins.

The volume opens with some brief memories of Ionesco's childhood and family life, which seems almost Proustian in the way smells, words, and things evoke the past. Still, for all the early reminiscences, *Past Present / Present Past* is essentially a chronicle of two years in the author's adult career—1940, when he was trapped against his will in Bucharest under the regime of the fascist Iron Guards, and 1967, when, already a well-established avant-garde playwright, he watched what he considered an equally threatening totalitarianism arising from the left. In a sense, *Past Present / Present Past* is a companion piece to Milan Kundera's *The Book of Laughter and Forgetting*. Both authors see themselves as puny individuals in the paralyzing grip of the mass state, using their art in an effort to speak truth to power.

As his title suggests, Ionesco is permitting his mind to wander back and forth over the uneven terrain of twenty-seven embattled years, as if these years were speaking to each other in a kind of historical dialogue. What he reveals in the process is a finely tuned intellect with a solid grounding in contemporary philosophical thought. Those interested in the origin and development of Ionesco's contempt for systems, as well as his hatred of theoretical constructions, will find ample biographical material here. In the theatre his anticonceptualism has established him as a comedian in the tradition of Molière, making intellectual pretension the target of scorching satire and biting humor. In contrast to his plays, however, his autobiographical prose is surprisingly somber, even morose, showing little of the playfulness encountered in *The Bald Soprano* or *Jack, or The Submission*. Still, the book confirms a suspicion, suggested in his plays, that behind this hater of theory lies an intellectual and a *philosophe*; Ionesco's anarchic humor is essentially grounded in political and philosophical anarchism, assuming it is possible to assign any ideological label to such an enemy of ideology. "I prefer disorder to tyranny," he declares in one of the more clarion moments in his book. He also seems to see chaos as the ultimate consequence of any falsely imposed conformity. From the moment Ionesco begins to describe, in simple declarative sentences, his memories of a threatening, authoritative father and of his own decaying first teeth, the feeling that "I am beginning to fall apart" becomes an image not only for his current state of mind but for the state of the entire world.

Throughout *Past Present*, in short, Ionesco is trying to defend the sanctity of the individual against the state. He shows us the origins of this individualistic faith in his hatred of his father, the ultimate apparatchnik, who always supported the dominant powers, whether they called themselves fascist, Communist, or democratic. Ionesco has no use for people who capitulate to the system—any system. Indeed, the armor-plated rhinoceros makes an early appearance in these pages, having become Ionesco's symbol for conformity long before he wrote his celebrated play. The problem with rhinos, to Ionesco's mind, is that for them "the state has become God." For Ionesco, on the other hand, all states, all revolutions, indeed all politics, are false, contemptible, and corruptible constructs. "Politics," he writes, "are no longer the organization of the City, they are the disorganization of the City. . . . Modern revolutions with their false religions are like the Christian revolutions that destroyed cultures; they are like the Moslem faith that destroyed Byzantium and the monuments of Athens. All revolutions destroy the libraries of Alexandria."

As he contemplates the tyranny of the new Algerian government, or the atrocities in the Sudan, or what he calls "the murderous anti-Israeli madness" (Ionesco is deeply upset by European anti-Semitism), he begins to exult in fantasies of total destruction. "Let everything collapse. I would like for there to be nothing at all." Like some of his theatrical predecessors—like Ibsen, for example, who was willing to torpedo Noah's Ark in order to make a fresh start for mankind, or like Strindberg, who fancied himself a "total incendiary," burning up the world in order to eradicate cant—Ionesco considers modern society so horribly regulated, so cruelly and stupidly managed that nothing can be set right without a completely new beginning. Ionesco is stupefied by the Communist concept of the Ideal City and enraged at those (particularly his archenemies Jean-Paul Sartre and Simone de Beauvoir) who still support it in the face of mounting evidence of atrocities. Every political utopia has been the occasion for unspeakable suffering, and every revolution merely reconstructs the old hierarchies. Ionesco looks forward almost eagerly to "the Great Explosion." But, awaiting the apocalypse, he will settle for a glass of alcohol to drown his rancor and regret.

Although Ionesco displays his seething rage and contempt throughout this book, he finds some respite from disgust in the contemplation of art and poetry, in the occasional ecstatic feelings that course through his spirit, and in his own domestic life, especially his close relationship with his little daughter. The morbid fulminations of *Past Present* are broken by four charming tales for "Children Less than Three Years Old." They seem almost to have been written by another author. These stories are remarkably sweet and naive, based on that bizarre disordering of the senses and surprising disconnection between words and objects that constitute Ionesco's primary verbal technique. Little Jacqueline learns that she mustn't call pictures "pictures," she must call them "pictures," that she walks with her ten eyes and looks with her two fingers, and so forth. In short, Ionesco is instructing his daughter to doubt the foolish symbology of language ("I have long felt lost in language," he moans) while also teaching her to doubt everything she will be taught, including his own instruction. These stories remind me of that fairy tale where a little child plays jacks with an ogre, who thereupon turns into a child himself. *Past Present / Present Past* is an act of contrition in which a raging, wounded animal, hurt to the brains, finds solace in the naive embraces of a little girl.

1997

The Sex Life of
Anton Chekhov

Anton Pavlovich Chekhov has always seemed the most generous, most selfless, most warmhearted of men—the paragon, as Richard Gilman calls him in his excellent study of Chekhov's plays, of "exemplary moral behavior and psychological good health." Although some critics, Gilman among them, have raised objections to the canonizing of Chekhov (biographies of the man often tend to blend into hagiographies), almost everyone agrees that Chekhov is one of the few modern writers one would like to have been friends with. He has certainly seemed a shining exception to the general run of modern dramatists, who are often inordinately hostile, predatory, or faithless in their relations with women. The thrice-married Strindberg, for example, accused the "third sex" (emancipated females) of being a coven of witches dedicated to emasculating and (in his case) electrocuting males. Bertolt Brecht maintained simultaneous relationships with five different mistresses while exploiting their money, labor, and talent (he also treated his wife, the brilliant actress Helene Weigel, like a kitchen slave). Bernard Shaw left a cold, unused marriage bed to conduct affairs with several actresses. Even the elderly Ibsen—the most domesticated of modern playwrights—had a courtship (though perhaps only epistolary) with an eighteen-year-old girl.

Ah, but Chekhov, who married only four years before he died, has always seemed almost monastic in his sexual relationships and entirely upright in his dealings with family and friends. True, biographers have noted his passing interest in such women as the children's story writer Lidia Avilova, who not only claimed to have been the model for Nina in *The Seagull* but nursed a passion for Chekhov throughout her life. This passion, however, like that of many of Chekhov's female admirers, was thought to be unrequited, leading biographers such as Ronald Hingley to conclude that Chekhov's "sexual temperature was low." Even Gilman, who disputes the common belief in Chekhov's erotic coldness, speculates that he "consummated no, or very few, love affairs, because he only had so much physical energy to give."

Now, just in time to compete for a prize in the Sexual Sweepstakes—the current publishing contest over who can expose the most secrets in the private lives of famous men—comes a new biography by Donald Rayfield that radically revises our estimate of Chekhov's sexual exploits, if not of his moral stature. In *Anton Chekhov: A Life*, Rayfield publishes the fruits of his prodigious research into many letters and documents, unrevealed till now because of the reticence of literary commentators or the puritanism of state bureaucrats. His untapped sources include Russian state archives, theatrical museums, and especially the writer's five thousand extant letters (which Chekhov carefully preserved), many of them published before only in bowdlerized form.

The result is a life, in Rayfield's words, that "was short, but neither sweet nor simple. [Chekhov] had an extraordinary number of acquaintances and liaisons (though few true friends and lovers)." Indeed, the number of sexual encounters retailed in this book suggests that Chekhov himself may have been the model for his first, unpublished play *Platonov* (sometimes called *Don Juan in the Russian Manner*). For like his Russian Don Juan, Chekhov went from woman to woman without ever being able to settle his affections. He spent a great deal of his free time in brothels. He suffered not only from diarrhea and hemorrhoids and the tuberculosis that killed him but from a serious case of clap. And despite his selfless devotion to humanity—most strikingly revealed in his humane medical practice and his arduous journey to the isolated convict colony of Sakhalin—he was a fairly indifferent friend.

Indeed, what most surprises the reader of this book is not the many sexual adventures Chekhov initiated—including a steamy threesome in the Hotel Louvre with two outspoken lesbians—but rather the coldness with which he treated old mistresses in need. "I am afraid of a wife and family life which will restrict me and as I imagine won't fit in with my disorderliness," he wrote to Suvorin.

"Anyway I don't love my mistresses any more and with them I gradually become impotent." Indeed, extreme sexual activity alternating with cold impotence seem to have been the pivots of his erotic temperament.

He could be bewitched by the sexual skills of the Japanese whores he met in a Blagoveshchensk brothel, but he barely recognized his early sweetheart, Sasha Selivanova, when she offered to come back into his life. He got himself engaged to a young Jewess, Dunia Efros (the model for Anya in *Ivanov*), and broke off the relationship, possibly because of her religion (Chekhov admired Jews—he later became a Dreyfusard—but felt them to be a race apart with what Rayfield calls "irredeemably unacceptable attitudes"). And after a long affair with the exquisite but ill-fated Lidia (Lika) Mizinova, he handed her over to his friend Potapenko, who was already married. Potapenko first impregnated and then deserted Lika, leaving her virtually penniless. Her anguished appeals to Chekhov for help in her distress are among the most moving things in Rayfield's book.

Chekhov responded either not at all or with frivolous banter—rather like Ibsen's Nora refusing to acknowledge that Dr. Rank is dying of syphilis. Lika, in her turn, was alternately forgiving and reproachful: "Your whole life is for others," she wrote, "and you don't seem to want a personal life of your own," grumpily adding, "Your promises to come are all rubbish. You will never move." Often he promised to meet her and didn't show, pleading muddy roads or missed trains. It was she, not Avilova, who was the true model for Nina in *The Seagull*—a woman seduced and abandoned by an artist. (In a bizarre foreshadowing of reality, Lika, like Nina, was later to lose her child as well.)

Responding to this tragedy, Chekhov finally agreed to meet with Lika in a hotel room where, rather like Dr. Dorn recommending valerian drops, he prescribed a sedative. A few hours after she left the room, he made love to another woman who had arrived seeking help with a manuscript.

Apart from the actress Olga Knipper, who was later to become his wife, the other major woman in his life was his sister Masha. Toward her Chekhov acted with varying degrees of selfishness and generosity. Rayfield leaves little doubt that Chekhov continually discouraged

Masha from marrying in order to preserve her role as his amanuensis. No wonder she shares her name with two of the most unhappy women in Chekhov's plays.

As for Olga Knipper, Rayfield implies that in her Chekhov had finally met his match. The biographer hints that she had earlier been the mistress of Nemirovich-Danchenko, the cofounder of the Moscow Art Theatre, and that this affair might have continued after her marriage. He also insinuates that her miscarriage might have actually been an ectopic pregnancy, conceived when she and Chekhov were eight hundred miles apart.

Like Chekhov with his former mistresses, Knipper was not very available when Chekhov needed her. She was often away working, sometimes for as long as four months. (Perhaps as a result of these long separations, he allowed that Knipper could take a lover if she so desired.) Exiled to Yalta for his health, coughing blood continuously, suffering from diarrhea, and trying to finish work on his last play, *The Cherry Orchard*, Chekhov struggled for breath in a state of depression and isolation. "My wife is either sick or travelling," he grumbled to a former mistress, "so we never make a proper go of it."

Knipper knew that her absence from Chekhov was causing talk. Justifying herself to Chekhov's sister, Masha, she wrote: "You must think very badly of me when you look at your life. . . . It's awfully hard for me to adandon my vocation. . . . I know you have different views and understand all too well if in your heart you condemn me." Nevertheless Knipper continued to pursue her career at the Moscow Art Theatre, provoking rivals into resigning from the company and carping at the performances of other actresses. She was not beloved by Chekhov's family either and tried to discourage his closeness to Masha (Masha grumbled: "My relations with my sister-in-law are still pretty bad"). Nevertheless, when Chekhov was dying in Germany, Knipper proved a tireless nurse and correspondent, sending regular bulletins to the family and to the Moscow Art Theatre. Nearing the end, Chekhov began devising stories and plays that sound very much like Beckett. In one of them, diners in a hotel wait for dinner, not knowing the cook has vanished. In another, passengers are stuck on an icebound ship. These were harbingers of death, and it was Knipper who eased him into it, administering morphine, cleaning up his messes, applying ice to his convulsive heart. But there must have been some residue of lingering resentment—Chekhov left the bulk of his estate to his sister Masha. Knipper got the equivalent of his second-best bed, a cottage in Gurzaf, and five thousand rubles. All of this makes for juicy reading, and perhaps those liquids are necessary to lubricate an essentially dryly written biography. Rayfield's "just the facts" commitment to the minutest details of Chekhov's life serve to fill in a lot of gaps. He has discovered some priceless letters by Chekhov's elder brother, Alexander, which cast this alcoholic clown in the role of the most Falstaffian member of the family. He is also interesting regarding Chekhov's relationships with Tchaikovsky and with Tolstoy (whose daughter Tatyana loved Chekhov from afar). But it is odd how little of the creative artist actually breaks through the crust and minutiae of everyday life. Like Martin Meyer's biography of Strindberg and John Fuegi's recent book on Brecht, Rayfield's *Anton Chekhov* uncovers a lot of clay around the feet of a major literary idol. But also like those books, it exposes the huge chasm that lies between diligent scholarship and imaginative criticism.

Rayfield cites each of Chekhov's stories in short synopses that capture nothing of their style or flavor. And his account of the plays is essentially limited to establishing their origins in Chekhov's past relationships, For a biography that is advertised as a complete account of this writer's career, there are surprising lacunae regarding Chekhov's attitudes toward the Moscow Art Theatre, particularly toward Stanislavsky, whom Chekhov believed to be ruining his plays. For that, and for a warmer sense of the man behind the work, one must turn to Ernest J. Simmons's engaging biography, which, though relatively silent about Chekhov's active sex life or his mistreatment of friends, gives us a much more complete sense of the writer's sympathetic humanity and his incomparable contributions to literature.

1998

Index

A NOTE ON THE AUTHOR

Robert Brustein is the founder and artistic director of the American Repertory Theatre at Harvard University, where he is also professor of English. He is theatre critic for *The New Republic* and the author of a number of distinguished books on theatre and drama. Mr. Brustein is the former dean of the Yale School of Drama and the founder and director of the Yale Repertory Theatre. He has twice been awarded the George Jean Nathan Award for dramatic criticism, in 1962 and 1987, and has also received the George Polk Memorial Award for outstanding criticism.